FELIX POMERANZ, CPA, has been concerned with government accounting and auditing issues since he served as Budget and Fiscal Officer, and instructor at the Finance School, U.S. Army in the early 1950s. He is a partner of Coopers & Lybrand, and Director of Accounting, Auditing, and SEC Technical Services. He has held executive positions at Westvaco Corporation and American Standard, Incorporated. A prolific writer on financial subjects, he is co-author of *Pensions: An Accounting and Management Guide,* the authoritative text dealing with the Employee Retirement Income Security Act (ERISA).

ALFRED J. CANCELLIERI, CPA, has been a manager in Coopers & Lybrand's Accounting, Auditing, and SEC Technical Services group since 1973 and has had more than fourteen years of public and private auditing experience. He is also a Certified Internal Auditor currently involved in the research and development of new auditing techniques in such areas as EDP, governmental auditing, and operational controls reviews; in addition, he has spearheaded the firm's task force that has created a series of operational controls review questionnaires pertaining to government functions. He has assisted in operational reviews at federal, state, and local levels.

JOSEPH B. STEVENS, CPA, has been with U.S. General Accounting Office since 1965 and is currently Assistant Director, Field Operations Division. His background includes supervising audits of major federal programs and activities; and more recently, he has been involved in the audits of large government corporations. During 1974-1975, he was associated with Coopers & Lybrand as a participant in the Presidential Executive Interchange Program. While with the firm, he assisted in the development of operational controls techniques for use in auditing state and local governments.

JAMES L. SAVAGE, CPA, is a partner of Coopers & Lybrand and chairman of the firm's Local Government Accounting Industry Committee. He is a member of the American Institute of Certified Public Accountants' Committee on Governmental Accounting and Auditing and has an extensive background of supervising audits of large governmental units. He currently is an Associate Professor of Accounting at Portland State University and is a co-author of the study, *Financial Disclosure Practices of the American Cities.*

AUDITING IN THE PUBLIC SECTOR

Efficiency, Economy, and Program Results

by

FELIX POMERANZ, CPA
Coopers & Lybrand

ALFRED J. CANCELLIERI, CPA
Coopers & Lybrand

JOSEPH B. STEVENS, CPA
U.S. General Accounting Office

JAMES L. SAVAGE, CPA
Coopers & Lybrand

WARREN, GORHAM & LAMONT
Boston

To the men and women
who, by auditing, enhance
productivity in government

1251 AVENUE OF THE AMERICAS
NEW YORK, NEW YORK 10020

Library of Congress Catalog No. 75-22798
ISBN 0-88262-123-8

PRINTED IN THE UNITED STATES OF AMERICA

Preface

This book is intended to be a practical guide to auditors and beneficiaries of auditing services in applying the *Standards for Audit of Governmental Organizations, Programs, Activities and Functions* prescribed by the United States General Accounting Office. States and municipalities have been confronted with the need to render an ever-increasing number of services to their citizens. Yet while the desirability of many of those services is accepted throughout the nation, funding has often lagged behind needs. Thus, the enhancement of productivity in government represents a challenge and an opportunity to government employees and to concerned citizens—especially to those of us who are members of the accounting and auditing profession.

The primary audience of this book is the men and women who perform audit services at the federal, state, and local levels. It is also directed toward those accountants in government who are concerned with following up on audit reports and with the monitoring of the resultant corrective actions. The book should also be of value to public accountants engaged in audits of public sector entities. And officials of government entities may well find the book of value as a "self-check" device; the numerous questions in this book are based on practices which the authors consider appropriate to good government. The government executive who compares his own practices to the practices considered preferred may well be in a position to come up with ideas that enhance productivity.

The standards of the United States General Accounting Office and the techniques which have been developed pursuant to those standards have deservedly projected a forward-looking image for the United States General Accounting Office. Yet Level II of the GAO's standards, which deals with the achievement of efficiency and economy, has not been widely applied at the state and local levels. And examples of successful Level III audits—audits directed toward the evaluation of the effectiveness of government programs—are rare. However, Level I audits, which are similar to the traditional financial audits by public accountants, are carried out frequently. For these reasons, we have decided to offer a comprehensive audit approach that might help to accelerate the rate at which the Level II and Level III standards are utilized in government audits.

On the practical side, our objective is to help reduce the extent to which individual auditors, faced with new demands on their professional skills, must redesign audit programs and approaches each time they face a new audit assignment. Thus, the structure of this book: The initial chapters primarily discuss the concepts, methods, and procedures involved in Level II and Level III auditing; Chapter 4 is concerned with the measurement of performance, using a technique to which we have given the term "dollarization"; and the remaining chapters concern major program or effort areas in government. The bulk of these chapters is devoted to individual function questionnaires. The questionnaires should eliminate the need for comprehensive advance surveys each time a new audit is contemplated. Questionnaires can be modified to fit unique situations.

We would like to acknowledge the advice, contributions, and encouragement of our associates in the Accounting, Auditing and SEC Technical Services Group of Coopers & Lybrand. Special credit is due to Ellen M. Spohn for her participation in researching and drafting portions of the manuscript and in critiquing numerous drafts. We also thank James E. Meredith, National Director of Government Services, for his guidance, suggestions, and constant support, and also those partners engaged in state and local practice who reviewed the operational controls questionnaires. Finally, we express appreciation to Norman E. Auerbach, Chairman and Chief Executive of Coopers & Lybrand, for his long-time recognition and support of innovative auditing concepts.

With respect to government, we commend Elmer B. Staats, Comptroller General of the United States, and Ellsworth H. Morse, Jr., Assistant Comptroller General of the United States, for their inspiring leadership in expanding the horizons of auditing. We commend H. L. Krieger, J. E. Thorton, and S. D. McElyea for their cooperation and efforts in maintaining an interchange of ideas and personnel between government and business.

Hopefully, this book will encourage interested parties, particularly organizations such as the General Accounting Office, the American Institute of CPAs, the Institute of Internal Auditors, the Association of Government Accountants, and the various federal, state, and local audit agencies to further research audit approaches and techniques. We also hope that the concepts outlined in this book will be of value to audit institutions abroad, particularly where auditors can—by improving the efficiency and economy of government operations—help to improve the quality of life of all citizens. In this way, we hope that the volume will make a small contribution toward international understanding.

FELIX POMERANZ
ALFRED J. CANCELLIERI
JOSEPH B. STEVENS
JAMES L. SAVAGE

New York, New York
November 1, 1976

Table of Contents

CHAPTER 1

Auditing the Public Sector

CHAPTER 2

Efficiency and Economy Audits–Concepts, Methods, and Procedures

CHAPTER 3

Program Results Audits—Concepts, Methods and Procedures

CHAPTER 4

Performance Measurement—Dollarization

CHAPTER 5

Operational Controls Review—Internal Audit

Part I—General Discussion

Part II—The Questionnaire

CHAPTER 6

Operational Controls Review—Budget Management

Part I—General Discussion

Part II—The Questionnaire

CHAPTER 7

Operational Controls Review–Personnel

Part I—General Discussion

Part II—The Questionnaire

CHAPTER 8

Operational Controls Review–Cash Management

Part I—General Discussion

Part II—The Questionnaire

CHAPTER 9

Operational Controls Review–Procurement

Part I—General Discussion

CHAPTER 11

Operational Controls Review–Maintenance

Part I—General Discussion

Part II—The Questionnaire

CHAPTER 12
Operational Controls Review–Grant Management

Part I—General Discussion

Part II—The Questionnaire

Appendixes and Bibliography

CHAPTER 1

Auditing the Public Sector

Standards of Government Auditing.
Levels of Audit.
  Level I—Financial and Compliance.
  Level II—Economy and Efficiency.
  Level III—Program Results.
The State of the Art.
Response by the Profession.

In recent years, government in the United States has grown in size and complexity. As illustrated by Figures 1-1 and 1-2, receipts and disbursements at all levels of government have more than doubled since 1960. Figure 1-3 shows that this trend is continuing: The federal government has budgeted receipts of $351 billion and disbursements of $394 billion for 1977.

As public-sector spending has accelerated, the public has become increasingly concerned about how this money is spent. (Figure 1-4 shows the sources and uses of the 1977 federal budget dollar.) Legislators and government management officials, as well as the general public, have become interested in more than financial accountability. They are now interested in determining if government is achieving its goals within the parameters of the law in an efficient and economical manner. As Ellsworth H. Morse, Jr., Assistant Comptroller General of the United States, said:

> Government programs and operations are big business and governmental expenditures are absorbing an ever increasing share of our national income. Government managers need all the help they can get to do an effective job.
>
> Public accountants have skills that can be adapted to improving the efficiency, economy, and effectiveness with which government operations are conducted. However, they need some sharpening to be more directly helpful to government managers and policy makers.

Government programs and their objectives are complex and they are conceived, financed and administered in a political environment. While there are some similarities, the framework of operations differs greatly from that of private enterprise. This means that if public accountants are to effectively contribute to better government, they must invest some effort in acquiring the necessary knowledge and skills to deliver what is wanted and what is needed.[1]

Figure 1-1

FEDERAL—BUDGET RECEIPTS AND OUTLAYS: 1960 TO 1974

(in Billions of Dollars)

Description	*1960*	*1965*	*1968*	*1969*	*1970*	*1971*	*1972*	*1973*	*1974*
Receipts	92.5	116.8	153.7	187.8	193.7	188.4	208.6	232.2	264.9
Outlays	92.2	118.4	178.8	184.5	196.6	211.4	231.9	246.5	268.4

SOURCE: U.S. Department of Commerce, *Statistical Abstract of the United States, 1975,* 225 (U.S. Government Printing Office 1975).

Figure 1-2

STATE AND LOCAL—TOTAL GOVERNMENTAL REVENUE AND EXPENDITURES: 1960 TO 1973

(in Billions of Dollars)

Description	*1960*	*1965*	*1970*	*1972*	*1973*
Revenue*	153.1	202.6	333.8	381.8	426.2
Expenditures**	151.3	205.6	333.0	397.4	432.6

* Excludes duplicative intergovernmental revenue. U.S. Bureau of the Census, *Governmental Finances,* reprinted in U.S. Department of Commerce, *Statistical Abstract of the United States, 1975,* 253 (U.S. Government Printing Office 1975).

** U.S. Bureau of the Census, Census of Governments: 1972, Vol. 6, No. 4, *Historical Statistics on Governmental Finances and Employment;* and *Governmental Finances,* reprinted in U.S. Department of Commerce, *Statistical Abstract of the United States, 1975,* 253 (U.S. Government Printing Office 1975).

[1] Morse, Jr., "Qualifications of Public Accountants to Audit Governmental Activities," paper presented at District of Columbia Institute of Certified Public Accountants Luncheon Meeting, Washington, D.C., Oct. 23, 1975, pp. 20–21.

The role of auditing in government is changing in response to these expectations. In the past, the quality of performance in government operations was monitored in essentially three ways:

- Financial audits;
- Managerial overview; and
- Special situation reviews and investigations.

While the traditional assessment methods provide reasonable assurance as to financial accountability, they provide little assurance about matters such as whether:

- An entity spends its money efficiently;
- It needs as much money as it uses; and
- It effectively accomplishes the purpose for which the money was appropriated.

The purpose of this book is to provide the means for addressing such issues. It provides the background for and explanation of the expanded concept of accountability in government. Most important, it provides a practical approach for auditing government entities in the current environment.

Standards of Government Auditing

In 1972, the Comptroller General of the United States issued a publication, entitled *Standards for Audit of Governmental Organizations, Programs, Activities and Functions*. The objectives of this document were to:

- Stimulate federal, state, and local government organizations to improve the quality of their auditing functions;
- Improve control over government entities; and
- Facilitate the evaluation of government entities.

These standards are applicable to audits of all government organizations, programs, activities, and functions, whether performed by internal auditors employed by federal, state, or local governments, independent public accountants, or others. The standards are also

Figure 1-3

FEDERAL—BUDGET RECEIPTS BY SOURCE AND OUTLAYS BY FUNCTION, 1970–1977

(In Billions of Dollars)

Description	Actual						Estimate	
	1970	1971	1972	1973	1974	1975	1976	1977
RECEIPTS BY SOURCE								
Individual income taxes	90.4	86.2	94.7	103.2	119.0	122.4	130.8	153.6
Corporation income taxes	32.8	26.8	32.2	36.2	38.6	40.6	40.1	49.5
Social insurance taxes and contributions	45.3	48.6	53.9	64.5	76.8	86.4	92.6	113.1
Excise taxes	15.7	16.6	15.5	16.3	16.8	16.6	16.9	17.8
Estate and gift taxes	3.6	3.7	5.4	4.9	5.0	4.6	5.1	5.8
Customs duties	2.4	2.6	3.3	3.2	3.3	3.7	3.8	4.3
Miscellaneous receipts	3.4	3.9	3.6	3.9	5.4	6.7	8.3	7.2
Total receipts	**193.7**	**188.4**	**208.6**	**232.2**	**264.9**	**281.0**	**297.5**	**351.3**
OUTLAYS BY FUNCTION								
National defense[1]	79.3	76.8	77.4	75.1	78.6	86.6	92.8	101.1
International affairs	3.6	3.1	3.7	3.0	3.6	4.4	5.7	6.8
General science, space, and technology	4.5	4.2	4.2	4.0	4.0	4.0	4.3	4.5
Natural resources, environment, and energy	4.0	4.9	5.5	5.9	6.6	9.5	11.8	13.8
Agriculture	5.2	4.3	5.3	4.9	2.2	1.7	2.9	1.7
Commerce and transportation	9.1	10.4	10.6	9.9	13.1	16.0	17.8	16.5
Community and regional development	3.2	3.6	4.3	5.5	4.9	4.4	5.8	5.5
Education, training, employment, and social services	7.9	9.0	11.7	11.9	11.6	15.2	18.9	16.6
Health	13.1	14.7	17.5	18.8	22.1	27.6	32.1	34.4
Income security	43.1	55.4	63.9	73.0	84.4	108.6	128.5	137.1
Veterans benefits and services	8.7	9.8	10.7	12.0	13.4	16.6	19.0	17.2
Law enforcement and justice	1.0	1.3	1.6	2.1	2.5	2.9	3.4	3.4
General government	1.9	2.2	2.5	2.7	3.3	3.1	3.5	3.4
Revenue sharing and general purpose fiscal assistance	.5	.5	.5	7.2	6.7	7.0	7.2	7.4
Interest	18.3	19.6	20.6	22.8	28.1	31.0	34.8	41.3
Allowances[2]	......	......	......	......	......	......	.2	2.3
Undistributed offsetting receipts	−6.6	−8.4	−8.1	−12.3	−16.7	−14.1	−15.2	−18.8
Total outlays	**196.6**	**211.4**	**231.9**	**246.5**	**268.4**	**324.6**	**373.5**	**394.2**

[1] Includes civilian and military pay raises for the Department of Defense.
[2] Includes allowances for civilian agency pay raises and contingencies for relatively uncontrollable programs and other requirements.

SOURCE: Office of Management and Budget, *United States Budget in Brief—Fiscal Year 1977*, 57 (U.S. Government Printing Office 1976).

applicable to internal audits and audits of contractors, grantees, and other external organizations.[2]

The GAO standards (see Appendix I: GAO Standards) conform to the generally accepted auditing standards of the American Institute of Certified Public Accountants for financial audits, but they go much further in their definition of auditing by:

- Including legal compliance within the scope of financial auditing; and
- Expanding the definition of auditing to include two additional elements or levels—efficiency and economy, and program results.

Not only do the standards recognize the value of and need for financial audits, they also recognize that audits of a broader scope are required to meet the needs of many users of government reports. In addition to expanding the audit scope, the standards call for the inclusion of recommendations for improvement in written audit reports.

Levels of Audit

Although the GAO standards do not prescribe specific methods and procedures to be used, they indicate audit objectives by separating audits into three distinct levels.

Level I—Financial and Compliance

> Level I. *Financial and compliance*—determines (a) whether financial operations are properly conducted, (b) whether the financial reports of an audited entity are presented fairly, and (c) whether the entity has complied with applicable laws and regulations.[3]

Basically, the purpose of the financial component of a Level I audit is to determine whether the financial statements of a government entity present fairly its financial position and results of operations in conformity with generally accepted accounting principles ap-

---

[2] U.S. General Accounting Office, *Standards for Audit of Governmental Organizations, Programs, Activities and Functions* 1 (U.S. Government Printing Office 1972).

[3] *Id.* at 2.

Figure 1-4

THE FEDERAL BUDGET DOLLAR

(Fiscal Year 1977 Estimate)

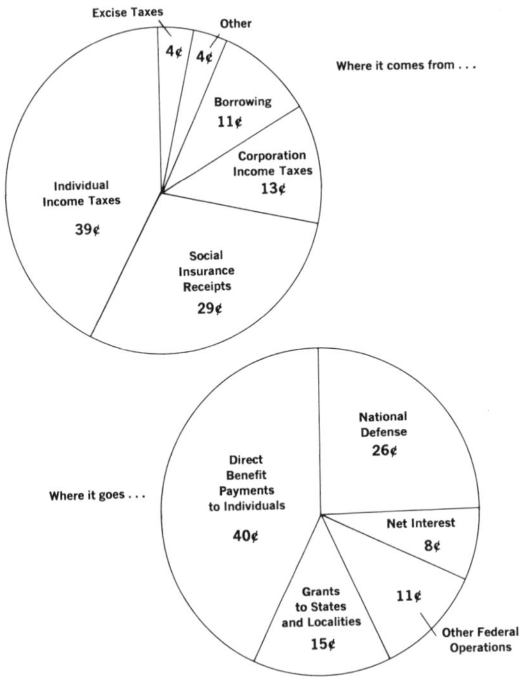

SOURCE: Office of Management and Budget, *United States Budget in Brief–Fiscal Year 1977,* inner cover (U.S. Government Printing Office 1976).

plied on a basis consistent with that of the preceding year. Obviously, this aspect closely parallels a financial audit in the private sector. The purpose of the compliance segment of Level I is to determine whether the entity has acted in accordance with applicable laws, regulations, policies, and procedures in handling its finances.

The AICPA's Committee on Relations With the General Accounting Office states the following in its publication, *Auditing Standards Established by the GAO—Their Meaning and Significance for CPAs:*

> Reviews of compliance with laws and regulations are not new to the accounting profession in that the independent accountant always has had to consider the financial effect of noncompliance on financial statements. Compliance reviews in nonfinancial

areas will require extensive data gathering and may be time-consuming and expensive. However, a substantial part of this can be done by the organization requesting the audit, thus limiting the auditor's involvement to the exercise of professional judgment in reviewing data accumulated. GAO states:

> "For many programs that are federally assisted, it would be neither practical nor economical to have every auditor at every level of government do his own background research on the laws, regulations, objectives, and goals of his segment of the program. Therefore, to provide the auditor with the necessary background information and to guide his judgment in the application of the accompanying standards, Federal or State agencies that request state, local, or other levels to make audits are expected to prepare broad, comprehensive audit instructions, tailored to particular programs or program areas.
>
> "The content of such audit guidance should include a digest of, or as a minimum, citations to applicable statutes, regulations, instructions, manuals, grant agreements, and other program documents; identification of specific audit objectives and reporting requirements in terms of matters of primary interest in such areas as program compliance, economy, and effectiveness; and other audit guidelines covering specific areas in which the auditor is expected to perform."

Several audit guides issued by governmental agencies currently require compliance reports in addition to reports on financial presentations. If the criteria for making such reviews have been incorporated in the audit guides, the report based upon such a review should conform to the recommendations contained in Section 641 of Statement on Auditing Standards No. 1 and the related interpretation thereof. In the absence of established criteria, it will be extremely difficult for an independent public accountant to render a report on compliance which does not include a disclaimer concerning the entity's overall compliance with appropriate laws, rules, and regulations.[4]

This book does not deal with Level I auditing, which, in the authors' view, has been addressed by a multitude of publications. (See Appendix II for Federal Audit Guides; see also the Bibliography.)

---

[4] Committee on Relations With the General Accounting Office, *Auditing Standards Established by the GAO—Their Meaning and Significance for CPAs* 5–6 (American Institute of Certified Public Accountants 1973).

Level II—Economy and Efficiency

> Level II. *Economy and efficiency*—determines whether the entity is managing or utilizing its resources (personnel, property, space, and so forth) in an economical and efficient manner and the causes of any inefficiencies or uneconomical practices, including inadequacies in management information systems, administrative procedures, or organizational structure.[5]

The purpose of a Level II audit is to identify ways to improve operations and reduce cost. Specifically, audits of efficiency and economy delve into such matters as the following:

> - Need for goods or services provided or procured.
> - Reasonableness of costs incurred or expenditures made.
> - Adequacy of safeguards over and care of resources acquired.
> - Proper utilization of resources.
> - Adequacy of revenue received for goods or services sold.
>
> Such matters are pursued primarily from the standpoint of improvements needed—usually by identifying avoidable costs or waste, possibilities for increased revenues, and alternative procedures for producing similar results at lower costs or better results at the same or lower costs.[6]

This level of government audit closely resembles the "operational controls review" performed in the commercial environment as an extension of a financial audit.[7] Obviously the identification of uneconomical practices and inefficiencies is as applicable to a government entity as it is to a commercial organization.

Level III—Program Results

> Level III. *Program results*—determines whether the desired results or benefits are being achieved, whether the objectives established by the legislature or other authorizing body are be-

---

[5] *Id.* at 2.

[6] U.S. General Accounting Office, *Answers to Frequently Asked Questions* 13 (U.S. Government Printing Office 1973).

[7] "Operational controls review" is Coopers & Lybrand's term for what is commonly referred to as "operational" or "management" auditing. This audit approach is described more fully in a booklet, *Auditing by Perception,* which may be obtained by writing the Coopers & Lybrand *Newsletter,* P.O. Box 682, Times Square Station, New York, N.Y. 10036.

ing met, and whether the agency has considered alternatives which might yield desired results at a lower cost.[8]

In a Level III audit, questions such as the following are asked:

- How successful is the program in accomplishing its intended results?
- Is the program succeeding within the cost framework originally anticipated?
- Are costs commensurate with benefits achieved?
- Have alternative programs or procedures been examined for their potential for achieving objectives with greater economy and efficiency?

The potential scope of a government audit is illustrated in Figure 1-5. The ideal audit encompasses all three levels. In practice, however, audits of each level may be performed separately. The GAO's standards state:

> In determining the scope for a particular audit, responsible officials should give consideration to the needs of the potential users of the results of the audit.
>
> This standard places on officials who authorize and prescribe the scope of governmental audits the responsibility for providing for audit work that is broad enough to fulfill the needs of all potential users of the results of such audits. The standard is not intended to prevent such officials from authorizing specific assignments of parts of the total scope of the audit work required by the standard or from authorizing special audits, nor is it intended to prevent auditors from performing such audits. However, those responsible for authorizing governmental audits are charged with the knowledge that, for most governmental programs, their full responsibility for obtaining audit work is not discharged unless the full scope of audit work set forth in the standard is performed.[9]

Where both Level II and Level III audits are to be performed, their planning should be carefully coordinated:

> Level II and Level III audits may be likened to a pyramid. Level II represents the base of the pyramid and Level III the apex. The auditor should start at the top of the pyramid; he

---

[8] *Standards for Audit of Governmental Organizations, Programs, Activities and Functions,* note 2 *supra,* at 2.

[9] *Id.* at 10.

Figure 1-5

THE POTENTIAL SCOPE OF A GOVERNMENTAL AUDIT

	COMPREHENSIVE AUDITS			
	FISCAL (FINANCIAL AND COMPLIANCE) AUDITS		PERFORMANCE OR OPERATIONAL AUDITS	
	FINANCIAL	COMPLIANCE	MANAGERIAL (ECONOMY AND EFFICIENCY)	PROGRAM RESULTS (EFFECTIVENESS)
Audit Focus or Thrust	Traditional	Legality Compliance With Regulation, Policies, Procedures, etc.	Economic Acquisition and Efficient Use of Material and Human Resources	Mission Accomplished and/or Progress Toward Objectives
	Financial Statements	External Constraints Internal Constraints	Personnel, Facilities, and Materials · Acquisition · Control · Utilization	Programs or Activities
			Management Representation: · May be made explicitly · May be implied	Performance Standards: · May exist · May be inferred · May be unavailable
Orientation of Audit Effort and Report	PAST	PRESENT AND FUTURE		
	OPINION(S)	JUDGMENTS, CONCLUSIONS, AND RECOMMENDATIONS		

SOURCE: Lynn & Freeman, *Fund Accounting—Theory and Practice* 773 (Prentice-Hall, Inc. 1974).

> should consider the entity's objectives in evaluating the overall criteria or goals. The auditor can work from the overall goals downward to detailed objectives and measurement criteria, many of which involve preferred practices. Alternatively, the auditor can move up from the base to evaluate the entity's practices in terms of preferred practices. He would then be in a position to draw conclusions about the entity's objectives. Stated differently, the deductive reasoning process which is applied to draw conclusions on the basis of details is complementary to the inductive process which explodes the mission goals into its components. Thus, Level II and Level III tend to be synergistic.[10]

Careful coordination is important for two reasons:

- The application of Level II audit procedures might provide insight to program effectiveness or facilitate the formulation of measurement standards.
- The application of Level III audit procedures can also serve as a measure of efficiency and economy.

It is not intended to suggest that audit procedures for Levels II and III must be combined. In some cases, Level III evaluations may be totally outside the areas examined in Level II procedures. Without advance clarification of the audited agency's objectives and the auditor's information needs, delays and repetition in audit performance may occur.

It is also important to recognize that the success an entity has in achieving its program objectives may be quite independent of how efficiently and economically it conducts its operations. Thus, an entity may be efficient and economical in spending its funds and yet fail to fulfill its objective.

For example, consider the case of a city administering the federal food-stamp program under state auspices. The city may dispense appropriated funds efficiently and economically to a limited number of eligibles and still fail to fulfill the program's overall objective, which is to provide food stamps to all the citizens within the jurisdiction who are eligible to receive them.

Conversely, a program may succeed in fulfilling its objective but be efficiently and/or uneconomically administered. For example,

---

[10] Pomeranz, "Evaluating the Results of Government Programs," address to Association of Government Accountants, Washington, D.C., Nov. 19, 1975.

a medicare program may be effective in providing health-care services to the elderly but may do so with low program efficiency and economy.

Distinguishing efficiency and economy from program effectiveness is important: Efficiency and economy can be audited by highly specific, detailed, and structured examinations, while program effectiveness involves subjective judgments.

With respect to Level II and Level III audits, distinctions may also be made between the techniques for recognizing a deficiency, documenting its impact on operations, and motivating improvement. A Level II reviewer may, using the techniques discussed in this book, arrive at a finding that identifies the problem and the inherent solution. In contrast, the Level III reviewer may well have no solution for a deficiency in program effectiveness. Consider again the hypothetical instance of the city's administration of the federal food stamp program. Suppose that (1) the success of the program was measured by the standard of having a high ratio of eligible citizens enrolled, and (2) the city failed miserably in meeting this standard. The failure may not be the city's responsibility. The state may be partially responsible because it did not provide a modus operandi for reaching and motivating eligible individuals to enroll. The reviewer would not be expected to propose such a modus operandi.

The State of the Art

Despite the benefits that can result from audits of efficiency and economy and program effectiveness, Level II and Level III audits are not widely performed. A study evaluating audit officials in fifteen states and ten federal agencies conducted by the GAO in 1974 indicated that many federal and state agency auditors felt limited in the resources they could allocate to Level II and Level III audits. State auditors in particular reported they would devote considerably more resources to Level II and III audits if they had adequate staff and legal authority.

From responses to an inquiry on how state auditors have applied audit resources in the past and how they would apply them in the future, the GAO obtained the following information [11]:

---

[11] U.S. General Accounting Office, *Increased Intergovernmental Cooperation Needed for More Effective, Less Costly Auditing of Government Programs* 17–19 (U.S. Government Printing Office).

	Percent of Resources	
	Past	*Future*
Financial and compliance	89	56
Efficiency and economy	8	23
Program results	3	21
	100	100

Both federal and state auditors told the GAO that, to expand the scope of their audits, they needed solutions to several problems, including the following:

1. The need for additional staff.

   Only 25 percent of the responding state auditors reported they had adequate funds and staff to expand the scope of their audits. Many state auditors reported that tight budgets made it difficult to obtain any fund increase for their organizations . . . According to 12 state auditors, legal requirements to make financial audits generally took all their available resources. Several state auditors reported they were from 2 to 5 years behind on financial and compliance audits.

   Both federal and state auditors anticipated a need for expertise in disciplines other than accounting.

2. Need for specific program objectives.

   To audit program results, the auditor must consider the relevance and validity of the criteria used by the audited entity to measure achievement of program results. [This requires entities to increase emphasis on the establishment of specific program objectives.]

The Comptroller General, in a message to Congress, has recognized the increasing number of instances in which legislation provides for evaluating program effectiveness as indicative of this interest but noted that more legislative emphasis on this area is needed.

3. The need for additional staff training.

   Both state and federal audit managers reported that making broad-scope audits as prescribed in the standards for audits of government programs was inhibited by the need for staff training. State auditors believed that, to perform more efficiency and economy and program results reviews, they would need additional staff training or experience.[12]

[12] *Id.*

Response by the Profession

While the GAO has provided new standards for what a government audit should accomplish, the task of implementing these standards is the responsibility of the accounting profession as a whole.

As shown in Figure 1-6, the profession has responded to this need. The authors have further responded through their participation in monographs, such as *Auditing by Perception* [13] and *The Expanded Scope of Government Auditing*.[14] As part of this commitment, a recently conducted joint study by Coopers & Lybrand and the University of Michigan, *Financial Disclosure Practices of the American Cities: A Public Report,* is available in booklet form.[15]

Auditing in the Public Sector is designed to provide a practical approach for performing Level II and III audits. The techniques presented can be used by government auditors at federal, state, or local levels, as well as by independent public accountants. Government leaders can use the techniques to identify areas requiring management attention and corrective action.

Chapter 2 deals with a technique for efficiency and economy audits. Chapter 3 provides a technique for program results audits.

The predominance in this book of Level II material over Level III material should not be construed as an indication of the importance the authors give the two areas. The disproportion is a result of the fact that examining efficiency and economy is more dependent upon observation of minute operational details. In some situations, improvements which can be achieved as a result of a Level III audit may be far greater than those achieved as a result of a Level II audit.

---

[13] Pomeranz, *Auditing by Perception* (Coopers & Lybrand 1973).

[14] Cancellieri & Enstrom, *The Expanded Scope of Government Auditing* (Coopers & Lybrand 1976). A copy of this booklet may be obtained by writing the Coopers & Lybrand *Newsletter,* P.O. Box 682, Times Square Station, New York, N.Y. 10036.

[15] *Id.* at 15.

Figure 1-6

RECENT PUBLICATIONS EXPLAINING AND SUPPLEMENTING THE GAO STANDARDS

GAO:

- *What GAO Is Doing to Improve Governmental Auditing Standards*
- *Auditors—Agents for Good Government*
- *Case Study—Illinois' Use of Public Accountants for Auditing State Activities*
- *Examples of Findings From Governmental Audits*
- *Questions and Answers on the Standards for Audit of Governmental Organizations, Programs, Activities and Functions*
- *Illustrative Report Prepared in Accordance with GAO Audit Standards*
- *Air Pollution Control Program, Sassafras County, Maryland*
- *Using Auditing to Improve Efficiency and Economy*
- *Case Study—How Auditors Develop Findings—Increasing the Productivity of City Water Meter Readers*
- *Audit Guidelines for Audits of Financial Operations of Federally Assisted Programs (Exposure Draft)*

AICPA:

- *Auditing Standards Established by the GAO—Their Meaning and Significance for CPAs*
- *Industry Audit Guide—Audits of State and Local Governmental Units*
- *Federal Financial Management: Accounting and Auditing Practices*
- *Guidelines for Participation in Government Audit Engagements to Evaluate Economy, Efficiency and Program Results (Exposure Draft)*

CHAPTER 2

Efficiency and Economy Audits–Concepts, Methods, and Procedures

As discussed in Chapter 1, the purpose of an efficiency and economy audit (Level II) is to determine whether a government entity is managing or utilizing its resources (personnel, property, space, and so forth) in an economical and efficient manner and, if not, to determine the impact inefficiencies or uneconomical practices have on operations. Efficiency and economy audits are performed primarily to assist management in improving future operations. By identifying costly deficiencies, such as antiquated budgeting systems and the lack of modern management methods for determining priorities and for planning and controlling operations, efficiency and economy audits often result in significant cost reductions.

Although the evaluation of an entity in terms of efficiency and economy is accomplished at the same audit level, the terms are not synonymous. The evaluation of economy requires an appraisal of management performance from a least-cost point of view, while the evaluation of efficiency involves an analysis of the relationship between benefits attained and costs incurred. Consider, for example, an entity that limits the amount of capital it invests in inventory. This entity is apparently acting economically in terms of the time value of money. If, however, the lack of inventory results in a delay in production, that entity's resources have not been managed efficiently.

The distinction between financial audits and efficiency and economy audits is illustrated in the following example:

> An entity paid a wide range of prices for lubricants, which were used in considerable quantity. The higher priced lubricants, costing 40 percent to 50 percent more than the others, contained additives, which were purported to be the source of special properties needed for certain applications. In ordinary financial auditing, the auditors would have been concerned with the pricing of the inventory and with the appropriateness of the supports for disbursements. An efficiency and economy audit, however, required testing the validity of the assumptions on which the higher prices rested. Accordingly, maintenance personnel were asked to draw up technical and performance specifications for lubricants used on particular jobs. When this was done, it became clear that the additives had no value for most of the uses to which they were put.[1]

Operational Controls Review

One approach to the conduct of an efficiency and economy audit involves an audit technique called an "operational controls review." As applied to a government entity, an operational controls review has six steps:

- Obtaining a working knowledge of the entity's purpose, systems, and operations;
- Identifying areas where efficiency and economy might be improved;
- Evaluating management practices in comparison with "preferred practices";
- Assessing departures from preferred practices;
- Formulating possible improvements and cost reductions; and
- Preparing a management letter describing findings and possible recommendations.

---

[1] Pomeranz, *Auditing by Perception* 6 (Coopers & Lybrand 1973).

Obtaining Working Knowledge of the Entity—Identifying Areas for Improvement

A good working knowledge of an entity's purpose, systems, and operations is a prerequisite to performing an efficiency and economy audit. To obtain this knowledge, the auditor should meet with key officials and employees, review physical operations, and review financial statements, budgets, policy and procedures manuals, and consultants' reports. (See Figure 2-1.) As this background and understanding are obtained, the auditor, using common sense and judgment, can focus on the areas having the greatest cost-reduction potential (for example, a department with appropriations of $1 million normally would have more potential for cost reduction than one with a $10,000 appropriation).

One indication of a cost reduction potential is an absence of supervisory controls. Supervisory controls provide the means for monitoring and correcting weaknesses. Without adequate supervision, even the best system of controls risks becoming undependable. Certain procedures or steps in the systems and controls may be left undone or unattended, or bypassed, or exceptions may be allowed to accumulate.

Lack of supervisory controls may be signaled by problems, such as an inordinate number of errors, backlogs, or instances of prescribed procedures that are not followed. If such problems proliferate and it appears that supervisory personnel are overly involved with the processing of details or lack adequate knowledge of their areas of responsibility, an auditor is on notice that he probably may not be able to rely on the continuity of other controls, no matter how well-designed.[2]

Preferred Practices

The next step—the heart of the operational controls review—is the comparison of the entity's operating or management practices with "preferred practices." A preferred practice is one that has been found successful (or a criterion that has been found optimal) through experience with, and study of, many entities over a period of years.

---

[2] Defliese, Johnson & Macleod, *Montgomery's Auditing* 74–75 (9th ed., Ronald Press Co. 1975).

Figure 2-1

BACKGROUND INFORMATION

Before beginning any audit (Level I, II, or III), the auditor should obtain and review the following background information:

(1) Obtain the most current financial statements for all funds.

(2) With the assistance of the entity's personnel, describe briefly the principal purpose of the entity, including, if practicable, estimates of the area and/or population it serves; the measure of value of the services it dispenses and/or its assets; and its resources. ....

....

....

(3) With the assistance of entity officials, summarize controlling legislation and any relevant regulatory requirements relating to the entity.

....

....

(4) Obtain a listing showing the key personnel of the entity by position level and work location.

Name	*Position*	*Location*
....	....	....
....	....	....
....	....	....

(5) Obtain an analysis, by major categories, of budgeted and actual results for the current and two prior years, and explanations for significant variances.

	Current Year			*Prior Year*			*Prior Year*		
Budget Categories	*Actual*	*Budget*	*Variance*	*Actual*	*Budget*	*Variance*	*Actual*	*Budget*	*Variance*
......	......	......	.....	......	......	.....	......	......	.....
......	......	......	.....	......	......	.....	......	......	.....
......	......	......	.....	......	......	.....	......	......	.....

Reason for variances: ....

....

....

(6) List all locations through which the entity operates.

Location	*Department or Division*	*No. of Employees*	*Activity*	*Value of Assets*
....	....	....	....	$...........
....	....	....	....	....
....	....	....	....	....
TOTAL		______		$ ______

(7) Obtain data on the number and cost of personnel authorized and employed.

Department or Division	*Number* *Authorized*	*Number* *Employed*	*Total Cost*
....	....	....	$............
....	....	....	....
....	....	....	....
TOTAL	______	______	$ ______

The failure to adhere to a preferred practice is an indication that resources may be, or at least may have been, wasted or inefficiently used.

Management actions are normally based on predetermined standards, rules, or practices. The effects of management actions (or inactions) are results which can be reviewed in terms of the favorable or unfavorable effect the actions have on operations. In an optimum situation, management actions are based on preferred practices. In any situation, preferred practices provide a basis for evaluating management actions. They represent a standard against which to be measured.

When a preferred practice question is answered "yes," the auditor must inspect evidence to corroborate the answer. The extent of evidence gathering, and subsequent supervisory review, should be proportionate to the significance of the control involved. The person performing the work should document the nature and source of all the evidence examined.

Within this frame of reference, we have developed a series of eight government-oriented operational controls questionnaires. The questionnaires serve as guides or "memory joggers" in the measurement of an entity's conformity to preferred practices. Although only selected areas are dealt with in the questionnaires, it should be remembered that an operational controls review can be applied to virtually any aspect of government operations.

The questionnaires have been prepared on the basis of functions, or areas of responsibility. Consequently, individual sections of the questionnaires may need to be assembled into a departmental program that crosses functional lines. Where the auditor encounters functional areas not covered in this book, he should construct his own approach. Appropriate questions should be selected from the operational controls questionnaires or developed to meet the needs of unique situations. (Additional examples of cost reduction opportunities are described in Appendices IV and V.)

The questionnaires, which appear in Chapters 5 to 12, provide preferred practice questions for the following areas:

- Internal audit;
- Budget management;
- Personnel;
- Cash management;
- Procurement;

- Public works;
- Maintenance; and
- Grant management.

Departures From Preferred Practices

When a preferred practice question is answered "no," the next step is to assess the significance of the deficiency. This can be done by systematically analyzing what can be described as the significant effects of the failure to follow a practice that is considered preferred. For example, if a government entity has no inventory stocking system for repeatedly used items, an analysis would be made to determine whether premium prices have been incurred for rush deliveries or whether operations have been impaired.

Formulating Possible Improvements and Cost Reductions—Dollarization

The process of expressing the effect of an operational controls deficiency in terms of money is called "dollarization." Basically, this technique enables a presentation of the cost of resources wasted through failure to adhere to a preferred practice. Dollarization also serves to quantify in dollar terms the magnitude of potential opportunities and/or alternatives.

Frequently, noncompliance with preferred practices is obvious, yet no corrective action is initiated until dollarization brings into focus the full impact of the delinquency. More commonly, management remains unaware of or disregards preferred practices, knowing only that the undesirable conditions exist.

The mechanics of various dollarization procedures are presented in Chapter 4. In the operational controls questionnaires, the preferred practice questions that generally should be considered for dollarization have been referenced to specific dollarization procedures in Chapter 4. It should be remembered, however, that the absence of such reference does not preclude the application of dollarization techniques in a given situation. The auditor should in all instances be aware of the impact, whether cost or other, of operational controls weaknesses. The inability to dollarize should not deter the auditor from reporting operational controls weaknesses to management.

Management Letter

Once an auditor has identified a deviation from a preferred practice and has quantified its effects on operations, he should present the problem to those persons with the authority to institute corrective actions. As discussed in Chapter 4, the communication of all weaknesses (Levels I, II, and III—dollarized and nondollarized) is generally made in the form of a management letter. If the auditor has obtained sufficient information as to why a preferred practice was not followed and he has determined that the cost/benefit relationship of instituting change is favorable, he might make a direct recommendation for remedial action in the management letter. If such information is not readily available to the auditor, he should describe the deficiency and suggest that the reason for not following the preferred practice be pursued and that a study of the cost versus benefit of using the preferred practice (or variation thereof) be performed.

All segments of an operational controls review should be adequately documented. The understanding of the entity's procedures, systems, and operations should be recorded, usually by means of flowcharts. A written "record of noncompliance with preferred practices" (for example, Figure 2-2) should be maintained. This record should document the nature of any deficiencies and the values involved. If an efficiency and economy audit is performed in conjunction with a financial audit, the auditor should ascertain that his audit program gives adequate consideration to all weaknesses identified in the "record of noncompliance with preferred practices."

Operational Controls Review in Action

To illustrate the use of the operational controls review technique, we will demonstrate the steps an auditor should take in answering a sample question. We have chosen the following preferred practice question from Chapter 9 as our example. Essentially, the same logic would be used in answering any preferred practice question.

In actually answering this question, the auditor would not necessarily encounter the detail of this illustration. Drawing on his past experience and his knowledge of the entity being reviewed, the auditor, in coordination with entity officials, would be able to evaluate rapidly whether or not a preferred practice is being adhered to.

Figure 2-2

RECORD OF NONCOMPLIANCE WITH PREFERRED PRACTICES

ENTITY: ....

Section: .... Sheet .... of ....

Ref.	*Discussed With Entity Officials*	*Nature of Weakness and Dollarized Effect on Financial Statements and/or on Efficiency of Operations*	*Could Material Error Arise?*		*Effect on Nature, Extent, and/or* Timing of Audit Procedures*		*Included in Management Letter?*		*Decisions/Actions of Entity Officials*
			Yes/No	*Justification*	*Audit Program Reference*	*Nature of Amendment Required*	*Yes/No*	*Date*	
(1)	*(2)*	*(3)*	*(4)*	*(5)*	*(6)*	*(7)*	*(8)*	*(9)*	*(10)*

* Applicable only if Level I audit is performed.

Does the purchasing agent actively solicit competitive bids from vendors:

(1) When required by law?

(2) When not required by law, but suggested by good business practice?

The answer is generally obtained by inspecting an entity's vendor and/or bid files. Solicitation of bids may not be appropriate in all situations; hence, the auditor must carefully evaluate the facts in each case, giving due consideration to the other shopping or negotiating techniques used by the entity. But if bids are not solicited in a situation in which bidding appears to be desirable (considering the commodities, markets, and services involved), there may be no incentive for vendors to compete. As a result, prices may be higher and quality, delivery, and service will suffer.

If the Answer Is "No"

When the auditor receives a "no" answer, the question should be considered for dollarization. (See Chapter 4, Dollarization Procedures 2: Bidding; and 19: Noncompetitive Buying.)

The auditor should seek an explanation of the deficiency from the entity personnel. The entity may offer at least two valid explanations for not seeking bids. (Situations (1) and (2).) Or the entity may have no explanation. (Situation (3).) With respect to each of the situations, we will discuss the facts, the action to be taken, and, at times, the nature of the management letter comment.

Situation (1)—Single Vendor

- *Comment:* Entity officials explain that they are buying a unique product protected by patents and obtainable from one vendor only.
- *Action:* The source of this information should be documented whenever possible, and the information should be considered for inclusion in a management letter.
- *Advice for writing the management letter comment:* If an entity is purchasing a product for which there is one source, the auditor should indicate the volume of purchases and advise the entity to consider substitute products to protect

against interruptions if the one source were to be eliminated.

Situation (2)—Product Is Competitively Priced

- *Comment:* The entity asserts that the product is competitively priced, i.e., that all vendors charge the same price.
- *Action:* When competitively priced purchases are significant, the auditor should question entity officials as to any special services rendered by the vendors. Such services may include service calls, warehousing, and delivery.
- *Advice for writing the management letter comment:* If the auditor, with the assistance of entity officials or by referring to bids obtained from the vendors, can price the special services, he can dollarize his findings.

Situation (3)—No Explanation

- *Comment:* Here, the entity gives no explanation for not seeking bids.
- *Action/advice for writing the management letter comment:* The auditor should compare prices for similar materials or compare prices actually paid to price lists of other vendors. The auditor should dollarize the cost of the deficiency and report his findings in the management letter.

If the Answer Is "Maybe"

Here, the auditor has the problem of determining which articles are purchased through bidding and which are not. In general, the distinction will arise by product line. Entity officials should be in a position to estimate the buying volume per product line; the auditor will then be able to break down a "maybe" answer into "yes" or "no" elements.

If the Answer Is "Yes"

When an auditor receives a "yes" answer, he must apply a healthy measure of skepticism, seek evidence whenever possible, consider the materiality of each transaction, and apply the preferred practice technique set forth in detail in this chapter. In our example, the auditor would be concerned with an evaluation of the competitive process which would involve questions such as: Are bids really competitive? How often are bids sought?

Are Bids Really Competitive?

- *Comment:* In order to be competitive, a minimum of three bids should be solicited. Thus, bids from only two vendors are considered unsatisfactory.
- *Action/advice for writing the management letter comment:* The auditor should evaluate a sample of bids to determine for how many transactions three or more bids were obtained, how many transactions two bids were obtained, how many transactions one bid was obtained, and how many transactions no bids at all were obtained.

How Often Are Bids Sought?

- *Comment:* Bids are usually obtained either for specific transactions or on a periodic basis. Bids will generally be waived either on grounds of materiality or because of emergency needs. (Situations (1), (2), (3), and (4).)

Situation (1)—Bids for Specific Transactions

- *Action:* The auditor documents the number of bids obtained for a series of specific transactions. He is cautious with respect to transactions that tend to be immaterial, but for which three or more bids are obtained. Excessive bidding activity reflects a misguided clerical effort or, worse, an attempt to create the appearance of activity. To document this problem, count the number of bids obtained for transactions of various dollar sizes.

Situation (2)—Periodic Submission of Bids

- *Action:* The auditor must ascertain that controls exist to prevent a bidder that performed unsatisfactorily in the past from continuing to bid. The auditor should examine contracts at their expiration dates (usually contracts should not be longer than one year) and determine that rebidding routines are applied. Documentation here involves a determination of how long particular contracts were in effect prior to rebidding.

Situation (3)—Bids Waived for Immateriality

- *Action:* Where bids are waived for immateriality, the auditor needs to use his common sense to see whether a reasonable determination has been made, subject to any pertinent entity procedures.

Situation (4)—Bids Waived for Emergencies

- *Action:* For bids waived for emergencies, the auditor should establish that valid emergencies existed. For example, many municipalities deal with snow removal and require chemicals in connection with this activity. It is not appropriate for a municipality to waive bidding on the procurement of snow removal chemicals. When an auditor encounters this problem, he should be alert to the possibility that emergency procurement is used as an excuse to circumvent bidding requirements. Documentation here simply consists of a list of "emergency" procurements, together with the volumes involved.

Efficiency and Economy Experiences

The following examples illustrate efficiency and economy findings.

Example 1

During an audit of a state's department of education (DOE), the auditors observed that the purchasing policies specified that one of the departmental purchasing office's duties was to "fix standards of quality and quantity and develop standard specifications after consultation with the proper authorities." There were no standards, however, for educational equipment. In their absence, individual schools and offices bought their own equipment on the basis of individual preferences as to make and model. Consider, for example, the following sample of equipment purchases made by thirty schools and their district office:

Equipment Description	*No. of Schools & Offices Making Purchases*	*Quantity Purchased*	*Cost*	*No. of Makes & Models Purchased*
Tape recorders:				
Cassette	30	300	$15,000	20
Reel to Reel	10	15	2,500	5
Projectors:				
Movie	30	40	20,000	15
Film/slide	15	40	5,000	15
Slide	10	15	2,000	14
Overhead	15	35	6,500	10
Typewriters	15	75	19,000	12
Television sets	5	25	3,000	3
Phonographs	15	60	5,500	15
Duplicators	15	25	20,000	12
Cameras	5	15	1,300	10

As shown in the table, numerous makes and models of each kind of equipment were purchased. The most extreme example is the purchase of fifteen slide projectors, which represent fourteen different makes and models. The auditors recognized that variations in the makes and models purchased would necessarily occur, to some degree, because of differences in equipment demands. Accommodating individual preferences and needs in equipment purchases, however, should be balanced against the economics of that practice.

With the expanding use of educational equipment, it was evident that standardization was essential. Standardization makes it possible to consolidate equipment purchases and buy in bulk. In one year, this DOE's equipment purchases totaled approximately $2.3 million. Clearly, bulk purchases make favorable purchase discounts and bid prices feasible, thus reducing equipment costs.

Bulk purchases usually make it easier to get service contracts because bulk buying generally means fewer brands of equipment are bought; the DOE had been having difficulty in securing service contracts. In addition, many products are also sold with attached warranty service, or warranty availability, and the vendors frequently obligate themselves to perform inspections or adjustments as part of that service. It is desirable that performance of these services be monitored to assure their performance within a realistic period of time. Obviously, the monitoring would be facilitated if fewer and more qualified vendors were selected.

In this particular case, the auditors understood that vendors were generally reluctant to provide repair and maintenance service under all-inclusive service contracts, because of the wide range of equipment brands used by the schools. For the fiscal year ended in 1972, the DOE's expenditures for equipment repairs and maintenance were approximately $336,000, of which only $58,000 was covered by service contracts. While, in some instances, service contracts are more expensive than ad hoc repairs, the DOE would almost certainly benefit from the favorable prices for repairs under these contracts.

Bulk purchasing would also offer the DOE the opportunity to obtain time-price contracts. These allow the purchaser to buy required equipment over a period of time at the bid price established in the contract, provided that a specified minimum number of items are purchased. Thus, equipment can be replaced at convenient intervals within the contract period at a fixed price. The purchase of fewer brands could enable the department to determine equipment life on a more uniform basis, making it easier to plan equipment replacements.

The auditors recommended that the department of education develop standards for specifications so that it could (1) purchase school equipment in bulk (the auditors emphasized that the department should continue to press for the necessary information from the various school districts to enable the department to implement a volume purchasing program) and (2) secure repair and maintenance service contracts on a wider scale.[3]

Example 2

In several cities, auditors found that the automatic data processing (ADP) department was not adequately planning and scheduling operations, bringing about both excessive operating costs and deficiencies in meeting the information needs of user departments. For these particular cities, the auditors' recommendations included:

- Developing comprehensive long-range data processing plans that would encompass the requirements of each city depart-

---

[3] Cancellieri & Enstrom, *The Expanded Scope of Government Auditing* 9–11 (Coopers & Lybrand 1976).

ment, in terms of relative priorities, hardware and systems needs, and level of staff training and experience.

- Establishing control procedures to enable city councils to properly review and make informed decisions about carrying out ADP plans. These procedures would allow the councils to monitor progress against plans and to decide on the commitment of future funds.
- Developing hardware and software compatibility with neighboring government units to disperse the development costs and promote processing flexibility.
- Delegating the responsibility to the internal audit function for reviewing proposed new applications for cost effectiveness before implementation. Involvement during the development phase also helps to ensure that appropriate accounting and operational controls are built into the new systems, thereby preventing later costly revisions.[4]

Example 3

An examination of a county's financial statements revealed duplications of check receipt listings and delays in depositing these checks, thus curtailing the amount of cash available for investment.

The cash application division received certain cash collections, prepared lists of the checks received, and sent lists and checks to the cashier's office. The cashier's office held the checks while awaiting notification from the cash application division of the proper account to be credited. After the cash application division had checked out all the receipts on the list of checks, a second listing, showing the proper account identification, was dispatched to the cashier's office. The receipts were then posted and included with that day's deposits.

The auditors noticed that the elapsed time between preparation of the list of checks and their actual deposit ran from five to seven days; the average dollar amount of a day's mail receipts ranged from $55,000 to $65,000. Therefore, undeposited checks on hand at all times approximated $360,000. Had the county treasurer invested that money at current rates, the county coffers would have been enriched by about $26,000 in yearly interest income.

The auditors recommended that the cashier deposit the cash collection as soon as it was received from the cash application divi-

---

[4] *Id.* at 9.

sion so that the treasurer could invest the money immediately. If necessary, the revenue could be temporarily posted to a suspense account until the proper coding had been determined.[5]

Implementation

As is the case with any organizational innovation, the acceptance and support of the operational controls review/preferred practice technique by government leaders is the key to its successful implementation. This support and commitment must begin with the higher echelons of government and permeate every management level.

The use of the operational controls review technique can guide leaders in assessing their own practices in an objective manner with the aim of operating more economically, effectively, and efficiently.

Auditing by means of preferred practices is effective, but management by preferred practices is dynamic.

---

[5] *Id.* at 11–12.

CHAPTER 3

Program Results Audits–Concepts, Methods and Procedures

Although an efficiency and economy audit may shed some light on program effectiveness, additional measures are needed to determine if program or activity objectives are being met. This represents a significant expansion of the traditional audit scope; it is, in effect, a redefinition of the auditor's role in government.

As discussed in Chapter 1, progress in the performance of program results audits (Level III) has been slow. One of the reasons why program results audits have not been used more widely is discussed in the AICPA's *Auditing Standards Established by the GAO—Their Meaning and Significance for CPAs:*

> Reviewing and reporting on program results, or effectiveness, is on the leading edge of what has been done in auditing. The state of the art is such that little has been established for audi-

tors in the way of precedent, evaluation guidelines, or measurement criteria. . . .[1]

Although the basic purpose of a program results audit is straightforward—the determination of whether a program has achieved what it was created to achieve—in practice there are obstacles to performing this type of audit. Specifically, the problems are these:

- Clearly defined goals and objectives are not always present in a given situation.
- Even where goals are adequately described, they may not be formally promulgated by the implementing agency as goals intended to be fulfilled.
- Goals may be misinterpreted at subordinate levels.
- Even where goals are explicit at each level, acceptable measurement criteria may not exist or may not be regularly and systematically applied and evaluated.

To determine if a program is effective, results have to be measured against goals and objectives that have been clearly defined. Unless goals are well defined, it may not be practicable or even possible for the auditor to ascertain whether a program is accomplishing its desired results or to what extent. How, for instance, can an auditor measure the effectiveness of a program whose ultimate goal is curing disease? How can the effects of a program in which inaction is often the best course of action be measured? Poorly defined goals or objectives invite confusion as to what constitutes a particular program's effectiveness.

For the auditor to perform a meaningful review, standards of measurement are essential. It is not the auditor's job to independently establish goals and objectives if management fails to do so. Therefore, it is extremely important that the author reach an agreement with the responsible agency on what its goals and objectives are before the audit begins.

The Auditor's Role

It is important to recognize a significant distinction between financial audits and program effectiveness audits. In the former, the

[1] Committee on Relations With the General Accounting Office, *Auditing Standards Established by the GAO—Their Meaning and Significance for CPAs* 9 (American Institute of Certified Public Accountants 1973).

auditor attests to the fairness of financial information. In the latter, he does not attest to program effectiveness, but rather reports what he finds, with constructive recommendations where he deems them appropriate.

Merely to identify inadequately defined goals, or even to demonstrate that adequately defined goals are not being met, is a public service in itself. Much has been made in recent years of social programs that have met objectives poorly. At least some of these programs have been unsuccessful because they were beyond the state of the art. In such cases, the auditor can no more make remedial recommendations than can the program administrators or the legislative body that initiated the program. His findings are nonetheless valuable, however, because as program effectiveness audits become more widespread, responsible agencies will be able to distinguish between the programs that work and the programs that do not work.

The auditor's role in auditing program effectiveness (as well as in auditing efficiency and economy) is to assist managers by providing information helpful in monitoring operations and in future planning. While the program results audit may detect problems, it should not be relied upon to provide detailed solutions to those problems.

Before describing the technique developed for program results audits, a discussion of the history and benefits of this level of audit (Level III) is in order.

Management by Objectives

Program effectiveness has a strong affinity with a management technique called "management by objectives" (MBO), a technique developed by Peter F. Drucker.[2] Basically, MBO can be defined as the conscious direction, over a given period of time, as specific actions toward a predetermined goal or objective. The essential elements or stages of the MBO cycle are:

(1) The *definition* of organizational goals by management.
(2) The *delegation* of such goals down the hierarchy.
(3) The *agreement* by superiors and subordinates as to the subordinates' responsibilities in the direction of the established goals.

---

[2] Drucker, *The Practice of Management* (Harper & Row 1954).

(4) The *implementation* of such agreements.
(5) A *review* of results.

Graphically, the MBO cycle may be shown as in Figure 3-1.

Figure 3-1

THE MBO CYCLE

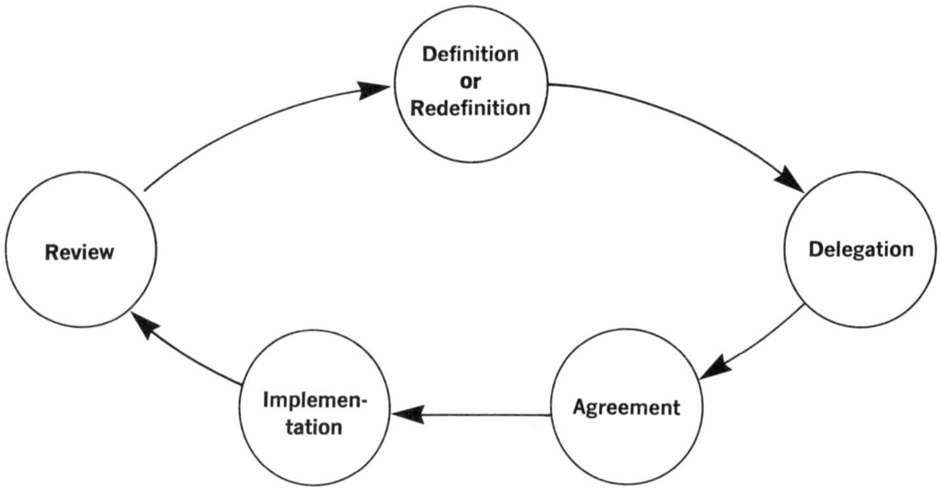

For purposes of understanding program effectiveness audits, it is useful to review each of the essential elements or stages of the MBO cycle.[3]

Stage 1—Definition

The establishment of objectives is the job of management. The objectives established should be specific and, where possible, measurable. They should be consistent with the social environment, and most important, they should be realistic and feasible.

In establishing objectives, care should be taken to:

- Define the objectives in writing;
- Define each objective in terms of measurable results;
- Specify the method of measuring the result;

[3] The following discussion is based in part on an explanation of the stages of MBO developed by Dr. James Owens in "The Values and Pitfalls of MBO," Mich. Bus. Rev. 11–14 (July 1974).

- Specify the time period within which the objective must be achieved;
- Include regular or routine objectives, as well as new or developmental objectives; and
- Assign priorities or weights to each objective.

In government, the objectives quite often will be set out by legislation and further defined by the hearing that precedes passage of the legislation. Optimally, the legislation will include provisions aimed at avoidance of duplication, elimination of conflicting objectives, and production of real and tangible benefits.

Stage 2—Delegation

The overall organizational goals should be analyzed by management at progressively lower levels of authority to produce groups of subgoals, which, through proper delegation and coordination, will support and achieve the ultimate goals of the entity. Decisions should be made as to which organizational units and subordinate personnel will be responsible for each aspect of the overall goals. As part of this process, management should consult with subordinates as well as with peers. As in the case of the primary goals, subgoals should be specific and, where possible, measurable.

Stage 3—Agreement

The agreement by the manager and subordinate on the subordinate's responsibility in the direction of the established goals is the core of MBO. Essentially, the agreement is the result of communication between the two parties in which each delineates his version of the subordinate's goals, functions, responsibilities, resource needs, and authority over a given period of time. The agreement serves as a standard against which the subordinate's efforts should be measured. It should be noted that an MBO program involves the coordination of many such agreements.

Stage 4—Implementation

At this stage, the various levels of management should help their subordinates fulfill the terms of their agreement. This means developing a mutual help relationship between the parties through counseling, coaching, and training.

Stage 5—Review

If MBO is functioning properly, the review process consists primarily of self-appraisal by the subordinate. If the subordinate falls short of his established goals, the reason for such failure should be investigated. If failure is due to a change in situation, or a shifting of priorities, the manager and subordinate should abandon the existing agreement and develop a new agreement that is in keeping with the realities of the new situation, i.e., they should redefine goals.

Figure 3-2 illustrates the use of MBO as it applies to a local government.

Benefits of Management by Objectives

The benefits of working toward management objectives (program results) are various:

- The pursuit of clearly perceived goals is effective in directing human energies. People with ill-defined objectives seldom produce and are rarely happy. People with definite goals are highly productive, energetic, and generally happy.
- The use of MBO permits fair evaluation of employee performance. The employee's participation in the development of his own goals favorably affects his morale, his self-esteem, and his commitment to agreed-upon goals, making it easier for him to accept criticism for failure to meet such goals.
- The use of MBO facilitates a sound manager-subordinate relationship.
- An MBO program often creates a team spirit through the organized and united pursuit of a common goal within the entity.

Management by Objectives Applications

Experience with MBO in the relatively few years of its application has varied. Some users have reported excellent results; others have expressed disappointment. There are many valid reasons for both success and failure of MBO, but the applicability of at least the basic MBO concepts to government operations is incontestable because of the degree of decentralization in government. Government programs originate in the legislature. They are administered by an independent executive agency, which in turn usually delegates the

Figure 3-2

GOVERNMENT BY OBJECTIVES FLOW CHART

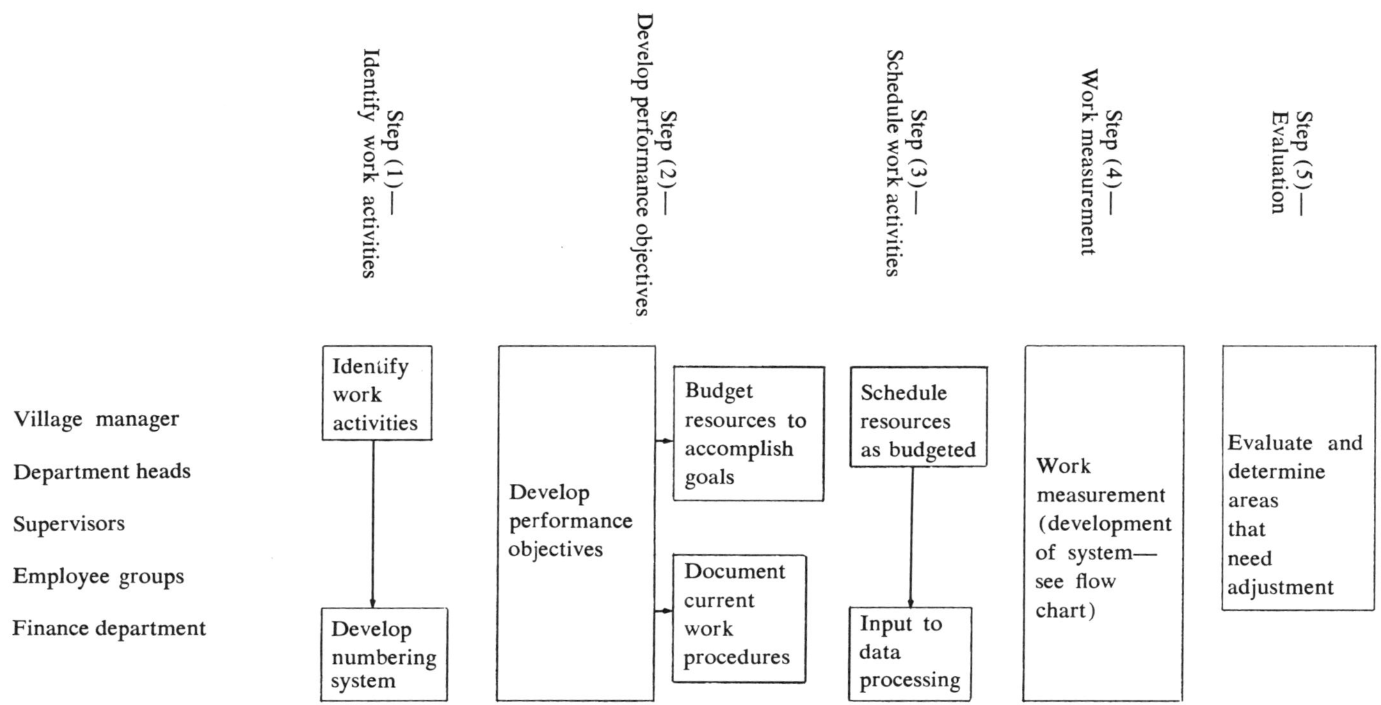

SOURCE: Maiben & Schwabe, "Government by Objectives: A Management System," Governmental Fin. 4 (Feb. 1974).

implementation to another separate and independent agency. Thus, objectives, administration, and implementation are completely divorced from each other.

In this context, MBO may be seen as a system for translating objectives into policies, policies into programs, programs into systems, systems into procedures, and procedures into results. In a cohesive entity, the flow from objectives to results is continuous and is continuously monitored. In an entity in which the process is discontinuous and is not monitored, the communication of program objectives is particularly important. MBO can preserve the integrity of the objectives throughout the descending chain of responsibility.

Although auditors and government officials may encounter difficulties in establishing quantitative measurement criteria, MBO can be a vital tool in helping clarify and perhaps improve government programs.

Program Effectiveness Experiences

Many government programs have fallen short of their goals. In most cases, the entities would have benefited from audits that identified problem areas at an early stage.

Here are two examples in which early audits might have resulted in program and policy changes.

Example 1

In January 1965, a state governor announced a five-year, $500 to $600 million program for the construction of health-care facilities. It was to include forty major projects, each valued at over $1 million. The total estimated cost for the major projects alone was approximately $320 million. These new units were to provide 14,500 patient beds, one-half of which were to be located in new state schools.

The announced overall objectives of this program were:

- Timely construction of facilities at reasonable cost;
- Relief of overcrowding;
- Modernization of facilities; and
- Location of mental hygiene facilities close to the people to be served.

Since these objectives did not lend themselves to precise evaluation, further specifics were developed in conjunction with a state audit. For example, the first objective—timely construction of facilities at reasonable cost—led to questions such as the following:

- Have projects been constructed according to the timetable set out in the 1965 plan?
- How does construction cost compare to the cost estimates set forth in the plans?
- As far as can be determined, have program costs been reasonable with respect to changes in plans and economic trends?

Among the major findings at the time of the audit's completion in September 1972, seven years after the governor announced the initiation of the construction program, were:

- Seventeen of the original projects had been canceled, involving the elimination of more than half of the planned beds.
- Delays ran up to forty-three months for completed projects, with a median delay of twenty months.
- Actual costs for the twenty-three surviving projects exceeded initial estimates by 50 percent. Even after taking into account the unusual inflation that had occurred during the six-year period from 1965 to 1971, the increase in the cost of the project was still intolerably high. When the Dodge construction index was applied, it was found that only 28 percent of the total cost increase was attributable to unanticipated inflation.[4]

This example emphasizes the need for the auditor, the legislature, and the local government to monitor program effectiveness. A timely audit could have brought to the attention of the proper authorities the failure to comply with state regulations, the failure to operate economically and efficiently, and the failure to attain program results.

Example 2 [5]

The Adult-Education Act of 1966 provides for federal assistance for programs whose purpose is to enable certain individuals to

[4] State of New York Legislative Commission on Expenditure Review, *Construction of Mental Hygiene Facilities* 1–6 (Oct. 1973).

[5] The following discussion is based on U.S. General Accounting Office, *The Adult Basic Education Program: Progress in Reducing Illiteracy and Improvements Needed* 1–30 (U.S. Government Printing Office 1975).

continue their education through secondary school. The basic program is designed to educate persons 16 years of age or older who are not in school and whose inability to speak, read, or write English impairs their ability to obtain or retain employment or to meet their responsibilities as adults. A person is considered to be literate, according to the Office of Education (OE), when he has achieved the equivalent of an eighth grade education.

Between the years 1966 and 1972, the number of persons attaining the eighth-grade standard through the program increased from 36,000 to 179,000. Federal cost for each adult-education enrollee fell from $83 to $59 from fiscal years 1965 to 1973. Despite these achievements, the program is not effective:

> . . . [I]t successfully reaches only a small fraction of those needing it—particularly among the more educationally deficient. In the Adult-Education Program's first 9 years, about 4.6 million adults enrolled. Only about 1 percent of the 57 million adults in the Adult-Education target population and 4 percent of the 15 million adults with less than 8 years of school have participated in any given year.[6]

The reason for the small impact the program has on illiteracy is basically the lack of clear, measurable objectives indicating what the program intends to accomplish. OE does not know whether it is making adequate progress in the reduction of illiteracy because it hasn't properly identified its target population:

> OE has relied almost exclusively on census data showing the number of years of formal school completed in identifying the program's population. . . . The census figures may not be a good indication of the size of the actual target population. According to the Director of OE's Division of Adult Education, grades completed do not necessarily measure a person's fundamental level because for many people actual functional levels are below the number of grades completed. . . .[7]

To summarize, this example demonstrates that a poorly defined objective will have a detrimental effect on the program in that:

- The amount of resources allocated to the program was disproportionate to the true target population.
- The program results could not be measured properly because of lack of an appropriate standard of measurement.

---

[6] *Id.* at i.
[7] *Id.* at 20.

Performing Program Effectiveness Audits

When requested to perform a Level III audit, the auditor must consider:

- The explicitness of the entity's objectives;
- The relevance and validity of the criteria used by the audited entity to judge effectiveness in achieving program results;
- The appropriateness of the methods followed by the entity in the evaluation of effectiveness in achieving program results;
- The accuracy of the data accumulated; and
- The reliability of the results obtained.

Such considerations should be made in light of a good working knowledge of the entity as a whole. To obtain such knowledge, the auditor should meet with key entity personnel, review physical operations, review financial statements, budgets, and policy and procedures manuals.

Figure 3-3 illustrates the decision process an auditor might use in performing an audit of program results. Following are some key questions an auditor would ask in connection with such decisions.

☐ *Does the entity have clearly defined objectives?* When the answer is "no," such objectives must be developed by the entity (or appropriate body—Congress, state legislature, etc.). When the answer is "yes," the auditor must determine whether they are realistic and feasible.

The second question to be asked is:

☐ *Have quantified and measurable criteria been identified?* If the answer is "no," the entity must identify meaningful measurement criteria for use in judging the effectiveness with which it is achieving desired results. The auditor should reach agreement with interested parties on the appropriateness of these measures.

The third question to be asked is:

☐ *Are the measurement criteria relevant and valid?* If the answer is "no," the entity must establish new criteria for use in judging its effectiveness.

Figure 3-3

FLOWCHART ILLUSTRATING DECISION TABLE FOR PROGRAM RESULTS

DESCRIPTION	STEP
Does the entity have clearly defined objectives?	1
Clearly defined objectives must be developed by the entity (or appropriate body – Congress, State, legislature, etc).	2
Have quantified and measurable criteria been identified?	3
The entity must identify measurement criteria for use in judging effectiveness	4
Is the measurement criteria relevant and valid?*	5

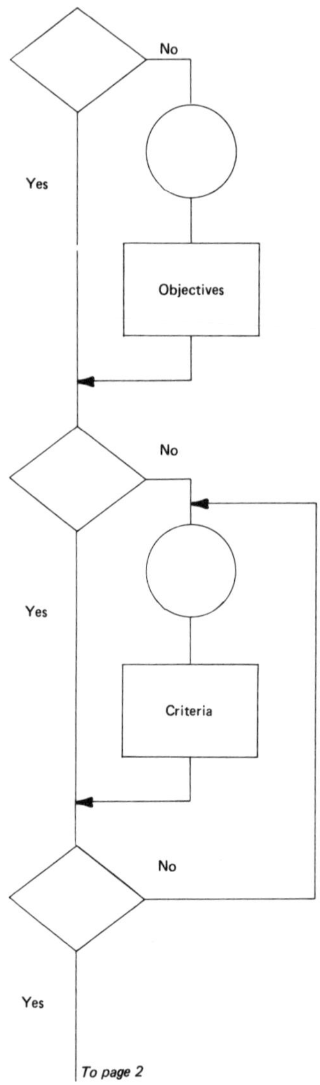

*If program results are to be evaluated by different persons on a coordinated basis, evaluation techniques should be uniformly prescribed. In the absence of uniform evaluation criteria, wide variations in the measurements applied to similar projects by different auditors may result in inefficiency in determining the effectiveness of the program as a whole.

[Page 2]

DESCRIPTION	STEP
Has data been accumulated for measurement against identified criteria?	6
The entity should accumulate data on: (1) Resources used (2) Results achieved.	7
Has accurate data been appropriately accumulated?	8
Analyze and evaluate data in relation to objectives and document finding.	9
Discuss finding with appropriate entity employees to: • Identify any additional factors that should be considered to place the finding in proper perspective • Enable the entity to take immediate corrective action if deemed necessary.	10

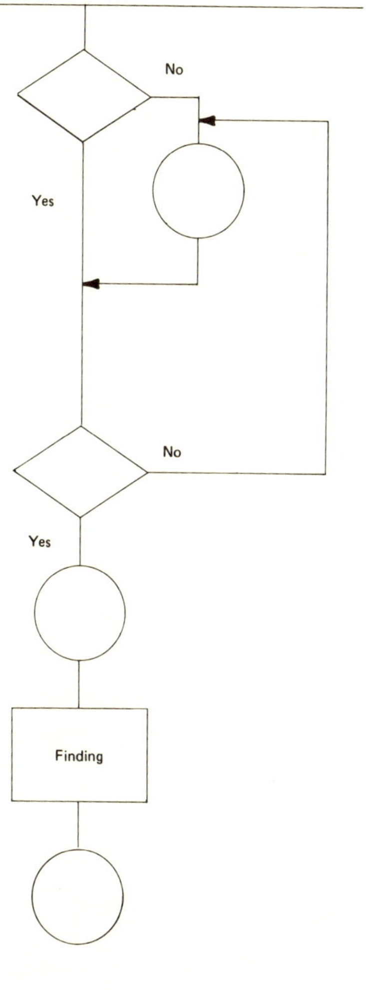

To Figure 4–1 Step 12

Legend

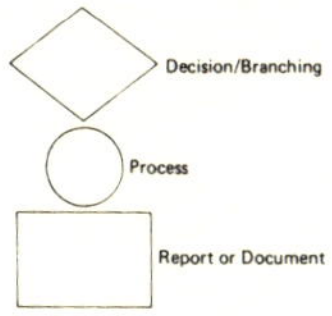

The fourth and fifth questions to be asked are:

☐ *Are program results to be evaluated by different persons on a coordinated basis? If so, Are evaluation techniques uniformly prescribed?* If the answer to the fourth question is "no," the auditor does not have to determine whether evaluation techniques are uniformly prescribed. If the answer is "yes," he must make this evaluation. If he finds that the techniques are not uniform, the auditor should request that the entity prescribe uniform evaluation techniques. Without uniform evaluation techniques, wide variations in measurements applied to similar projects by different auditors may result in inefficiencies in determining the effectiveness of the program as a whole.

The sixth and seventh questions to be asked are:

☐ *Have data been accumulated for measurement against identified criteria? If so, have accurate data been appropriately accumulated?* When the answer to the sixth question is "no," the auditor should direct the entity to accumulate data on the resources used and the results achieved. If the answer is "yes," the auditor must determine the appropriateness of the methods followed and the accuracy of the data accumulated.

Enhancing Program Effectiveness

Federal, state, and local government entities must be encouraged to take an aggressive and coordinated part in the planning, implementation, administration, and management of government programs. Legislation by objectives is needed to establish effectiveness of program results.

Government leaders should define and legislate goals and work through the government network to implement these goals. For implementation to be effective, legislation must include provisions for adequate funding and must be free of restrictions that could inhibit the attainment of goals. How, for instance, can an entity be effective in carrying out its goals if it doesn't have authority over an activity it is directed to monitor?

Goals must be delegated downward through the levels of government. This is not to say that each government agency will be striving for the same apparent objective. The pursuit of a better life for all men, for instance, is accomplished in various ways by numerous agencies; one agency may be working for equal employment opportunity, another for the freedom to enjoy a quality education. The essence is not sameness of immediate goals, but rather of philosophy.

Government entities must enlist the involvement of subordinates by restating objectives at each descending level of implementation in functional terms, and, if at all possible, identifying measures of performance. It is often only in this way that progress in the attainment of seemingly remote objectives can be assessed.

Clearly, cooperation must prevail in such an environment. Divergent interests must be reconciled and conflicts narrowed. Emphasis must be placed on compromise. Government, like the human body, functions only as well as its weakest member.

In 1832, students of the German philosopher Georg Hegel published the master's lectures posthumously under the title of *The Philosophy of History*. Hegel's message remains pertinent:

> The adoption of rules by a government must be preceded by a long struggle to understand, before what is really appropriate can be discovered. . . . Reason governs the world and, consequently, has governed history.[8]

The evaluation of the results of government programs has indeed required a prolonged struggle of understanding. Yet we must have the ambition to persevere in obtaining that understanding not only for the sake of the present but also for future generations.

---

[8] Hegel, *The Philosophy of History* 8-26 (J. Sibree transl., Wiley Book Co. 1964).

CHAPTER 4
Performance Measurement–Dollarization

Dollarization

As defined in Chapter 2, a preferred practice is a practice that has been found successful (or a criterion that has been found optimal) through experience with and study of many entities over a period of years. The failure to adhere to a preferred practice is an indication that resources may be, or at least may have been, wasted.

In performing an operational controls review, if a preferred practice question is answered "no" and there is no alternative or compensating control, there is a deficiency. The next step is to assess the significance of the deficiency. Dollarization is the process of expressing the effects of a deficiency in terms of money.

Benefits of Dollarization

Dollarization provides:

- An effective stimulus for management action;
- An aid in assessing the cost versus benefit of proposals for corrective action;

- A ranking of alternative corrective actions in terms of their cost;
- A quantification of opportunities and alternatives; and
- Improved auditor insight into the problems of management.

Various dollarization techniques are presented in the latter part of this chapter. Within the operational controls questionnaires presented in Chapters 5 through 12, the preferred practice questions that generally should be considered for dollarization are referenced to specific procedures in this chapter. It should be remembered, however, that the techniques presented here are not all-inclusive, and the absence of reference to a dollarization procedure within a questionnaire does not preclude the application of dollarization. The auditor should always be aware of the impact, whether cost or otherwise, of a weakness in operational controls.

Decision to Dollarize

A decision to dollarize is influenced by the following:

- The apparent importance of the finding;
- The cost versus benefit of dollarizing;
- The availability of records; and
- The entity's willingness to assist in dollarizing.

To be beneficial, dollarization must meet the following criteria:

- There should be a reasonable relationship between the benefits to be achieved through dollarization and the effort and cost involved.
- The technique used must be reasonable in the light of the finding. In other words, if the dollarization technique is illogical or reflects poor judgment, the finding is likely to receive little attention.
- A dollarization analysis should be completely and readily understandable. A complicated analysis is time-consuming for the auditor and unintelligible to the entity.
- Unwarranted conclusions should not be drawn from dollarization. Dollarization normally should not be extrapolated to an entire universe unless the technique used has statistical validity.

Generally an entity's personnel can assist in dollarization by:

- Helping to focus on problem areas;
- Providing appropriate documents and reports;
- Making informed estimates;
- Agreeing to the appropriateness of the dollarization techniques used; and
- Assisting in the development of the dollarization analysis.

Wherever possible, employee verbal statements should be verified through inspection of evidence; if such verification proves impractical, the finding will necessarily have to be qualified.

Dollarization sources should be explained as part of a finding. Some common sources are the following:

- Financial statements;
- Statistics;
- Internal auditors' reports;
- Consultants' reports;
- Ledger accounts;
- Work orders and maintenance logs;
- Payroll journals and time tickets;
- Vendor catalogs; and
- Equipment utilization schedules.

Figure 4-1 illustrates a basic approach to dollarization. It should be remembered that at times dollarization can be a two-edged sword. For example, say it has been noted that an agency buys retail, rather than wholesale. If negligible inventories are maintained, an arrangement to buy in large quantities, at a discount, could result in higher average inventories and increased cost.

Drafting the Management Letter

The expression of an operational controls deficiency in terms of money is very effective for motivating remedial action. When an operational controls questionnaire is completed, significant findings (both dollarized and nondollarized) should be presented to appropriate officials within the audited entity. This communication is generally made in the form of a management letter.

Figure 4-1

FLOWCHART ILLUSTRATING A BASIC APPROACH TO DOLLARIZATION

DESCRIPTION	STEP
Record finding based on understanding of response to preferred practice question. (See Chapter 2)	1
Discuss finding with appropriate entity employees to: • Identify any compensating controls • Identify any additional factors that should be considered to place the finding in proper perspective • Enable the entity to take immediate corrective action if deemed necessary	2
Does the finding affect costs, expenses or revenues?	3
Can the finding be dollarized?	4
Is it clearly evident that the amount – if dollarized – would not be material?	5
Determine the dollarization technique to be used (See Page 55 Dollarization Procedures Index).	6

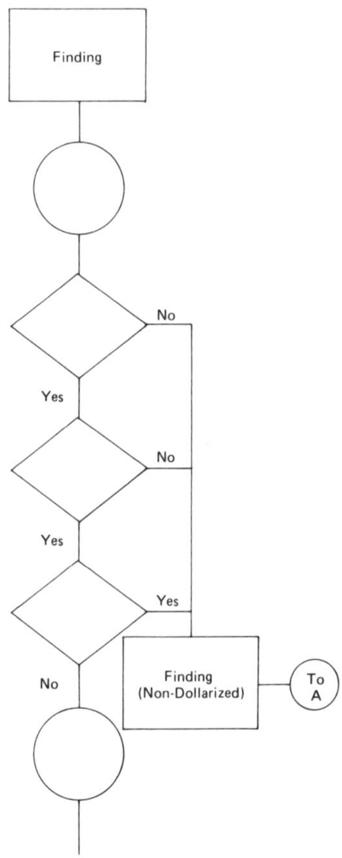

To page 2

[Page 2]

DESCRIPTION	STEP
Perform dollarization procedure (With assistance of entity employees if appropriate).	7
Is it appropriate to extrapolate finding, usually based on statistical validity or other logic?	8
Extrapolate or project finding to entire area reviewed.	9
Are there offsets to dollarized finding?	10
Amend finding to reflect offsets.	11

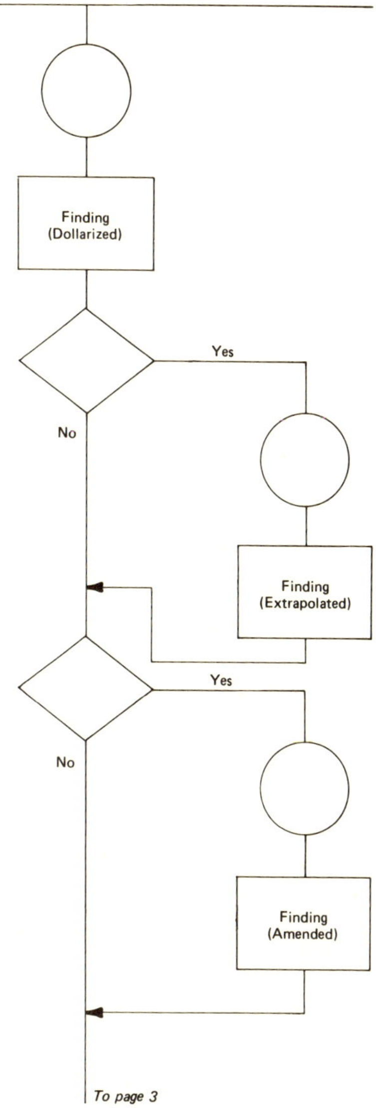

[Page 3]

DESCRIPTION	STEP
Consider all findings (Levels I, II and III – dollarized and non-dollarized) for inclusion in management letter. (See Figure 3–3)	12
Draft management letter.	13
Review draft of management letter with appropriate entity officials.	14
Do the entity officials agree with facts, methods, and conclusions contained in the draft management letter?	15
Review and investigate descrepancies and amend draft management letter if necessary.	16
Issue final management letter.	17

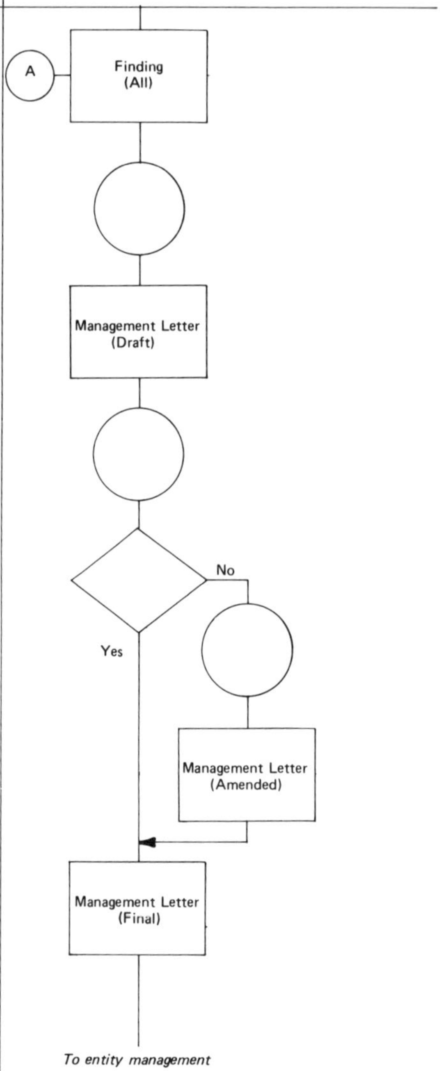

Legend

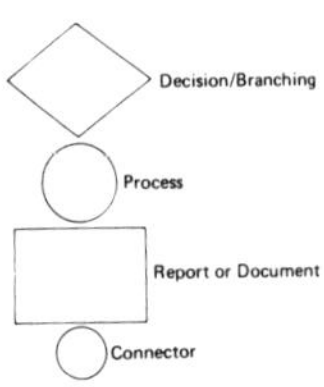

Comments should be logical and clearly expressed. The extent or scope of the review generating the comments should be stated in the letter. All comments contained in the management letter should be adequately documented and reviewed with appropriate operating officials before the letter is issued. The auditor should be available to discuss the management letter with entity officials and should state this in the letter. The management letter should be transmitted to appropriate entity officials as soon as possible after its review.

As stated, both dollarized and nondollarized findings should be communicated to management. If it is not possible to dollarize a finding, an explanation as to how the deficiency reduces the effectiveness of the system or could have a potentially adverse dollar effect should be presented in the management letter. Dollarization should be performed wherever possible, however, since it provides a tangible basis for evaluating a finding.

See the "Dollarization Procedure Index" immediately following for a list of the various dollarization procedures applicable to the operational controls questionnaires in Chapters 5 through 12. Again, it should be remembered that the absence of reference to a specific procedure does not preclude the application of dollarization. In every situation, the auditor must rely on judgment and common sense.

Dollarization Procedures Index

Procedure No.	
1	Personnel Allocation
2	Bidding
3	Equipment Downtime Evaluation
4	Computer Utilization
5	Personnel Utilization Evaluation
6	New Machine Feasibility
7	Cost of Idle Funds
8	Establishing Credit Terms/Progress Payments
9	Delinquency Penalties
10	Untimely Invoicing
11	Undeposited Receipts
12	Cash Maintenance
13	Cash Discounts
14	Cash Investment
15	Investment Expenses

Procedure No.	
16	Multiple Stocking
17	Extra Cost for "Rush" Deliveries
18	Excessive Inventories
19	Noncompetitive Buying
20	Lost Quantity Discounts
21	Repair Versus Replace
22	Purchase Order Completeness
23	Estimated Billings
24	Billing Frequency
25	Equipment Utilization Review
26	Lease Versus Purchase
27	Deficient Inventory Control

Dollarization Procedure 1: Personnel Allocation

(a) With the assistance of the entity's personnel, compile the following data for a given period. (It may be necessary to expand this schedule to provide detailed analyses of certain departments or divisions.)

Department/ Division	*Permanent Employees*		*Output*	
	No.	*% of Total*	*Quantity/Time**	*Per Employee*
....	...	....	....	....
....	...	....	....	....
....	...	....	....	....
....	...	....	....	....
....	...	....	....	....
		100%		

Department/ Division	*Hours Worked*							
	Regular		*Overtime*		*Temporary*		*Total*	
	Hours	*% of Total*	*Hours*	*% of Total*	*Hours*	*% of Total*	*Hours*	*% of Total*
....	......	.....	......	.....	......	.....	......	.....
....	......	.....	......	.....	......	.....	......	.....
....	......	.....	......	.....	......	.....	......	.....
....	......	.....	......	.....	......	.....	......	.....
....	......	.....	......	.....	......	.....	......	.....
		100%		100%		100%		100%

(b) Discuss any apparent imbalance in the allocation of personnel, as evidenced above with an appropriate entity representative. Document the comments of the representative.

Name: .... Title: ....

Comments of representative: ....

....

....

....

....

....

* For example, number of tons of garbage collected in a week.

(c) Compile the following for a category of work:

Month	*Total Hours Worked by Temporary Personnel*	*Amount Paid to Temporary Personnel*	*Average Rate Per Hour Temporary Personnel*	*Average Rate* Per Hour Permanent Personnel*	*Difference Per Hour*
(1)	....	$.........	$............	$............	$........
(2)	....	....	....	....	....
(3)	....	....	....	....	....
(4)	....	....	....	....	....
(5)	....	....	....	....	....
(6)	....	....	....	....	....
(7)	....	....	....	....	....
(8)	....	....	....	....	....
(9)	....	....	....	....	....
(10)	....	....	....	....	....
(11)	....	....	....	....	....
(12)	....	....	....	....	....
	══════	$ ══════			

The amount paid to temporary employees is generally more than that paid to permanent employees to allow for contractors' profits; temporary employees are sometimes less conscientious. Thus, if there is a trend evidenced above, it may be to the entity's benefit to hire more employees and dispense with the temporary workers.

* Including fringe benefits.

Dollarization Procedure 2: Bidding

(a) Select a sample of purchases on the basis of invoice values grouped into various ranges. Classify each of the acquisitions on the basis of the number of bids obtained. Complete the following schedule.

(1) *Dollar Range of Purchase*	*(2)* *Number of Purchase Transactions in Sample*	*(3)* *Number of Bids for Transactions in Sample*			
		0	*1–2*	*3–5*	*6 and Over*
0–$50	....	...	...	...	....
....	....	...	...	...	....
....	....	...	...	...	....
....	....	...	...	...	....
....	....	...	...	...	....
....	....	...	...	...	....
....	....	...	...	...	....
....	....	...	...	...	....
....	....	...	...	...	....
....	....	...	...	...	....
Over $......	....	...	...	...	....

(b) The results of this analysis should be reviewed in terms of legal requirements, if any, which determine the minimum number of bids, and in terms of the cost versus benefit of bid solicitation. For all but insignificant dollar purchases, 3 to 5 bids should be obtained. In cases where less than three bids are obtained, the entity may be purchasing at a noncompetitive price. Where more than five bids are obtained, the entity may spend excessive effort with little or no benefit.

Dollarization Procedure 3: Equipment Downtime Evaluation

Department/ Division	*Downtime Hours*	*Average Wage Rate*	*Total Amount*
....	....	$...........	$.........
....	....	....	....
....	....	....	....
....	....	....	....
		TOTAL	$.........

(a) In reviewing downtime hours, be sure to exclude those hours attributable to other factors such as preventive maintenance, work stoppages, materials shortages, power failures, etc. Only those hours lost as a result of equipment failure should be used.

(b) Review computation with entity's personnel to assure only appropriate amounts have been used. Document name and title of entity's personnel consulted.

Name: .... Title: ....

Dollarization Procedure 4: Computer Utilization

	Hours	*Percent*
Total hours available (exclusive of preventive maintenance)		
Less:		
Testing (debugging)		
Other (explain):		
....		
....		
....		
	___	___
Available for production		
Reruns (give reasons):		
....		
....		
....		
	___	___
Downtime (give reasons):		
....		
....		
....		
	___	___
Net utilization, represented by applications		%
	===	===

Dollarization Procedure 5: Personnel Utilization Evaluation

(a) With the assistance of the entity's personnel, compile the following data:

(1)	*(2)*	*(3)*	*(4)*	*(5)*	*(6)*
		*Idle Hours**		*Overtime Hours*	
Period	*No. of Employees*	*No.*	*Amount*	*No.*	*Amount*
1	....	...	$......	...	$.......
2	....	...	....	...	....
3	....	...	....	...	....
4	....	...	....	...	....
5	....	...	....	...	....
	TOTAL		$		$

* Idle hours should be determined based upon a large number of work/no work observations. It may be desirable to have skilled observers take these readings. To determine the number of idle hours, first develop a ratio of idleness. For example, if 1,200 observations show no work in 710 cases, the idle hours would be determined by multiplying the available hours by 710 over 1,200 or 59.17 percent. To determine the amount paid for idleness, use the average pay rate for personnel for a particular month and multiply by the number of idle hours as computed previously. Also, list any premium paid for overtime.

Dollarization Procedure 6: New Machine Feasibility

(a) With the assistance of entity personnel, compile the following:

- *Old machine:*

Estimated Useful Life	*Estimated Output Per Year*	*Total Estimated Output*		*Estimated Cost of Production*	*Estimated Cost of Production Per Unit*
			Material	$	$
			Labor		
			Overhead		
			TOTAL	$	$

(b) By reference to invoices or by interview with appropriate entity personnel, estimate the expected cost and output of a new machine and its estimated life. Compile the following:

- *New machine:*

Estimated Useful Life	*Estimated Output Per Year*	*Total Estimated Output*		*Estimated Cost of Production*	*Estimated Cost of Production Per Unit*
			Material	$	$
			Labor		
			Overhead		
			TOTAL	$	$

(c) Compare the estimated cost of production per unit using the old machine to the estimated cost of production per unit using a new machine.

(d) Estimate the number of units to be produced in a year and apply the difference in unit price calculated above.

Note: The auditor is advised that many additional factors such as the following will need to be considered in equipment replacement decisions:

- Need for the additional output generated by a new machine;
- Financing charges and depreciation expenses;
- Repair versus replace decisions (see Dollarization Procedure 21: Repair Versus Replace); and
- Maintenance cost.

Dollarization Procedure 7: Cost of Idle Funds

(a) Prepare a schedule showing:

Description	*Present Fund Balance*	*Minimum Fund Balance**	*Idle Portion*
. . . .	$.	$.	$. . . . . .
. . . .	. . . .	. . . .	. . . . . .
. . . .	. . . .	. . . .	. . . . . .
. . . .	. . . .	. . . .	. . . . . .
. . . .	. . . .	. . . .	. . . . . .
	$	$	$

* The minimum fund balance should be based upon seasonal cash needs of a particular fund with due allowance for compensating balance requirements adjusted by the float of unclaimed checks. The lowest experienced balances, as shown on bank statements, may offer a clue as to realistic minimum balances.

(b) Select and indicate an applicable rate of return based upon either the rate obtained on the entity's existing cash investments (or borrowings) or other appropriate target rate established by the entity.

This information can be obtained through interviews with entity personnel and review of the entity's investment data. If such information is not readily available, a realistic investment yield can be obtained by reference to prevailing money market rates offered on the class of instruments which suits the entity's needs and satisfies the applicable statutory constraints. The existing rate offered on U.S. Treasury bills, for example, might present a logical choice. The basis of the rate of return chosen should be documented as to source and date.

(c) Calculate the obtainable investment revenue:

$$\text{Idle Portion} \times \text{Rate} \times (\text{Days} \div 360) = \text{Revenue}$$

In cases where compound interest is applicable, consult the appropriate reference table.

Dollarization Procedure 8: Establishing Credit Terms/Progress Payments

(a) Through inquiry of entity personnel, determine the earliest possible due date based upon local regulation for the collection of an account receivable and compute the number of days from the earliest possible due date to the billing date being used by the entity.

(b) Using the entity's records, schedule the total amount of revenue for the year subject to the credit terms mentioned in (a) above.

(c) Determine the prevailing interest rate during the period on short-term investments, such as U.S. Treasury bills, or the borrowing rate, if entity is not in an excess cash position. Convert to a daily rate.

(d) Complete the following computation, using the information obtained:

(1) Aggregate annual revenue	\$........
(2) Difference between due dates in number of days	....
(3) Cost of money—per day	% ....
Estimated annual savings (1 × 2 × 3)	\$______

Note: The above computation assumes that all revenue would be collected even with a shorter credit period. Accordingly, the conclusions should be tempered by qualifying language or by building into the computation the actual collection experience of the entity.

Dollarization Procedure 9: Delinquency Penalties

(a) Obtain copies of the entity's aged accounts receivable trial balance for the last twelve months and compute the total past due balance for each month.
(b) Obtain the percentage charged by the entity on delinquent accounts, if any.
(c) Select a realistic alternative interest rate to be charged on delinquent balances. (The prime interest rate is a good possible choice, but, depending on economic conditions and the financial condition of the entity, the appropriate interest rate may be 1 to 1½% over prime.)
(d) Perform the calculations below using the information obtained.

Past due accounts receivable balances:

(1)	$........	(7)	$........
(2)	....	(8)	....
(3)	....	(9)	....
(4)	....	(10)	....
(5)	....	(11)	....
(6)	....	(12)	....
		TOTAL	$ ________

Divide: Total ÷ 12

(1)	Average past due balance		$........
(2)	Penalty rate: Per entity	........%	
(3)	Proposed*	........%	
(4)	Excess (2 – 3)		........%
(5)	Estimated cost of low penalty rate (1 × 4)		$ ________

* Proposed rate should be discussed with entity personnel.

Dollarization Procedure 10: Untimely Invoicing

(a) Select a number of invoices. Summarize the amount of these invoices that were billed late.

(b) Based on discussions with entity personnel, estimate the average lag between the date the invoices should have been issued and the date they were actually issued.

(c) Determine prevailing interest rate available during the period on short-term investments, such as U.S. Treasury bills, or the borrowing rate if entity is not in an excess cash position. Convert to a daily rate.

(d) Compute the following:

(1) Dollar amount of late invoices	$........
(2) Time lag in number of days	....
(3) Cost of money (per day)	.... %
(4) Total cost for period tested (1 × 2 × 3)	$
(5) Number of periods in year	....
Estimated annual costs (4 × 5)	$

Dollarization Procedure 11: Undeposited Receipts

(a) Compute the average amount of funds received by outside agencies which are not remitted on a timely basis to the central office of the entity.

(b) With the assistance of entity personnel, estimate to what degree the amount of undeposited receipts could be reduced. (There are a number of techniques for minimizing undeposited receipts, e.g., lock boxes.)

(c) Compute the amount of revenue lost by not promptly depositing receipts as follows:

$$\text{Amount} \times \text{Rate} \times (\text{Days} \div 360) = \text{Revenue}$$

The rate used in this formula should be based on the rate obtained by the organization on its short-term investments (or borrowings) or, if such data is not readily available, on an appropriate standard, such as the average Treasury bill rate in effect during the period.

Dollarization Procedure 12: Cash Maintenance

(a) Prepare a schedule showing the personnel costs related to the specific cash management functions (i.e., segregation of incoming cash, maintenance of balances, preparing transfers, etc.) under consideration. It may be necessary to expand the schedule to provide detailed analyses of specific locations.

(b) For each function, attempt to identify the service cost applicable to the performance of the service by a bank.

Typical techniques that reduce clerical effort include:

- Zero/automatic balance accounts;
- Imprest accounts;
- Lock boxes;
- Special purpose accounts; and
- Centralized payables processing.

Estimates related to the cost of such items can be obtained by referring to local banking practices.

Function	*Personnel Cost*	*Related Bank Service*	*Bank Service Cost*	*Cost Differences*
. . . .	$.	. . . .	$.	$. . . . .
. . . .	. . . .	. . . .	. . . .	. . . .
. . . .	. . . .	. . . .	. . . .	. . . .
. . . .	. . . .	. . . .	. . . .	. . . .
. . . .	. . . .	. . . .	. . . .	. . . .
. . . .	. . . .	. . . .	. . . .	. . . .
. . . .	. . . .	. . . .	. . . .	. . . .
TOTAL	$ ______		$ ______	$ ______

Dollarization Procedure 13: Cash Discounts

(a) Select a number of purchase invoices.
(b) Prepare a schedule showing:

  (1) Credit terms;
  (2) Amount and date actually paid;
  (3) Amount which could have been paid if any available discounts were taken; and
  (4) The difference between (2) and (3) above.

(c) Assuming a valid sample, project the estimated annual savings that could be achieved by the entity if cash discounts were taken, bearing in mind the interest paid by the entity.
(d) Evaluate the potential cost reduction keeping in mind that cash withdrawal should be delayed until the latest possible date.

Dollarization Procedure 14: Cash Investment

(a) Calculate the annual yield derived from the prior year's cash management program.

Where the required information is not already available via management reports, the actual yield should be estimated with the assistance of entity employees.

(b) Compare the yield to that derived from a suitable benchmark rate.

	Average Invested Amount (In Thousands)	*Return (Dollars)*	*Rate (%)*
Actual	$....................	$.........	....
Projected	$....................	$.........	....

Dollarization Procedure 15: Investment Expenses

(a) Based upon examination of the entity's records, determine the dollar amount of investment expenses applicable to the investment program. Consider such items as management fees, advisory fees, custodian fees, commissions, etc.

(b) Ascertain whether an adverse trend is developing with respect to such expenses:

	19—		*19—*		*19—*	
Expense	*Dollar Amount*	*% to Total Average Invest-ment*	*Dollar Amount*	*% to Total Average Invest-ment*	*Dollar Amount*	*% to Total Average Invest-ment*
Management fees	$......	......%	$......	......%	$......	......%
Advisory fees	......	......	......	......	......	......
Custodian fees	......	......	......	......	......	......
Commissions	......	......	......	......	......	......
	......	......	......	......	......	......
	......	......	......	......	......	......
	......	......	......	......	......	......
TOTAL	$	100%	$	100%	$	100%

Dollarization Procedure 16: Multiple Stocking

(a) With the help of the entity's purchasing personnel, identify materials and supplies that are purchased to accomplish similar tasks but that vary only on the basis of brand or trade name. Examples are bearings that are fully interchangeable and appropriately referenced for interchangeability; number one fuel oil, which is a standard grade description provided by many different manufacturers; tires, which must conform to federal standards. Be sure to consider items stored at various locations.

(b) Determine the aggregate stocks and aggregate usage of the items described in (a) above, and compute the number of months' supply on hand. (See Dollarization Procedure 18, Excessive Inventories, for further explanation.)

(c) Where similar articles differ substantially in price, compute the differential between the lowest priced article and the others available, and apply the differential to the quantities purchased.

A similar effect may be achieved by referring to price lists to determine a quantity discount price that might have been obtainable had the items been combined. (See Dollarization Procedure 20: Lost Quantity Discounts.)

Dollarization Procedure 17: Extra Cost for "Rush" Deliveries

(a) Through discussion with entity's personnel, determine whether higher purchase prices have been experienced as a result of a requirement for delivery on a rush basis. (Some vendors, but not many, indicate on the invoice the amounts charged for rush delivery. Most will include this charge as extra minimums or "setups," or simply as higher prices.)

Name: .... Title: ....

		Price		
Commodities	*Volume*	*Actually Paid*	*Lowest Available*	*Estimated Delivery Premium Dollars*
....	......	$......	$.......	$..............
....	......	....	....	....
....	......	....	....	....
....	......	....	....	....
....	......	....	....	....

Dollarization Procedure 18: Excessive Inventories

(a) Determine whether the entity has any report indicating the relationship of the quantities on hand to usage—for example, "number of months' supply on hand."

(b) Develop the following classification, either by reference to available reports or by a sampling of inventory records. (The results of a sampling may be projected to the entire inventory if statistically valid selection procedures are employed.)

Dollar value of items that have shown no movement during the past year	$........
Dollar value of items for which there is a year's supply, or more, on hand	....
Dollar value of items for which there is less than a year's supply, but more than six months' supply	....
Dollar value of stock with six months' supply or less	....
TOTAL VALUE TESTED	$

Computation of months' supply can be made by the following formula:

$$\text{Inventory} \div \frac{\text{Annual Usage}}{12} = \text{Number of Months' Supply.}$$

This data can be obtained either from a summary of usage in the inventory records or by taking the opening inventory receipts and adjustments and subtracting returns and the ending inventory. If it is difficult to obtain annual usage, a shorter term usage can be employed, provided that periodic usage neither fluctuates nor is distorted by factors such as seasonality.

(c) Calculate the dollar effect of dormant inventories by multiplying the "dead" stock by a rate representing variable annual carrying cost, say 10 to 15 percent.

Dollarization Procedure 19: Noncompetitive Buying

(a) Determine whether the entity has experienced any loss as a result of noncompetitive buying. (See Dollarization Procedure 20: Lost Quantity Discounts.)

(1) Identify a significant number of commodities the entity purchases from different vendors.

(2) Prepare a schedule showing:

- Commodity description;
- Current annual usage;
- Vendors;
- Quantities bought, dates, unit prices, total dollars;
- Difference between the unit price charged by the lowest priced qualified vendor and the actual prices paid; and
- Potential savings (quantities extended by price difference).

Note: Be sure that (1) prices are adjusted for freight and (2) all vendors are qualified from the standpoint of delivery and quality.

(b) Review your schedule with the appropriate entity personnel.

Name: .... Title: ....

Comments: ....

....

....

....

....

....

....

Dollarization Procedure 20: Lost Quantity Discounts

(a) In conjunction with the entity's purchasing personnel identify a representative number of commodities that result in significant expenditures and that are purchased repetitively.

(b) Have the entity's personnel prepare a schedule for these commodities, showing:

- Commodity description (see Dollarization Procedure 16: Multiple Stocking);
- Current annual usage;
- Vendors used in past year (by location);
- Quantities bought, dates, unit prices, total dollars;
- Difference between the unit price charged by the lowest priced qualified vendor (or the lowest price obtainable per catalog) and actual prices paid; and
- Potential saving (quantities extended by price difference).

(c) Test this schedule by reference to vendor invoices and catalogs.

Record the results noting any factors compensating for differences in price: ....

....

....

....

....

....

(d) With entity personnel estimate the aggregate potential saving from more effective combination of purchases (see Dollarization Procedure 16: Multiple Stocking):

Commodity Group	*Cost Reduction* Method*	*Estimated*			
		Current Annual Usage		*Cost Reduction*	
		Quantities	*Dollars*	*Dollars*	*%*
....	....	....	$.....	$.....	...
....	....	....	.....	.....	...
....	....	....	.....	.....	...
....	....	....	.....	.....	...

Name: .... Title: ....

* For example, standardization.

Dollarization Procedure 21: Repair Versus Replace

	Asset or Asset Group
(1) Replacement cost	$
(2) Repair and maintenance costs for the current year	$
(3) Percentage of 2 to 1	%

(a) Replacement cost should be determined as of the most recent balance sheet date.

(b) Information on replacement cost could be obtained by reference to invoices for actual purchases of similar items, by reference to vendor price lists, or by interviews with entity personnel.

Note: The above does not take into account machine productivity and labor or material cost reductions. In addition, in making repair versus replace determinations, a comparison should be made of the useful life of a new machine and the expected useful life of an old, repaired machine. (See Dollarization Procedure 6: New Machine Feasibility.)

Dollarization Procedure 22: Purchase Order Completeness

Determine whether purchase orders are complete, thereby reflecting the "striking of a complete bargain" between buyer and seller.

(a) Select a number of recently completed purchase orders.
(b) Indicate the incidence of missing data.

	Number
Purchase orders lack:	
Price	....
F.O.B. point	....
Routing	....
Cash discount	....
Sales tax exemption certificate or other appropriate reference	....
Delivery date	....
TOTAL PURCHASE ORDERS TESTED	....

Note: The significance of these omissions varies widely from one entity to another. The omission of prices need not mean much if goods are bought at prices as of the date of delivery; routing may not be significant if goods are bought on a "delivered" basis and if there is plenty of time for delivery. On the other hand, delivery dates are often highly important for expediting purposes and vendor evaluation.

(c) Determine whether the entity has experienced loss as a result of failure to price purchase orders.

Have the entity's personnel prepare a schedule covering articles on unpriced purchase orders showing:

- Commodity description;
- Current annual usage;
- Vendors;
- Quantities bought and dates;
- Difference between the unit price charged by the lowest priced

qualified vendor or the lowest obtainable quantity price, per vendor catalog, and the actual prices paid; and

- Potential saving (quantities extended by price difference).

Note: Be sure that:

(1) Schedule does not include articles subject to pricing at time of delivery.
(2) Prices are adjusted for freight.
(3) All vendors are qualified.

Test entity's schedule by reference to vendor invoices and/or catalogs.

Record the results of this review: ....

....

....

....

....

....

....

....

....

(d) As to loss from failure to take cash discounts:

Take a sampling of invoices and determine from the purchasing agent whether the vendors permit cash discounts. Trace the payment of the invoice to determine if such cash discounts were taken by accounting. (See Dollarization Procedure 13: Cash Discounts.)

(e) See Dollarization Procedure 2: Bidding.

Dollarization Procedure 23: Estimated Billings

(a) With the help of the entity's personnel, determine for a given period (a week, month, etc.) the dollar amount of billings whose collection could be accelerated by the use of estimated billings. (Such estimate could be based on a prior period's billing.)

(b) Calculate the approximate interest that could be earned on the collection of the estimated billings. The rate obtained by the entity on its short-term investments (or borrowings) should be used, or if such data is not readily available, an appropriate standard, such as the average Treasury bill rate in effect during the period.

(c) Deduct the approximate cost of billing more frequently from the amount calculated in (b) and annualize the resulting amount. (See Dollarization Procedure 24: Billing Frequency.)

Note: The above computation assumes that all revenue would be collected even with a shorter credit period. Accordingly, the conclusions should be tempered by qualifying language or by building into the computation the actual collection experience of the entity.

Dollarization Procedure 24: Billing Frequency

(a) With the help of the entity's personnel, determine the amount collected for low cost services in a three-month period and calculate the approximate interest that could be earned on the collection of such amount if monthly billings were made. The rate available on the entity's short-term investments (or borrowings) could be used, or if such data is not readily available, an appropriate standard such as the average Treasury bill rate in effect during the period.

(b) With the help of the entity's personnel, determine the approximate cost of billing these services on a monthly basis and on a quarterly basis.

(c) Compare the additional cost of billing on a monthly basis to the loss of income caused by billing on a quarterly basis and determine the most favorable alternative.

Note: The above computation assumes that all revenue would be collected even with a longer credit period. Accordingly, the conclusions should be tempered by qualifying language or by building into the computation the actual collection experience of the entity.

Dollarization Procedure 25: Equipment Utilization Review

Asset or Group of Assets	*Utilization Rate*		
	Budgeted	*Actual*	*Variance*
....	....	....	....
....	....	....	....
....	....	....	....
....	....	....	....
....	....	....	....

(a) Usage should be designated in whichever units are most appropriate, e.g., machine-hours, mileage, etc.

(b) Information derived from completion of this schedule should be discussed with entity personnel to explore any items that may be unusual.

Note: For ADP equipment, see Dollarization Procedure 4: Computer Utilization.

Dollarization Procedure 26: Lease Versus Purchase

(1) Total purchase price	\$........	
(2) Total estimated carrying cost (maintenance, insurance, etc.)	....	
(3) Total (1 + 2)		\$........
(4) Present value of total lease payments		....
Excess (3 – 4)		\$

(a) The above schedule assumes that certain carrying costs incident to ownership, such as maintenance and insurance, are included in the lease payment.

(b) Present value equals $R\left(\frac{1-(1+i)^{-n}}{i}\right)$, where R equals the amount of each rent payment, i equals the interest rate, and n the number of payments.

Note: The auditor must also consider factors such as scrap value and depreciation recapture in the above calculation.

Dollarization Procedure 27: Deficient Inventory Control

(a) With the assistance of the entity's personnel, compile the following data for major inventory categories through review of reports. This data should be compiled for a period of time long enough to evidence any developing trends.

Type of Inventory (Property, Supplies, Equipment)	*Period 1*		*Period 2*		*Period 3*		*Period 4*	
	Dollar Amount	*% of Total*	*Dollar Amount*	*% of Total*	*Dollar Amount*	*% of Total*	*Dollar Amount*	*% of Total*
....	$......	.....	$......	.....	$......	.....	$......	.....
....	......	.....	......	.....	......	.....	......	.....
....	......	.....	......	.....	......	.....	......	.....
....	......	.....	......	.....	......	.....	......	.....
	$	100%	$	100%	$	100%	$	100%

(b) Consider developing certain information that may indicate problems in inventory control, such as:

(1) The ratios of certain inventory costs to labor hours;
(2) The change, over a period of time, in the inventory cost per unit served; or
(3) The change, over a period of time, in inventory cost as a percentage of labor costs.

Presentation of the dollar amount of inventory used, over which there is no system of internal controls, may be helpful in demonstrating to the entity that an effective controls system is needed.

(c) Discuss the above information with appropriate entity personnel to determine the reasons for any evident trends. It should be remembered that, while some of the information may indicate negative patterns, consideration must be given to the extent to which normal business pressures, (e.g., inflation) have created such trends.

Name: .... Title: ....

Comments of Representative: ....

....

....

....

CHAPTER 5

Operational Controls Review–Internal Audit

Part I—General Discussion

Part II—The Questionnaire

Part I—General Discussion

The primary purpose of an internal audit department is to assist management in evaluating the functioning of systems and controls. In government, as in the private sector, the size and scope of internal audit departments and the degree to which they aid management vary widely. If government internal auditors function as the General Accounting Office (GAO) prescribes, they perform audits on each of the three levels discussed in the preceding chapters. At times, however, they may devote much of their time to special projects or even to record-keeping.

The services that internal auditors provide vary primarily because of differences in management needs. However, differences in operations, organizational structures, quality of personnel, management concepts, and availability of funding also contribute to the diversity of internal audit services provided. Although the full scope of a government audit is set forth in the first general standard in Appendix I, not every audit will be this extensive. Internal audit work must be tailored to each situation so that the needs of management are met.

Role of Internal Auditing

The role of internal auditing in government was described in 1974 by the Comptroller General of the United States:

> Information needed by management may come from direct observation; from routine and periodic operating, accounting, statistical, and analytical reports; and from functional or staff reviews. Another important source of information is the internal audit organization which conducts independent examinations and makes reports on its findings and appraisals of operations and performance. The internal audit function uniquely supplements routine management checks through its independent approach and methods of review. This function is one of the essential tools of management, complementing all other elements of management control.

Nature of Internal Auditing

> The overall objective of internal auditing is to assist agency management in attaining its goals by furnishing information, analyses, appraisals, and recommendations pertinent to management's duties and objectives.
>
> Internal auditing is a staff and advisory function, not a line-operating function. Thus, the internal auditor should not have authority to make or direct changes in his agency's procedures or operations. His job is to independently and objectively analyze, review, and evaluate existing procedures and activities; to report on conditions found; and, whenever he deems it necessary, to recommend changes or other actions for management and operating officials to consider.
>
> An internal auditor should not be given direct operating responsibilities. Rather, he should be expected to concern himself primarily with the performance of others, to retain an independent outlook in all of his work, and to direct particular attention to matters requiring corrective action. His function is

to present his views and suggestions constructively in such a manner as to stimulate or encourage action on his suggestions by others.

Benefits of Internal Auditing

Management has found that services rendered by the internal auditor in the form of constructive recommendations supported by unbiased, relevant information have aided in meeting many of the problems of both large-scale and decentralized operations. The numerous, complex administrative problems of large organizations impose on management the necessity of delegating a large degree of operating authority within the organizational structure. Management must keep informed on what is happening in the organization at its various levels. Internal auditing is an important means by which management can provide itself with such information and related evaluations.

Management also benefits from timely information on problems on which remedial measures can be taken before the functioning of the organization is impaired. These problems, once they have been examined and appraised, often lead to opportunities for achieving lower costs, increased efficiency, and faster ways of getting things done.

Internal auditing can be of special benefit to the management of smaller organizations, or of small segments of large organizations, where the customary division of duties among employees is not always economical or practical. The internal auditor can often provide additional internal checks and controls required for effective and efficient management.

By reason of his knowledge of management policies and procedures and his contacts with officials and employees at all organizational levels, the internal auditor can render a valuable service by promoting better communications within an agency. He can obtain first-hand observations on the usefulness or effectiveness of prescribed policies and procedures and he can bring to top management's attention those needing modification, explanation, and interpretation. This type of service can contribute greatly to good management control.

Scope of Internal Audit Work

To be of maximum usefulness, the scope of the internal auditor's activity should not be restricted. It should extend to all agency activities and related management controls.

The duties of the internal auditor should be clearly stated by the head of the agency, and information concerning these duties should be disseminated throughout the agency to insure full recognition of the nature of his functions at all levels.

Appraising Performance

> A necessary function of management is to establish and prescribe policies, plans, and procedures for carrying out programs and activities in pursuit of the objectives of the organization and to establish organizational or management systems for review of operations.
>
> The internal audit function can provide a highly valuable service to management by reviewing, appraising, and reporting on the extent and nature of internal compliance with management's policies, plans, and procedures as well as with applicable legal and external regulatory requirements.
>
> The internal auditor's work should include the review of the operation of the whole system of management controls over operations and resources to ascertain whether they are functioning in accordance with their design and are functioning effectively. In organizing his work, particularly in large agencies, he should consider making comparative examinations of similar functions which are performed in the various organizational components of the agency.
>
> In making such examinations, the internal auditor should be alert to possibilities for improving operations and identifying opportunities for bringing about greater efficiency and economy.
>
> As a result of his familiarity with management plans and policies, intra-agency relationships, and procedures and with the manner in which they are working out, the internal auditor should also report observations as to their adequacy and effectiveness in relation to top management objectives together with such recommendations for improvement he considers appropriate.[1]

Coordinating the Audit Functions

Sometimes internal audit departments of the city, state, and federal government are jointly given the responsibility for auditing a particular entity or activity. To avoid the cost of duplicated effort, each audit group must know the scope of the audit being conducted by the other audit groups involved.

In determining the nature, timing, and extent of their own procedures, independent auditors must assess the extent to which information developed by an internal audit department is useful and rele-

---

[1] U.S. General Accounting Office, *Internal Auditing in Federal Agencies* 1–4 (U.S. Government Printing Office 1974).

vant, and the extent to which the internal auditor may be used in performing the independent audit. The AICPA Statement on Auditing Standards No. 9, *The Effect of an Internal Audit Function on the Scope of the Independent Auditor's Examination,* provides guidance on the factors that affect an independent auditor's consideration of the work of internal auditors in an examination made in accordance with generally accepted auditing procedures.

Part II—The Questionnaire

Background Information

In developing an understanding of the internal audit department, the reviewer should focus on organization, independence, competence, reporting, and accomplishments. To facilitate this understanding the following information should be obtained:

(1) Obtain a listing of recipients of audit reports. . . . .

. . . .

. . . .

. . . .

. . . .

. . . .

(2) Obtain a listing showing the key personnel of the internal audit staff by position level and work location.

Name	*Position*	*Location*
. . . .	. . . .	. . . .
. . . .	. . . .	. . . .
. . . .	. . . .	. . . .
. . . .	. . . .	. . . .

(3) Determine the qualification level of the internal audit department:

	Number	*Degree(s)*	*CPAs*	*CIAs*
Auditors	. . . .	. . . .	. . . . . .	. . . . . .
Other professionals (e.g., engineers, statisticians, ADP personnel, etc.)	. . . .	. . . .	. . . . . .	. . . . . .
Clerical	. . . .	. . . .	. . . . . .	. . . . . .
TOTAL	. . . .	. . . .	. . . . . .	. . . . . .

(4) With the assistance of the internal auditors, prepare a schedule showing the distribution of the audit workload.

	Staff Years	*% of Time*
Type of audit:		
Entity audits	......	....
Functional audits	......	....
Special reviews:		
ADP—preinstallation	......	....
ADP—postinstallation	......	....
Other	......	....
	......	....
		100%
Level of audit:		
I—financial/compliance	......	....
II—efficiency and economy	......	....
III—program results	......	....
		100%

Internal Audit Questionnaire

The internal audit questionnaire should be used when an internal audit department is being evaluated or when a degree of reliance is intended to be placed on its activities. Because the auditor may find the work of the internal audit department useful in conducting certain aspects of his audit, he should evaluate the internal audit department first. Thus, he should apply the internal audit questionnaire before the others.

The auditor usually finds few opportunities for using dollarization techniques in evaluating an internal audit department. He should nevertheless advise management of any significant weaknesses to stimulate remedial action and enhance the efficiency and effectiveness of the department.

The internal audit questionnaire consists of four sections:

- Section I: Organization and Independence;
- Section II: Professional Skills;
- Section III: Audit Performance; and
- Section IV: Reporting Practices.

Section I: Organization and Independence

The organization of an internal audit department will deeply affect its functioning. Unless the department is sufficiently independent to assure the impartiality of audit opinions, conclusions, judgments, and recommendations, it cannot be effective.

Organization

	Yes	*No*
(1) Is the internal audit department authorized under a statute or other formal enactment?	☐	☐
(2) Does the internal audit department operate within its own budget appropriation?	☐	☐
(3) Is the internal audit department a separate organizational unit with no responsibility that is inconsistent with appropriate segregation of duties?	☐	☐
(4) Are the internal auditors allowed access to all operations?	☐	☐
(5) Is the internal audit department given the funding to perform full scope audits?	☐	☐
(6) Have steps been taken to avoid duplication of the audit department's activities by other audit agencies at the same or different levels of government?	☐	☐
(7) Is the internal audit department responsible directly to the governing board or legislative body?	☐	☐
(8) If so, does it report to such body regularly?	☐	☐
(9) Is the head of the internal audit staff appointed (or confirmed) and terminated with the approval of the governing board or legislative body?	☐	☐
(10) Is the internal audit staff organized by position level and/or audit task teams to allow recognition of responsibilities and performance?	☐	☐
(11) Are specific audit procedures delegated to other audit groups where possible and practical, sub-		

	Yes	*No*
ject to the maintenance of appropriate control over work quality?	☐	☐
(12) Does the internal audit department have		
(a) Goals and objectives?	☐	☐
(b) A policy and procedures manual?	☐	☐
(c) Written audit programs?	☐	☐
(d) Standards of field work?	☐	☐
(e) Job descriptions?	☐	☐

Independence

(13) Have policies been established to determine that the internal audit staff is free of conflicts of interest, including		
(a) Related-party transactions (see Statement on Auditing Standards No. 6)?	☐	☐
(b) Partisan political offices?	☐	☐
(c) Participation in employee bargaining groups?	☐	☐
(14) Do policies require that internal auditors periodically update and sign conflict-of-interest statements?	☐	☐

Section II: Professional Skills

A full-scope government audit requires an adequate staff of competent, experienced personnel. The internal auditors not only must be knowledgeable about accounting and auditing principles and procedures, but also must be informed on such matters as the purposes and objectives of the entities they are auditing, and regulatory legislation. The auditor must be able to communicate audit results to management in a constructive manner.

(1) Has the internal audit department established entry level qualification standards?	☐	☐
(2) Is the internal audit staff composed of full-time career people with adequate professional credentials and apparent capacity for advancement?	☐	☐

	Yes	*No*
(3) Do the working papers and reports of the internal audit staff reflect a degree of competence in		
(a) Financial accounting?	☐	☐
(b) Auditing procedures?	☐	☐
(c) Accounting systems review?	☐	☐
(d) Automatic data processing (ADP) controls review of both installations and applications?	☐	☐
(e) Knowledge of applicable laws and regulations?	☐	☐
(f) Statistical sampling?	☐	☐
(4) Does the collective expertise of the audit staff include the potential for performing		
(a) Financial/compliance audits?	☐	☐
(b) Efficiency and economy audits?	☐	☐
(c) Program results audits?	☐	☐
(5) Does the internal audit staff have available to it, as needed, the services of resource personnel in the areas of		
(a) ADP auditing?	☐	☐
(b) Quantitative audit techniques?	☐	☐
(c) Civil engineering?	☐	☐
(d) Industrial engineering?	☐	☐
(e) Actuarial services?	☐	☐
(6) Is the performance of the internal audit staff periodically evaluated?	☐	☐
(7) Is the staff given demonstrable opportunities for		
(a) Career development?	☐	☐
(b) Training?	☐	☐
(c) Advancement?	☐	☐
(8) Is the internal audit staff compensated at apparently competitive salary scales?	☐	☐

Section III: Audit Performance

Adequate planning is essential for an effective internal audit department. Audit plans should identify the areas to be audited to enable effective scheduling of work and to maximize the use of personnel. Audit plans should be responsive to changing circumstances, however, to provide the best service to management.

	Yes	*No*
(1) Are the internal audit activities planned and conducted under project management or scheduling control, as follows:		
(a) Is audit work coordinated with external auditors?	☐	☐
(b) Do the individuals assigned to each audit have the education and experience necessary for the audit work to be performed?	☐	☐
(c) Is the number of supervisors adequate?	☐	☐
(d) Are outside consultants used where appropriate?	☐	☐
(e) Is on-the-job training provided to inexperienced personnel?	☐	☐
(f) Is there a written program of work to be performed?	☐	☐
(g) Is an entrance conference held to discuss the audit?	☐	☐
(2) Are assignment priorities submitted to and approved by audit management?	☐	☐
(3) If so, are such priorities based on professional judgments?	☐	☐
(4) Are audits planned so that complete systems or departments are covered rather than small segments?	☐	☐
(5) Are audit tasks guided by programs, objectives, or audit guides?	☐	☐
(6) Are internal audit programs, objectives, and/or audit guides revised to reflect changing conditions?	☐	☐
(7) Are the internal audit activities directed toward audit assignments, rather than clerical tasks?	☐	☐
(8) In developing programs, is use made of available programs of other agencies where appropriate?	☐	☐

	Yes	No
(9) Are the internal auditors able to cover significant facilities and functions within a reasonable time cycle?	☐	☐
(10) Is evidence examined to ensure that operational and accounting controls are functioning effectively?	☐	☐
(11) Does the audit work include the examination of sufficient, accurate, and relevant evidence to afford a reasonable basis for the auditors' opinions, judgments, conclusions, and recommendations?	☐	☐
(12) Is the internal audit staff instructed to alert the head of the internal audit department at once of any serious breakdown in control?	☐	☐
(13) Is the head of the internal audit department instructed to make an immediate review when a serious breakdown in control is reported and to report to higher authority so that corrective action can be taken?	☐	☐
(14) Does policy require that the internal auditors investigate		
(a) Potential conflicts of interest?	☐	☐
(b) Related-party transactions?	☐	☐
(c) Acceptance of gifts?	☐	☐
(d) Borrowing at preferred rates?	☐	☐
(e) Failure to record transactions?	☐	☐
(15) Do the internal auditors periodically review the maintenance of conflict-of-interest statements?	☐	☐
(16) Does the audit staff become involved in reviews of new systems early in their development stage?	☐	☐
(17) Does the entity have an effective audit committee?[2]	☐	☐

[2] For further information regarding audit committees, see *Audit Committee Guide* (2d ed., Coopers & Lybrand 1976).

	Yes	*No*
(18) Does the audit committee		
(a) Participate in the selection of the independent auditors?	☐	☐
(b) Review the prospective internal and external audit approaches?	☐	☐
(c) Review audit findings?	☐	☐
(d) Monitor corrective action?	☐	☐

Section IV: Reporting Practices

Audit reports and management letters are of paramount importance to the internal audit function because they are the means by which the auditor communicates his findings, observations, conclusions, and recommendations to the audited entity. The distribution of audit reports in government varies. Reports may go to a governor, legislature, legislative committees, or to the general public.

Management support of the internal auditors' conclusions and recommendations is critical. Lack of support may result in the continuation of uneconomical or inefficient practices.

	Yes	*No*
(1) Are reports issued identifying weaknesses and recommendations for improvement?	☐	☐
(2) Are reports issued on a timely basis?	☐	☐
(3) Is the content of the audit reports		
(a) As concise as possible, yet clear and complete enough to be understood by the users?	☐	☐
(b) Objectively presented?	☐	☐
(4) Is the report in a format that facilitates management action?	☐	☐
(5) Are the audit reports reviewed by the		
(a) Supervisor of internal audit?	☐	☐
(b) Manager of internal audit?	☐	☐
(6) Are the audit findings supported by adequate working papers?	☐	☐

	Yes	*No*
(7) Are the audit working papers reviewed periodically by the		
(a) Supervisor of internal audit?	☐	☐
(b) Manager of internal audit?	☐	☐
(8) Are the findings dollarized where practicable?	☐	☐
(9) Are the findings usually accepted?	☐	☐
(10) Where appropriate, are recommendations made?		
(11) Are such recommendations usually accepted?	☐	☐
(12) Do reports require a response from the agency?	☐	☐
(13) Are reports followed up to determine whether deficiencies are corrected and recommendations considered?	☐	☐
(14) Is an exit conference held to discuss the findings and recommendations of the audit?	☐	☐

CHAPTER 6

Operational Controls Review–Budget Management

Part I—General Discussion

Part II—The Questionnaire

Part I—General Discussion

The public demands accountability over the government's expenditure of appropriated funds. Typically, accountability is achieved through the budgetary process:

> Defined in its most general sense, a budget is a plan of financial operation embodying an estimate of proposed expenditures for a given period of time and the proposed means of financing them. In contemporary public financial administration, there

> are two types of budgets: long-term budgets and annual budgets. The first of these represents estimates of public expenditures for a period of several years . . . and the proposed means of financing such expenditures. Frequently, such a long-term budget is restricted to major capital outlays only, in which case it is referred to as a capital improvement program or capital budget. The second type of budget, sometimes referred to as the current operating budget because it authorizes and controls current financial operations, is the annual budget applicable to each fiscal year. It is the latter budget which the Committee recommends for adoption, whether required by law or not, and which should be integrated with the accounting system to provide a workable system of budgetary accounting and control. . . .[1]

With the growth of government in recent years and the increase of government spending and services, the budgetary function has assumed increased importance. In most instances, even the smallest political subdivisions are required by law to adopt a budget and report comparisons of budget to actual expenditures.

Figure 6-1 outlines the eight fund categories prescribed by the National Committee on Government Accounting in *Governmental Accounting, Auditing and Financial Reporting* (GAAFR). Budgeting requirements, also illustrated in Figure 6-1, generally differ between the various funds. (Figure 6-1 appears on pp. 104–105.)

GAAFR Principles 3 and 13 relating to budgeting are as follows:

> GAAFR Principle 3
>
> An annual budget should be adopted by every governmental unit, whether required by law or not, and the accounting system should provide budgetary control over general governmental revenues and expenditures.[2]
>
> GAAFR Principle 13
>
> Financial statements and reports showing the current condition of budgetary and proprietary accounts should be prepared periodically to control financial operations. At the close of each fiscal year, a comprehensive annual financial report covering all funds and financial operations of the governmental unit should be prepared and published.[3]

---

[1] National Committee on Governmental Accounting, *Governmental Accounting, Auditing and Financial Reporting* 5 (Municipal Finance Officers Association 1969).

[2] *Id.* at 5.

[3] *Id.* at 13.

The budget serves as an important communicative link between an entity's chief executive and its operating departments. It provides the departments with a convenient channel through which they can communicate upward their proposed plans and programs for consideration. Conversely, it provides the chief executive with a tool for overseeing and controlling the entire entity.

Methods of Budgeting

GAAFR defines the three basic methods of budgeting as follows:

> *Traditional Budget.* A term sometimes applied to the budget of a governmental unit wherein expenditures are based entirely or primarily on objects of expenditure.[4]
>
> *Program Budget.* A budget wherein expenditures are based primarily on programs of work and secondarily on character and object. A program budget is a transitional type of budget between the traditional character and object budget, on the one hand, and the performance budget, on the other.[5]
>
> *Performance Budget.* A budget wherein expenditures are based primarily upon measurable performance of activities and work programs. A performance budget may also incorporate other bases of expenditure classification, such as character and object, but these are given a subordinate status to activity performance.[6]

Traditional Budget

The AICPA has described the traditional budget approach as follows:

> The traditional budget emphasizes the planned input of resources into a given organizational unit for particular objects of expenditure, such as salaries, supplies, equipment, maintenance, etc. In its present form it is oriented to the organizational structure for the primary purpose of imposing accounting and administrative responsibility upon department or division heads who expend appropriated funds. Without modification, it will not measure total expenditures for specific services, functions, or activities.

---

[4] *Id.* at 171.
[5] *Id.* at 166.
[6] *Id.*

Figure 6-1

GOVERNMENT FUNDS—CHARACTERISTICS AND BUDGET REQUIREMENTS

Types of Funds	*Budgeting Characteristics and Requirements by Funds*
The following eight types of funds are prescribed for use in accounting for governmental financial operations as indicated.[1]	Budgeting requirements differ among the eight funds prescribed in GAAFR.[2]
(1) *The general fund*—to account for all financial transactions not properly accounted for in another fund.	*The general fund* and special revenue funds have annual budgets, each with its own estimated revenues and appropriations. Normally, the sources of revenues and the functions, activities, and objects of expenditure would be classified in the budget.
(2) *Special revenue funds*—to account for the proceeds of specific revenue sources (other than special assessments) or to finance specified activities as required by law or administrative regulation.	*Special revenue funds* require careful consideration because their revenues may have particular restrictions. For example, a motor fuel tax fund might require budgetary approval by the state agency which distributes the motor fuel tax revenue to the local unit.
(3) *Debt service funds*—to account for the payment of interest and principal on long-term debt other than special assessment and revenue bonds.	*Debt service funds* normally originate by reason of a general obligation bond issue and will be governed by the terms of the issue. The two principal types of bond issues are serial bonds and term bonds, the former being more common. A debt service fund for serial bonds operates almost exactly like a special revenue fund. Term bonds, in contrast, may require accumulation of a sinking fund under specified conditions. There may be several debt service funds in existence at any one time. Typically, there will be a voter referendum approving the project and the related financing. The approved referendum would be implemented by a bond ordinance or resolution, which in effect results in a legal contract between the voters and the bond holders. Consequently, the financial needs for the entire life of the bond issue are provided for at the origin of the issue. As a result, the control factors inherent in an annual budget are satisfied by the terms of the bond resolution or ordinance. Including a budget comparison in the financial statements of a debt service fund provides little information or control, as there should be few variations between budgeted and actual expenditures because the budget for each year should conform with the terms of the indenture agreement.
(4) *Capital projects funds*—to account for the receipt and disbursement of monies used for the acquisition of capital facilities other than those financed by special assessment and enterprise funds.	*Capital project funds* account for resources appropriated for the construction or acquisition of fixed assets. Most governmental units maintain forward moving long-range plans of five or more years in advance. Such planning would give rise to annual authorizations for individual projects, which might be financed by bond issues, intergovernmental grants, or by other means. The project approvals would authorize expenditures not to exceed a given amount for the specific purpose, and would authorize the means of financing, subject to voter referen-

dum or appropriate legal action. These project approvals are then incorporated each year into the formal budgets of the individual unit. Generally, annual operating budgets are not legally required for capital project funds because most projects are not completed within one year. Capital project budgets (for the life of the project) are generally adopted. There may be more than one project in process at any one time, with the result that a separate budget for each project may be adopted; however, projects financed from the same source are usually combined in a single capital budget.

Where a unit utilizes recurring annual revenues to finance smaller capital improvements or projects, generally under a "pay as you go" financing program, the annual budget is more appropriate. Such a fund is also more appropriately titled "capital improvements funds."

(5) *Enterprise funds*—to account for the financing of services to the general public where all or most of the costs involved are paid in the form of charges by users of such services.

For *enterprise funds*, legal requirements vary among jurisdictions as to use of formal budgets. The adoption of a budget providing for estimates of operating revenues and expenses is recommended as an aid to good management and sound financial planning. However, for purposes of achieving flexibility in management and financial planning, authorities generally recommend that such budgets be retained in memorandum form and not be subjected to formal budgetary accounting and control.

(6) *Trust and agency funds*—to account for assets held by a governmental unit as trustee or agent for individuals, private organizations, and other governmental units.

If budgets are used for *trust and agency funds*, an annual budget is appropriate. An example of a trust fund for which a budget may be useful would be a public library given to a municipality by a private foundation that meets part of the library's operating costs, while the remainder is met by tax revenues.

(7) *Intragovernmental service funds*—to account for the financing of special activities and services performed by a designated organization unit within a governmental jurisdiction for other organization units within the same governmental jurisdiction.

Intragovernmental service funds, such as central stores or central garages, perform services principally for the general and special revenue funds. Charges for such services are set at break-even levels as such funds are not intended to generate a profit. Normally, such funds will not have revenue and expense budgets unless required by law. One reason many jurisdictions do not require budgets for such funds is because the principal expenditures which such a fund can incur are limited by the direct appropriations of the various departments it serves.

(8) *Special assessment funds*—to account for special assessments levied to finance public improvements or services deemed to benefit the properties against which the assessments are levied.

Special assessment funds are used to finance and account for the construction and financing of certain public improvements that are to be paid for wholly, or in part, from special assessments levied against benefited property. . . . Unless required by state or local law or ordinances, budgets normally are not adopted for special assessment funds. However, where legally required, the project type budget is the more appropriate.

[1] National Committee on Governmental Accounting, *Governmental Accounting, Auditing and Financial Reporting* 7-8 (Municipal Finance Officers Association 1969).

[2] Committee on Governmental Accounting and Auditing, *Audits of State and Local Governmental Units, Industry Audit Guide* 30-32 (American Institute of Certified Public Accountants 1974).

> The traditional budget is a legal financial plan which involves an estimate of the revenue needs; the planning of spending requirements (which would justify the raising of revenue); legal action, by tax levy ordinance or otherwise, to fulfill these requirements—generally by funds, followed by the legal action of appropriation, again by funds. Generally, original planning is performed by the executive branch, but the final budget is a legislative enactment. . . .[7]

The program budget approach and the performance budget approach each have been described as follows:

Program Budget

> Program budgets deal principally with broad planning and the costs of functions or activities. A *full* program approach to budgeting would require that the full cost of a function, e.g., juvenile delinquency control, would be set forth under the *program* regardless of the organizational units that may be involved in carrying such programs into execution. Thus, in the juvenile delinquency "program," certain activities of the welfare agency, the police department, the juvenile courts, the law department, and the district attorney would be included. . . .
>
> A *modified* program budget approach would be organized solely within major organizational units, e.g., departments.[8] [Emphasis added.]
>
> As the term is used here, "program budgeting" refers to a *planning-oriented* approach which emphasizes programs, functions and activities—with lesser emphasis upon evaluation or control. Performance measurement is not, therefore, a prerequisite to program budgeting, though it may be a useful adjunct. Too, the program approach is *communication-oriented,* with budgetary requests and reports summarized in terms of a few broad programs rather than in a myriad of object-of-expenditure or departmental activity details—though such details may be provided in the executive budget and the final appropriation may be on a line-item basis.[9]

Performance Budget

> This [the performance budget] approach embodies a shifting of emphasis from objects of expenditure to "measurable per-

---

[7] Committee on Governmental Accounting and Auditing, *Audits of State and Local Governmental Units, Industry Audit Guide* 26–27 (American Institute of Certified Public Accountants 1974).

[8] Moak & Killian, *Operating Budget Manual* 11–12 (Municipal Finance Officers Association 1963).

[9] Lynn & Freeman, *Fund Accounting—Theory and Practice* 73 (Prentice-Hall, Inc. 1974).

> formance of activities and work programs." The primary focus is on *evaluation* of the efficiency with which existing activities are being carried out; its primary tools are cost accounting and work measurement. The gist of this method may be summarized as (1) classifying budgetary accounts by function and activity, as well as by organization unit and object of expenditure, (2) investigating and measuring existing activities in order to obtain maximum efficiency and to establish cost standards, and (3) basing the budget of the succeeding period upon unit cost standards multiplied by the expected number of units of the activity estimated to be required in that period. The total budget for an agency would be the sum of the products of its unit cost standards multiplied by the expected units of activity in the upcoming period. The enacted budget is viewed somewhat as a performance contract between the legislative branch and the chief executive.[10]

The auditor will encounter combinations of these three basic approaches. A commonly used combination, the "planning-programming-budgeting" concept (PPB), integrates the three elements in a single budget. The federal government attempted to establish PPB as a federal standard in 1965, but results were not consistent and the requirement was withdrawn. PPB approaches are used in some large state and local governments, but its use by small entities is limited.

Organization and Management

In most large government entities, the budget function is part of the office of the chief executive. The function is usually headed by an administrative or budget officer, who may be supported by a budget staff or committee, depending on the size of the government. In small government entities, the chief executive may serve as the budget officer. In these situations, the chief executive is responsible for the initial preparation of the budget, which he then submits to the legislature or council for review, revision, and final approval.

Some small council-oriented governments provide little power to the office of the chief executive for the overall management of the government. In this environment, the budget function often is the responsibility of the council and is performed by a budget committee appointed by the council.

In both large and small governments, the central budget staff may be supported by smaller budget and planning staffs in major

---

[10] *Id.* at 70.

departments and offices. The central staff is responsible for coordinating and consulting with the department staffs to ensure that the department budgets are in line with the objectives of the government entity, that they are adequately justified, and that they fall within funding constraints established by the council or chief executive.

The following are basic elements of a budgetary process:

- Budget formulation;
- Legislative consideration and adoption of budget; and
- Budget execution.

Budget Formulation

As already stated, budget formulation is usually the responsibility of the chief executive—through the budget officer or committee—and is accomplished by conforming expenditure estimates to anticipated revenues. A necessary part of this process is the budget calendar, which shows estimates of the time required for completion of the various phases of the formulation process and identifies all organizational units covered by the budget. The calendar highlights critical target dates and steps of the formulation process and is prepared by the budget officer or committee.

The budget officer usually initiates the formulation process by providing instructions, schedules, and worksheets to the operating departments to be used in the development of their proposals. When the department heads receive this material, they document their departmental objectives, taking into consideration their long-range work programs, and they determine the materials and personnel required to accomplish their objectives. Because governments generally are faced with limited resources, departments are often required to prepare an alternative budget based on the possibility of funding limitations. When faced with the possibility of funding limitations, it is especially important for each department to establish a priority system for its programs and to identify the impact that funding limitations will have on the effectiveness of the department and its programs.

Once a department has completed a preliminary budget, the document is forwarded to the central budget staff—budget officer or committee—for review. The staff checks the preliminary budget for completeness, accuracy, and compliance with instructions, and evaluates it in terms of the entity's overall financial and program goals and objectives. This involves considerable consultation with department heads.

The staff compiles a budget for the entire entity using the preliminary budgets submitted by the departments. Once a workable budget has been developed, the budget officer meets with the chief executive to present the overall budget. The recommendations of the executive are incorporated in the budget, and then it is resubmitted to the chief executive. When the chief executive has approved the budget, he submits it to the legislative body.

Legislative Consideration and Adoption of Budget

The chief executive's budget package—often referred to as the budget document—includes summary schedules of proposed expenditures for the fiscal year and the official estimate of revenues, supplemental schedules detailing revenues and expenditures, and the chief executive's budget message. The budget document should be detailed enough to be understood by the general public, as well as by the legislature.

In his message, the chief executive should outline the administration's policy, general objectives, and financial status of the government, highlight major new programs or changes to current ones, and discuss problem areas.

Once the legislative body has reviewed the budget, a series of hearings are conducted to examine the budget in detail. Department heads may be asked to explain their sections of the budget and their requests for funds. Private citizens or groups should be given an opportunity to express their views on the budget.

On the basis of the hearings and budgeting sessions, the legislature makes whatever amendments to the budget it deems appropriate. The revised budget is drawn up and presented at a public session of the legislature.

Budget Execution

The responsibility for successful execution of the budget ordinarily rests with the chief executive and the department heads. For successful execution of the budget, the entity must have a system for providing expenditure authority to departments or programs. The chief executive allots expenditure authority to programs, organizational units, or other expenditure classes on a periodic basis, e.g., monthly or quarterly. The purpose of the system is to ensure that funds are available when needed by each organizational element and that control is maintained. In most jurisdictions, legal requirements are established to preclude the organizational elements from spending in excess of the amounts allotted to them. However, most governments have established legal and administrative procedures to provide for emergency fund allotments and transfers.

The allotment system must be supported by a sound accounting system and management reporting system. Separate budget accounts and control ledgers should be established for all budgeted and alloted funds. All expenditures should be approved at an appropriate level and supported by adequate documentation.

Periodic reports on the status of department programs are essential for management control. These reports show the financial status of the programs, including expenditures and encumbrances compared to appropriations, reasons for variances, and suggested revisions to the allotment process.

The financial reports should be supplemented by performance reports that compare actual program results with planned results. These reports provide an overall assessment of the department programs and of the impact that funding constraints, if any, have on program performance.

Department heads use the financial and performance reports to evaluate and measure the operations under their control. The chief executive uses the reports to measure department operations and to assign responsibilities. Managers at all levels use the reports to see that the goals and objectives of their organizational elements are accomplished in an effective and efficient manner.

Part II—The Questionnaire

Background Information

Before using the budget management questionnaire, the auditor should obtain and review the following background information:

(1) Obtain a copy of the budgetary system and procedures manual.

(2) Obtain an analysis by major categories of budgeted and actual results for the current and two prior years, and explanations for significant variances.

Budget Cate-gories	*Current Year*			*Prior Year*			*Prior Year*		
	Actual	*Budget*	*Variance*	*Actual*	*Budget*	*Variance*	*Actual*	*Budget*	*Variance*
......	......	......	......	......	......	......	......	......	......
......	......	......	......	......	......	......	......	......	......
......	......	......	......	......	......	......	......	......	......
......	......	......	......	......	......	......	......	......	......
......	......	......	......	......	......	......	......	......	......

Reasons for variances:

....

....

....

....

....

....

....

(3) With the assistance of budget department officials, summarize controlling legislation and any relevant regulatory requirements relating to the budgetary process. ....

....

....

....

....

....

(4) Obtain a listing showing the key personnel of the budget department by position level and work location.

Name	*Position*	*Location*
....	....	....
....	....	....
....	....	....
....	....	....
....	....	....
....	....	....

Budget Management Questionnaire

Since budgeting is integrated throughout most government operations, use of the budget management questionnaire at an early audit stage is frequently advantageous, since it provides good insight into the workings of an entity.

The budget management questionnaire includes the following categories:

- Section I: Organization and Management;
- Section II: Budget Formulation;
- Section III: Legislative Consideration and Adoption of Budget; and
- Section IV: Budget Execution.

Section I: Organization and Management

Budgeting is important to government because of the critical nature of services provided (for example, fire, police, and education); the complex economic environment; and the public's involvement through elected officials. An effective budgeting process cannot be instituted successfully, however, until the government entity recognizes the need to give budgeting a top place in the organizational structure. Because budgeting embraces all major elements of an organization, it must be directed by a chief executive with sufficient authority to get the job done effectively.

The budgeting function must have a defined organizational structure with appropriate lines of authority and an intelligent grouping of tasks. The structure should be documented with an organization chart and an operations manual.

Normally, the budgeting function is headed by a budget director or officer who reports directly to the chief executive. The size and complexity of the director's organization generally vary with the size of the government.

Executive Planning

	Yes	*No*
(1) If the entity has an executive planning function, does it provide overall goals and objectives for use in the budgeting process?	☐	☐
(2) Does the executive planning group		
(a) Have representation from the various organizational elements?	☐	☐
(b) Formulate and revise the long-range plans to accomplish organizational goals and objectives?	☐	☐
(c) Reconcile the organizational long- and short-range plans with those of the individual departments?	☐	☐
(d) Require the budget to be developed in a manner which is consistent with each fund's method of accounting?	☐	☐

Budget Organization

(3) Does the entity have an identifiable organizational function responsible for the overall budgeting process?	☐	☐
(4) If so, is this function		
(a) Separate from the accounting function?	☐	☐
(b) Accountable to an appropriate management level, preferably the chief executive?	☐	☐
(c) Directed by a budget director or budget officer?	☐	☐
(d) Coordinated with the financial department?	☐	☐
(5) Has the budgeting group developed and implemented a formal budget procedures manual?	☐	☐

	Yes	*No*
(6) If so, do the procedures follow an established budget approach (traditional, program, or performance)?	☐	☐
(7) Has the entity evaluated various budget approaches to determine the one that best meets its needs?	☐	☐
(8) Does the entity's organization provide for an objective review of the budget by an individual knowledgeable in applicable accounting principles?	☐	☐

Section II: Budget Formulation

Budget formulation is usually the responsibility of the chief executive—through the budget officer—and is accomplished by the correlation of financial data and the projected requirements of the various functions and activities of the entity. During the preparation period, the budget director and the various organizational units continuously exchange information, proposals, and evaluations of budgetary requests.

The organizational units must prepare their estimates of revenue and/or expenditures early enough in the cycle to permit appropriate review and consolidation by the budget director. The budget preparation effort should be completed in sufficient time to enable the adoption of the budget before the beginning of the period covered.

Budget Calendar

	Yes	*No*
(1) Is a budget calendar used?	☐	☐
(2) If so, does the calendar		
(a) Detail the completion dates for each phase of the budgeting process?	☐	☐
(b) Identify the organizational units involved in each phase of the process?	☐	☐
(c) Permit time for management review at each organizational level?	☐	☐
(3) Is the calendar based on prior experience modified for anticipated events?	☐	☐

	Yes	*No*
(4) Does the chief executive or budget officer monitor the budgeting process to ensure that each step is accomplished in a timely manner?	☐	☐
(5) Is the budget calendar flexible enough to permit consideration of unforeseen events, e.g., passage of emergency legislation?	☐	☐
(6) Is the budget prepared in accordance with statutory requirements and consistent with each fund's method of accounting?	☐	☐

Revenue Planning

Estimating revenue has as many facets as there are types of revenue. Normally, a government's major source of revenue is taxes. Estimates of tax revenue can generally be derived by applying to the appropriate tax bases the tax rates set by the legislative body. The auditor must ascertain, however, if the entity has considered the relevant determining factors—increases in building activity, rises or declines in unemployment, economic development, new regulations, etc.—in determining the tax bases.

Other revenue sources include licenses and permits, fines and penalties, intergovernmental grants, and shared revenue. The basis for estimating revenue from these sources varies with the type of revenue being considered.

(7) Are estimates of revenue developed before the budget is formulated?	☐	☐
(8) Does the entity have adequate procedures for identifying new sources of revenue?	☐	☐
(9) Are the revenue estimates supported by detailed analyses?	☐	☐
(10) Do revenue estimates give consideration to		
(a) Actual revenues of prior years?	☐	☐
(b) Scheduled funding of grants?	☐	☐
(c) Reimbursement of funds expended?	☐	☐

	Yes	No
(11) Are management's assumptions concerning significant increases or decreases in revenue realistic?	☐	☐
(12) Have those assumptions given consideration to		
(a) New sources of revenue that will be effective in the new year?	☐	☐
(b) Changes in policy or conditions that may affect revenue items?	☐	☐
(c) Anticipated surplus carryovers from prior years?	☐	☐
(d) Anticipated deficit carryovers from prior years?	☐	☐
(e) Reliable estimates of delinquent revenue?	☐	☐
(f) Revenue programs scheduled to end during the budget period?	☐	☐
(g) The effect of pending legislation?	☐	☐

Expenditure Planning

Estimates of expenditures normally fall into two major categories: (1) those covering general expenses that are not the responsibility of any one department, such as interest maturing during the period on general obligation bonds; and (2) those covering operations of the various departments.

Departments prepare their expenditure estimates or budget appropriations in accordance with the governmental budget approach (i.e., traditional, program or performance). To ensure uniformity in the estimates, the budget officer normally issues detailed instructions to the departments before the budget cycle begins.

Budget procedures:

(13) Have forms been developed for departments to use in preparing their expenditure estimates?	☐	☐
(14) Are these forms compatible with the entity's		

		Yes	*No*
	overall budget approach to facilitate consolidation of the estimates into the final budget?	☐	☐
(15)	Are instructional packages sent to all departments in the initial stage of developing the expenditure budget?	☐	☐
(16)	Do these instructional packages include		
	(a) The budget calendar?	☐	☐
	(b) An executive statement concerning goals, policies, and expectations for the upcoming budget period?	☐	☐
	(c) Instructions for completing the budget forms, including comments on required documentation?	☐	☐
	(d) Analysis of the previous year's activities?	☐	☐
(17)	Do the executive policy statement and related policy documents included in the budget package provide		
	(a) A translation of broad goals and policies into detailed requirements for the various departments?	☐	☐
	(b) Positive goals rather than negative ones?	☐	☐
	(c) Measurement criteria?	☐	☐
	(d) The general level of revenue and expenditures for the projected budget period?	☐	☐
	(e) Estimates of expected cost reductions for the year by department?	☐	☐
	(f) Organizational plans for new, improved, or expanded services?	☐	☐
	(g) Notice of new administrative regulations and guidance in their application?	☐	☐
	(h) Comments as to the impact of economic conditions on services and programs?	☐	☐

Department budget formulation:

(18)	Do the department budgets include goals and objectives in line with those in the chief executive's policy statements?	☐	☐

	Yes	*No*
(19) Do the policy statements indicate how the goals and objectives should be measured?	☐	☐
(20) Are the department programs and services consistent with these goals and objectives?	☐	☐
(21) Is department workload data compiled and used to produce and support the budget request?	☐	☐
(22) Are the unit costs and workload data based on actual performance results with consideration given to anticipated events that will affect those measurements?	☐	☐
(23) Does the department budget provide estimated performance results at various levels of funding as well as the department's final recommended budget?	☐	☐
(24) Are the department budget estimates broken out by organizational subunit, e.g., branch or division?	☐	☐
(25) Does the budget officer receive budgets from all departments and institutions over which the entity has jurisdiction?	☐	☐
(26) Are the budgets and supporting data received no later than the date designated in the budget calendar?	☐	☐
(27) Are the department submissions		
(a) In conformance with the overall budget approach?	☐	☐
(b) Adequately supported?	☐	☐
(28) Is the chief executive promptly informed of key decisions made during the department's development of the budget?	☐	☐

	Yes	No
Budget review staff:		
(29) Does the chief executive use program specialists or consultants in the review of department requests?	☐	☐
(30) Is the chief executive's budget review staff of sufficient size to ensure effective review and appraisal of the department submissions?	☐	☐
(31) Does the budget review staff		
(a) Correlate the budget requests with the short- and long-range plans of the department and the governmental entity?	☐	☐
(b) Review the department assumptions to make certain that all factors (wage increases, for example) that influence the estimates are incorporated into the budget?	☐	☐
(c) Verify the adequacy and accuracy of the data submitted by the departments?	☐	☐
(d) Coordinate the review with each department to ensure that budget requests are fully understood and supported?	☐	☐
(e) Verify that department procurements and services are not duplicated by another department?	☐	☐
(32) In preparing the budget data for the chief executive's review, does the review staff		
(a) Prepare or request additional information that will facilitate the chief executive's review?	☐	☐
(b) Prepare a comprehensive budget package, including recommendations for action?	☐	☐
(c) Determine that the chief executive's policy statements have been recognized in the budget package?	☐	☐
(33) Does the budget officer keep the chief executive		

		Yes	*No*
	informed of the review staff's actions and key decisions?	☐	☐
(34)	Are the major revisions proposed by the review staff approved by the chief executive?	☐	☐
(35)	Does the budget officer and/or review staff assist the chief executive in		
	(a) Preparing the final budget document?	☐	☐
	(b) Responding to legislative inquiries on the budget, including the development of additional support data where needed?	☐	☐
	Submission of budget for chief executive's review:		
(36)	Are the department budget requests consolidated into a budget summary for the chief executive's review?	☐	☐
(37)	Is the summary and supportive data sufficient for the chief executive to prepare his recommendations to the legislative body?	☐	☐
(38)	During his review of the expenditure budget, does the chief executive have an up-to-date estimate of revenue?	☐	☐
(39)	Are the departments given an opportunity to support their requests through hearings or by providing additional data before the chief executive's revision of the budget?	☐	☐
(40)	Does the chief executive refrain from making arbitrary adjustments to expenditure requests?	☐	☐
(41)	Before reducing expenditure requests, does the chief executive evaluate the impact the reduction will have on services or in creating revenue, such as matching grant funds?	☐	☐

Section III: Legislative Consideration and Adoption of Budget

When the chief executive has completed his review, the budget document is prepared for submission to the legislative body for its consideration and adoption. Normally, the document includes a summary budget schedule, detailed statements, and a message from the chief executive. The detailed statements reflect past operations, debt summaries, a statement of debt limits, and a comparative statement of tax levies and collections.

After the legislative body receives the budget, it initiates the review process preparatory to its final adoption. For large entities, committees within the legislative body review the budget before it is considered by the full legislative body.

	Yes	*No*
Budget Document		
(1) Does the budget document submitted to the legislative body contain		
(a) A message from the chief executive?	☐	☐
(b) A budget summary showing estimated revenues and expenditures for each fund?	☐	☐
(c) Detailed schedules of revenues by fund and source and expenditures by fund and function/program?	☐	☐
(d) Schedules of nondepartmental program expenditures by fund?	☐	☐
(e) An appropriate level of detail for expenditures? (Minor expenditures and programs should be consolidated to avoid excessive detail.)	☐	☐
(2) Does the chief executive's statement explain the major budget items, current financial status of the entity, and recommendations for the coming year?	☐	☐
(3) Do the revenue statements provide data on revenue earned and resources carried over from the prior year?	☐	☐
(4) If short-term borrowing is contemplated, does the document contain schedules of current borrowing and proposed borrowing for the coming year?	☐	☐

	Yes	*No*
(5) Are proposed programs or revisions to old ones adequately justified and supported in the budget document materials?	☐	☐
(6) Are variances between budgeted and actual results for prior year revenues and expenditures adequately explained in the document?	☐	☐

Legislative Review

(7) Does the legislative body's system provide for a review of the budget?	☐	☐
(8) Are the chief executive and department heads given an opportunity to justify their requests to the legislative review committee and/or legislative body?	☐	☐
(9) Are public hearings conducted on the proposed budget?	☐	☐
(10) Is publicity given to the public hearings?	☐	☐
(11) Is appropriate legislative action taken to ensure that new sources of revenue are effective in time to finance expenditures?	☐	☐
(12) Does the chief executive prepare or participate in the preparation of the legislative documents, i.e., appropriation acts or ordinances and tax-levy ordinances?	☐	☐
(13) Does the entity's system permit expedient response to legislative program changes and related requests for alternative financial proposals?	☐	☐
(14) Is the entity able to respond in a timely manner to the legislative body's requests for additional support and explanation?	☐	☐
(15) Are department heads made aware of potential changes to their programs?	☐	☐

	Yes	*No*
(16) Do the appropriation acts or ordinances		
(a) Agree with the final approved budget?	☐	☐
(b) Permit the chief executive some flexibility in administering the budget?	☐	☐

Section IV: Budget Execution

The budgeting process does not stop with the adoption of the budget by the legislative body. Suitable procedures and controls must exist to ensure that the budget is executed properly.

Proper control over budget execution encompasses the allotment procedure, a sound budgetary reporting system, and expenditure control. Although budget execution is directly related to the accounting function, operational controls must exist to restrict expenditures to the amounts allotted to each fund and to identify budget variances and their cause.

Allotment Procedures

The appropriation act or ordinance generally does not specify the rate at which expenditures are to be made throughout the year. Therefore, the chief executive in most government entities divides the budgeted appropriations between the various departments by time period or by particular project or activity.

This process is intended to achieve an effective and orderly use of funds. In some jurisdictions, it may be a violation of law for a department or agency of a government entity to incur obligations or make expenditures in excess of the allotted amounts. The allotment process provides the chief executive with a control device that can be used to ensure that expenditures are made as needed and that expenditures correspond with the flow of revenue. In any event, the control process should be evaluated to determine if the cost of control is greater than the benefits derived.

(1) After the legislature approves the budget, are all departments provided with an approved operating budget?	☐	☐
(2) Using the funding parameters established by the budget, are fund allotment forecasts developed for each department?	☐	☐

	Yes	*No*
(3) Does the funding schedule		
(a) Show the intradepartmental distribution of funds to activities or functions?	☐	☐
(b) Contain a monthly analysis of how the funds will be obligated and expended?	☐	☐
(4) In developing his funding schedule, does the department head		
(a) Consider increases or decreases in the rate and volume of activities (for example, the opening of a new municipal building would increase the workload of the public works department)?	☐	☐
(b) Consider seasonal variations in activity (for example, funding park services)?	☐	☐
(c) Allow lead time for review of the schedule by the chief executive and budget director?	☐	☐
(5) Is the annual funding schedule supplemented by monthly or quarterly requests for funds from the departments to the chief executive?	☐	☐
(6) Are the periodic requests reviewed by the budget director or chief executive to assure compliance with		
(a) The department budget?	☐	☐
(b) The funding schedule?	☐	☐
(7) When department allotment limits are reached before the end of an interim period (month, quarter, etc.), does the system		
(a) Provide for the discontinuation of funding?	☐	☐
(b) Require that the department submit data to support the need for increased funds?	☐	☐
(c) Require the chief executive's approval for additional funds?	☐	☐
(8) Are appropriate management actions initiated when allotment limits are exceeded without chief executive approval?	☐	☐

	Yes	*No*

Budget Reporting

Management should use an effective budget reporting system to control the implementation of the budget. The reporting system should provide management with data on financial and program performance results.

Reporting system:

	Yes	No
(9) Has the entity established a results-oriented reporting system which provides		
(a) Financial results?	☐	☐
(b) Performance results?	☐	☐

Financial reports:

	Yes	No
(10) Does the financial aspect of the reporting system provide for the issuance of		
(a) Revenue and expenditure statements?	☐	☐
(b) Balance sheets?	☐	☐
(11) Are the financial reports		
(a) Prepared on a periodic basis?	☐	☐
(b) Prepared for all funds?	☐	☐
(c) Generated as a part of the basic accounting system?	☐	☐
(12) Do the financial statements provide full disclosure of		
(a) Anticipated deficits or surpluses?	☐	☐
(b) Encumbrances through the end of the budget period?	☐	☐
(c) Current conditions of appropriations?	☐	☐
(d) Actual versus estimated revenues and expenditures?	☐	☐
(e) Reasons for revenue and expenditure variances?	☐	☐

	Yes	No
Performance reports:		
(13) Do the performance reports generated by the reporting system		
(a) Show actual results in the same format and period as the budgeted estimates?	☐	☐
(b) Contain explanations for variances from the budget?	☐	☐
(c) Provide an analysis of the causes and effects of the variances?	☐	☐
(d) Contain revised estimates when actual results differ substantially from anticipated results?	☐	☐
(e) Forecast needs and anticipated results through the end of the budget period?	☐	☐
(f) Provide the data needed by management to evaluate the execution of the budget?	☐	☐
(g) Provide meaningful measurement of actual performance?	☐	☐
(14) Are the performance reports timely?	☐	☐
(15) Are the performance reports accurate?	☐	☐
(16) Are needs for additional funding identified soon enough to permit time for required legislative action?	☐	☐
Management review of reports:		
(17) Does the entity have procedures for continuous report review by responsible and knowledgeable staff?	☐	☐
(18) Is the review group experienced in the entity's overall operation?	☐	☐
(19) In performing its review responsibilities, does the staff		
(a) Evaluate department requests for additional funds?	☐	☐
(b) Provide guidance to departments when ad-		

	Yes	No
ditional funds are needed or when action is required to correct budget variances?	☐	☐
(c) Evaluate department assumptions used to forecast budget needs for the remainder of the budget period?	☐	☐
(d) Respond to budget variations by determining the causes and effects and either taking appropriate corrective action or recommending such action to the chief executive?	☐	☐
(20) In reviewing performance, does the review staff		
(a) Assure that the departments submit budget reports (financial and performance) on a timely basis?	☐	☐
(b) Keep the executive informed of actual operational results on a timely basis?	☐	☐
(c) Develop proposals and make recommendations to resolve budget conflicts?	☐	☐
(d) Follow up on executive recommendations to the departments on budgetary matters to ensure they are being implemented?	☐	☐
(21) On a broader scale, does the review staff periodically evaluate the cost versus benefit of the entity's programs and services (for example, the group might evaluate the cost versus benefit of the summer-in-the-parks-program)?	☐	☐
General:		
(22) Does top management (chief executive and department heads) respond to the recommendations of the review staff?	☐	☐
(23) Does management respond in a timely manner?	☐	☐
(24) When significant revisions are made to the budget, are long-range plans revised?	☐	☐
(25) Has the reporting system been reviewed and evaluated recently?	☐	☐

	Yes	No
Expenditure Approval		
Under most government budgeting systems, expenditures and obligations have to be approved before the actual disbursement is made. Some government entities may require approvals only for major expenditures, while others require that all expenditures be approved.		
(26) Do procedures require approval of		
(a) Encumbrances?	☐	☐
(b) Expenditures?	☐	☐
(27) Has this approval function been assigned to an appropriate management level, e.g., chief accounting officer?	☐	☐
(28) Does the approval function include		
(a) Determination that the expenditure does not exceed the allotment limit?	☐	☐
(b) Determination that the purpose of the expenditure is in line with the purpose detailed in the budget?	☐	☐
(c) Proper coding of the expenditure to facilitate recording in budget accounts?	☐	☐
(29) For planned contract obligations and expenditures, does the approval function		
(a) Obtain certification from the procurement function that all prior contracting requirements from the same vendor or source have been met?	☐	☐
(b) Make certain that progress payments comply with the contract, including any provisions for the retention of a percentage of the payment?	☐	☐
(c) Obtain evidence that the contracted results have been accepted before final payment is made?	☐	☐

	Yes	No
(30) For major purchases, does the approval function		
(a) Ensure that the purchase has been properly authorized?	☐	☐
(b) Ascertain that the item has been inspected and accepted before payment?	☐	☐
(c) Ensure that available discounts are taken?	☐	☐
(31) Are major obligations or expenditures forwarded to the chief executive for his review and approval?	☐	☐

CHAPTER 7

Operational Controls Review–Personnel

Part I—General Discussion

Part II—The Questionnaire

Part I—General Discussion

Effectiveness in government is largely dependent on the quality and responsiveness of the people that carry out operations. The importance of people as a factor in public administration and the magnitude of labor costs make it essential that human resources are employed efficiently. The purpose of this chapter is to provide guidelines for evaluating the effectiveness of a government entity's personnel function. The preferred practice questions contained herein are designed to evaluate the means by which employees are selected and to evaluate the extent to which the needs of both management and its employees are met subsequently.

The overall goal of any personnel function should be

> . . . to identify people with management potential early in their careers; to encourage the growth and development of all employees; to provide jobs that enable the jobholder to experience a sense of satisfaction and achievement; and to supply the organization with a continuing supply of competent, imaginative, well qualified management people.[1]

Within this frame of reference, we will discuss the components of an effective personnel function.

Personnel Structure

One of the primary responsibilities of a personnel function/department is the development and maintenance of a personnel structure for the organization. Basic requirements for a satisfactory personnel structure include a position classification system and clearly defined personnel requirements and policies.

Position Classification System

One of the requisites of an effective personnel structure is a position classification system. A position classification system defines particular jobs in terms of the functions and responsibilities they entail, and the skills and capabilities needed for the job. The use of a position classification system greatly facilitates staffing because it simplifies the matching of candidate qualifications with job requirements. It also provides a proper balance of supervisory and staff positions, which can serve as an important control on the performance of individuals and groups within an organization. It ensures that appropriate levels of supervision are available to all employees and provides top management with a means to delegate responsibilities and to evaluate performance.

A classification system should be reviewed periodically and updated by both operating and personnel managers. The personnel managers also must coordinate their efforts with the chief executive of the entity so that the system established is responsive to the plans and policies of top management. For example, the chief executive must communicate anticipated budgeting and other funding con-

---

[1] *Staffing Systems–Managerial and Professional Jobs, Report No. 558* 118 (The Conference Board 1972).

straints to the personnel manager so that the appropriate revisions can be made to personnel forecasts.

Personnel Requirements and Policies

As discussed in Chapter 3, the pursuit of clearly perceived goals is particularly effective in directing human energies. People with ill-defined objectives seldom produce, while people with definite goals are often highly productive. In keeping with this philosophy, it is extremely important that employees are aware of what is expected of them in day-to-day operations, based on management policy. "A policy is a predetermined, selected course established as a guide toward accepted goals and objectives."[2] Policy is an expression of how management proposes to attain its objectives or, in other words, a guideline as to what is expected.

With regard to the management of personnel, clearly defined guidelines or policies should be developed for functions such as the following:

- Recruiting;
- Hiring;
- Training and development;
- Performance appraisal and promotion; and
- Compensation and related benefits.

Personnel policies, of course, vary from entity to entity as well as within the framework of authorizing laws and regulations. The essential consideration is that appropriate policies are established and effectively implemented.

Recruiting

Because of the importance of people as a factor in public administration, care must be taken to ensure that job vacancies are filled with the best-qualified individuals. Because employment commitments in most government entities are long-term and involve long-range benefits, an effective recruiting system must be used to attract those individuals who will enhance operations.

The recruiting process begins by defining personnel needs from the standpoint of the positions to be filled and the skills required. In

---

[2] Yoder, *Personnel Management and Industrial Relations* 26 (6th ed., Prentice-Hall, Inc. 1970).

defining needs, the personnel department must work closely with the requesting department in order to gain an understanding of the type of individual to be recruited.

Once personnel needs have been defined, a judgment must be made as to where the prospective candidates are likely to be found. Sources include the following:

- College recruitment;
- Minority recruitment;
- Placement services;
- Vocational or trade schools; and
- Announcements in newspapers, trade journals, etc.

Hiring

The next step is to determine how the actual selection is to be made. The first action should be to obtain sufficient information on the candidates and their work and educational backgrounds. With regard to candidates applying for technical positions, it may be useful to evaluate the quality and reputation of the trade school or other training received by the candidate. Much of the data required can be supplied by requiring each candidate to complete a written application form and, if the position demands, a resumé detailing work history and other biographical information. In those situations that demand more data, written references can be requested from former employers of the candidate. For most positions, however, the use of the organization's standard application form should suffice.

In order that the application form can be applied on a broad scale, the form should ask only for the data needed to make an employment judgment. It should not ask for unduly sensitive or personal information.

Some positions require that the candidate be subjected to skill tests. The tests should be designed to make certain all applicants are given a fair opportunity to demonstrate their skills.

Probably the most widely used and at the same time the best process for screening prospective candidates is the personal interview conducted by the personnel manager and/or the operating manager. Both employer and applicant benefit from an interview because the exchange of information enables both parties to learn things that facilitate the important decision to be made.

Training and Development

No organization can afford to ignore the educational and career development needs of its employees if it is to maintain the level of competence required for effective operations. Employee training and development must begin the first day an individual reports to work and must continue throughout his career. The intensity of the training and development depends on the nature of the job.

Each new employee should participate in a basic orientation program to familiarize him with the organization and its goals and provide the instruction necessary to perform the job. The program should provide the new employee with administrative requirements such as hours of operation and time reporting procedures. The job assignment instructions normally should come from the new employee's supervisor. Not only does this help the person understand his duties as the supervisor sees them, it also gives the parties the opportunity to get acquainted and reduce the tension generated by such situations.

Many organizations have found it useful to employ training directors for orientation programs and other formal training required on an organization-wide basis. The director's primary duties are to define the training needs of the entity; obtain the necessary funding for the programs; administer desired programs; and carry out a continuous study and evaluation of the entity's training needs. To accomplish the training objectives, the director must work closely with the operating managers to ensure that the appropriate training is provided, and that it is available at appropriate stages in the employees' career development.

Training is a costly investment and should not be taken lightly by management. It is important that all alternatives be considered before embarking on a particular program. For example, it may be less costly to use a local college or university to provide the desired training than to develop a course in-house. The use of outside agencies and consultants also should be considered and evaluated.

Performance Appraisal and Promotion

Another important aspect of employee development and promotion is the appraisal of performance. Employees should be provided with an effective system whereby their performance is appraised both on an informal and formal basis. It is imperative that the organization provide a channel for communicating this evaluation to the employee and for the employee to have an opportunity to react to the evaluation.

The informal performance appraisal, in most instances, comes from the employee's immediate supervisor. Thus, the occurrence and nature of such appraisals are often determined by the attitude of each supervisor.

The formal appraisal process should provide for the completion of standard appraisal or counseling forms. These forms should be prepared on a periodic basis, reviewed by the appraiser's supervisor, discussed with the employee, and made a part of his personnel file. The system should allow for a response from the employee verifying that he has accepted the appraisal.

In developing standard appraisal forms, most organizations have found it desirable to have different, specialized forms for various staff levels, trades, and skills. This increases the usefulness of the forms, since they can be designed to relate more specifically to the employees' job assignments. Regardless of the appraisal system used —informal, formal, or a combination of both—the important factor is the organization's recognition of the need for using an appraisal system.

Compensation and Related Benefits

Most government organizations have found it necessary to provide their employees with services and benefits in addition to their basic salaries. Many of these, such as working facilities, insurance and health programs, and other fringe benefits have become so significant to the employee that they often are the determining factors in the employment selection. If the organization is to compete in the labor market, it must develop a viable program of employee services and benefits.

Employee benefit programs can be costly, so management should carefully define the organizational needs in relation to the cost of meeting these needs. From the auditor's perspective, the important factor is to make certain that management has adequately defined what employee services and benefits are provided and has given attention to the costs versus benefits of such programs. Each employee service and benefit program must have clearly defined objectives, and management should periodically assess the degree to which the programs achieve these objectives. The key consideration is that management maintain control over these programs and carefully evaluate the cost versus benefit before embarking on any new programs.

Part II—The Questionnaire

Background Information

Before initiating the review of a personnel department, the following background information should be obtained:

(1) Obtain data on the number of employees authorized and employed.

Department or Program	*Operating*		*Administrative*	
	Authorized	*Employed*	*Authorized*	*Employed*
....	....	....	....	....
....	....	....	....	....
....	....	....	....	....
....	....	....	....	....
....	....	....	....	....
....	....	....	....	....
TOTAL				

(2) Obtain a five-year summary of personnel costs.

Year	*Operating*	*Administrative*	*Total*
.....	$..........	$..............	$..........
.....	....	....	....
.....	....	....	....
.....	....	....	....
.....	....	....	....
TOTAL	$	$	$

(3) Obtain a five-year summary of the employee turnover rate.

Year	*Turnover Rate (%)*		
	Operating	*Administrative*	*Total*
.....	....	....	....
.....	....	....	....
.....	....	....	....
.....	....	....	....
.....	....	....	....

(4) Obtain a listing showing the key personnel of the personnel department by position level and work location.

Name	*Position*	*Location*
....	....	....
....	....	....
....	....	....
....	....	....
....	....	....
....	....	....

Personnel Questionnaire

This questionnaire should be used as a guide for reviewing a personnel department. The questionnaire contains the following sections:

- Section I: Personnel Structure;
- Section II: Filling Personnel Needs;
- Section III: Training and Promotion; and
- Section IV: Working Conditions.

Section I: Personnel Structure

Basic requirements for a satisfactory personnel structure include a position classification system and sound and clearly defined personnel policies.

	Yes	*No*
(1) Does the personnel department have		
(a) Clearly defined goals and objectives?	☐	☐
(b) Criteria to measure their accomplishment?	☐	☐
(2) Are results		
(a) Documented?	☐	☐
(b) Compared to goals and objectives?	☐	☐
(3) Are the department's lines of authority and responsibility clearly defined?	☐	☐
(4) Does the department have clearly defined, written personnel policies?	☐	☐
(5) Are personnel policies adhered to?	☐	☐

	Yes	*No*
(6) Has the personnel department developed a position classification system for all major departments, programs, and activities?	☐	☐
(7) If so, does the system differentiate between levels of responsibility and complexity of work?	☐	☐
(8) Has an analysis of job and skill requirements been made?	☐	☐
(9) Does the classification system include		
(a) Position descriptions?	☐	☐
(b) Skill level analysis?	☐	☐
(c) Performance requirements?	☐	☐
(d) Salary ranges?	☐	☐
(10) Are the position descriptions periodically reviewed and updated?	☐	☐
(11) Are job assignments consistent with the job descriptions?	☐	☐
(12) Are applicable laws, regulations, and union contracts adhered to?	☐	☐
(13) Has the department projected the government entity's short- and long-range personnel needs?	☐	☐
(14) If so, do these projections give consideration to		
(a) The short- and long-range plans of each department?	☐	☐
(b) Attrition?	☐	☐
(c) Promotions and transfers to other departments?	☐	☐
(d) New skills that may be required?	☐	☐
(e) Transfers or other dispositions of excess employees?	☐	☐
(f) Innovations that may reduce personnel needs (for example, automatic data processing equipment)?	☐	☐

(15) Does the personnel department interact with the

	Yes	*No*
operating departments periodically to determine if duplication of activities occurs?	☐	☐
(16) Does the department use personnel pools for seasonal, emergency, and temporary assignments (see Chapter 4, Dollarization Procedure 1: Personnel Allocation)?	☐	☐

Section II: Filling Personnel Needs

The first step in effectively managing the personnel function is a careful evaluation of current and prospective personnel requirements and capabilities. An effective recruiting system must exist to ensure that adequate numbers of qualified employees are available when needed.

	Yes	*No*
(1) Are periodic analyses made to determine if work being done is essential?	☐	☐
(2) Are positions filled when a need exists rather than when a vacancy occurs?	☐	☐
(3) Does the department have an effective recruiting system?	☐	☐
(4) If so, does the recruiting system provide for		
(a) Use of position descriptions?	☐	☐
(b) Use of financial advancement as incentive?	☐	☐
(c) Consideration of present staff to fill open positions through promotion or transfer?	☐	☐
(d) Contact with educational, professional, and vocational agencies to seek qualified applicants?	☐	☐
(e) Public announcement of positions available?	☐	☐
(f) Controls to ensure compliance with		
(i) applicable laws and regulations?	☐	☐
(ii) the personnel budget?	☐	☐
(5) Does the recruiting system include		
(a) Completion of standard application forms?	☐	☐
(b) Testing of applicants for technical positions?	☐	☐

	Yes	*No*
(c) Evaluation of applicants' qualifications and prior experience?	☐	☐
(d) Personal interviews?	☐	☐
(e) Verifying references?	☐	☐
(f) Bonding procedures?	☐	☐
(g) Final review and approval by management?	☐	☐
(h) Documentation of the process?	☐	☐
(6) Are pertinent federal, state, and local equal employment opportunity regulations adhered to?	☐	☐
(7) Does the personnel department periodically evaluate the effectiveness of the government entity's equal employment opportunity program?	☐	☐
(8) Are new employees given a medical examination?	☐	☐
(9) Has the department established procedures for the selection and use of consultants?	☐	☐
(10) If so, do the procedures provide for		
(a) An evaluation process that establishes a definite need		
(i) for skills not available in-house?	☐	☐
(ii) for skills to supplement fully utilized in-house skills?	☐	☐
(b) A selection process designed to obtain the most qualified individual or group?	☐	☐
(c) Guidance as to fee limitations?	☐	☐
(d) A system of follow-up to evaluate a consultant's performance?	☐	☐
(e) Competitive bidding (see Chapter 4, Dollarization Procedure 2: Bidding)?	☐	☐
(f) Audit of contract terms?	☐	☐

Section III: Training and Promotion

The training and development of people must be a major activity of any entity that strives to operate efficiently. People, like any other resource, must be developed to enable them to make their maximum contribution toward the achievement of an entity's objectives.

	Yes	*No*
(1) Does the department have an orientation program for new employees?	☐	☐
(2) If so, does the program include		
(a) A general description of the program and how the new employee relates to the total program?	☐	☐
(b) An adequate description of job specifications?	☐	☐
(c) A description of administrative requirements (work hours, timekeeping procedures, etc.)?	☐	☐
(d) A description of duties (normally given by the immediate supervisor)?	☐	☐
(e) Formal training if required?	☐	☐
(3) Does the department follow up on the performances of new employees to determine if they are achieving job standards?	☐	☐
(4) Do present employees meet the stated job specifications?	☐	☐
(5) Are periodic staff meetings conducted to keep employees informed of department activities?	☐	☐
(6) Are performance rating reports used?	☐	☐
(7) Are performance rating reports used in determining promotions and pay adjustments?	☐	☐
(8) Do promotion and transfer procedures include		
(a) Comparison of position requirements with employee qualifications?	☐	☐
(b) Testing of employees where appropriate?	☐	☐
(c) Competition for openings for all employees who meet the minimum qualifications?	☐	☐
(9) Are employees made aware of and encouraged		

		Yes	*No*
	to participate in training programs that will assist them in advancing to higher positions?	☐	☐
(10)	Does the personnel department monitor and follow up on		
	(a) Absences?	☐	☐
	(b) Excessive time off?	☐	☐
	(c) Chronic lateness?	☐	☐
	(d) Failure to work a full day?	☐	☐
	(e) Actual or expected vacancies?	☐	☐
(11)	Do the various departments maintain a program to monitor		
	(a) Quantity of work performed (see Chapter 4, Dollarization Procedure 1: Personnel Allocation)?	☐	☐
	(b) Individual or unit productivity data (see Chapter 4, Dollarization Procedure 1: Personnel Allocation)?	☐	☐
	(c) Machine downtime data (see Chapter 4, Dollarization Procedure 3: Equipment Downtime Evaluation)?	☐	☐
	(d) Processing time data (see Chapter 4, Dollarization Procedure 4: Computer Utilization)?	☐	☐
	(e) Premium time data (see Chapter 4, Dollarization Procedure 5: Personnel Utilization Evaluation)?	☐	☐
(12)	Are work output requirements established?	☐	☐
(13)	Have performance standards been established?	☐	☐
(14)	If so, do they include standards as to		
	(a) Quality of service?	☐	☐
	(b) Timeliness of service?	☐	☐
	(c) Quantity of service?	☐	☐
(15)	Are performance standards adhered to?	☐	☐
(16)	Are quality control techniques used?	☐	☐

	Yes	*No*
(17) Are work measurements or similar techniques used?	☐	☐
(18) Are error rates established for each job?	☐	☐
(19) Are error ratios acceptable for economical and efficient performance?	☐	☐
(20) Do personnel department managers recognize that they are responsible for the use of effective personnel methods and procedures?	☐	☐

Section IV: Working Conditions

Appropriate personnel policies regarding the health, safety, security, and comfort of employees are important if the government entity is to attract and retain high-caliber individuals.

Health and Safety

	Yes	*No*
(1) Are employees provided with clean, well-lighted, and well-ventilated working facilities?	☐	☐
(2) Does the entity have an active health and safety program?	☐	☐
(3) If so, does the program provide		
(a) Written guidance to employees?	☐	☐
(b) Special precautions for employees in dangerous work areas?	☐	☐
(c) Training seminars?	☐	☐
(d) Periodical medical examinations?	☐	☐
(e) Compliance with grantor requirements where individuals and animals are used as research subjects?	☐	☐
(4) Does the entity have a formal safety reporting system?	☐	☐
(5) Are first-aid stations and other medical facilities available to employees?	☐	☐

	Yes	*No*
(6) Are accident reports reviewed by management to determine causes and identify trends?	☐	☐
(7) Does management take action to promote safety in high-risk areas and areas with recurring accidents?	☐	☐
(8) Does the entity have		
(a) A fire-prevention program?	☐	☐
(b) A fire-drill schedule?	☐	☐
(c) A sufficient number of fire extinguishers?	☐	☐
(9) Are employees covered by workmen's compensation or similar plans?	☐	☐

Employee Benefits

(10) Does the entity have a hospitalization and group life insurance plan for the employees?	☐	☐
(11) Does the entity have a retirement plan for employees?	☐	☐
(12) If so, has a qualified actuary determined whether it is adequately funded?	☐	☐

Administration

(13) Does the personnel function periodically conduct productivity analyses of the various departmental functions and activities (see Chapter 4, Dollarization Procedures 1: Personnel Allocation; and 5: Personnel Utilization Evaluation)?	☐	☐
(14) Do the analyses consider the potential for using more modern equipment and techniques to increase productivity at less cost (see Chapter 4, Dollarization Procedure 6: New Machine Feasibility)?	☐	☐
(15) Does the entity have an awards program for recognizing superior performance?	☐	☐

		Yes	*No*
(16)	Is there a system whereby employees can make cost reduction or other suggestions?	☐	☐
(17)	If so, are suggestions reviewed and appropriately acted upon by management?	☐	☐
(18)	Are employees rewarded for suggestions used by management?	☐	☐
(19)	Have employee conduct standards been established and communicated to all employees?	☐	☐
(20)	Are counseling services available to employees?	☐	☐
(21)	Are new employees briefed as to their responsibility for security?	☐	☐

CHAPTER 8

Operational Controls Review–Cash Management

Part I—General Discussion

Cash management is one operating area in which efficiency and economy become one and the same thing: If money is not spent as efficiently as possible, it is not spent as economically as possible.

The preferred practices contained in this chapter are designed to promote an effective cash management system in a government entity. Cash flow must be planned to ensure that cash is available during periods of peak need and to maximize earnings on idle funds during periods of surplus. The effects of inefficient cash management may often seem to be negligible, but in agencies receiving and disbursing millions of dollars a year, poor cash management can result in serious losses.

Emphasis must be placed on practical steps to counter at least some of the effects of inflation. Effective anti-inflationary systems must start by seeking to improve or protect the cash position. Reducing monetary items, such as cash or accounts receivable, is crucial in minimizing the effects of eroding purchasing power. Other ways to lessen the effects of inflation are to improve the yields on investments, speed up the flow of receipts, and delay the flow of disbursements. (See Appendix VI: Anti-Inflation Tactics.) The subject of operational policies for a period of inflation is, of course, a large one, and we do not intend to give it comprehensive coverage here. Rather, we hope to touch on usable ideas, both as reminders and perhaps as new techniques gleaned from our own day-to-day experiences.

Management Methods

The principal tools of effective cash management are forecasts and budgets. A financial forecast is a statement presenting the most likely outcome of a given set of assumptions. A cash budget is an aggregation of forecasted revenue and expenditures for a given period of time. Its purpose is to determine the timing and magnitude of projected cash requirements and availability.

The high predictability in government of receipts (taxes, grants, assessments) and disbursements (wages, other operating costs, capital expenditures) facilitates cash budgeting. By using this technique, an entity can plan for the investment of any surplus funds and can minimize expensive short-term borrowing.

Essentially, a well-managed cash-flow system results from the adherence to a few basic rules:

- Cash must be brought under control as quickly as possible. This depends on fast and accurate processing, including daily bank deposits, lock-box systems, and timely, accurate grant requests.
- The amount of cash not generating income must be kept at a minimum. The cash balance maintained must be determined with reference to the compensating balance requirements imposed by commercial banks as well as an entity's forecast of cash needs.
- Disbursements should be postponed to the latest possible date.

Part II—The Questionnaire

Background Information

In developing an understanding of an entity's cash management function, an auditor must have insight into the entity as a whole. He must focus on the organization and management of the receipts and disbursements systems, banking relations, forecasting and budgeting procedures, and the general use of funds. To develop this understanding, the following information should be obtained:

(1) Obtain summary data on the entity's banking arrangements. Indicate type of account (i.e., savings, demand deposits, etc.) and the compensating balances required, if any. For other services, indicate type and fee arrangement. (Use figures for latest available year.) Group similar accounts and services together.

	Bank	*Account Service Type*	*Purpose*	*Interest Rate*	*Compensating Balance/Service Fee*
(A)	......	....	....	....	$.................
(B)	......	....	....	....	....
(C)	......	....	....	....	....
(D)	......	....	....	....	....
(E)	......	....	....	....	....
(F)	......	....	....	....	....
(G)	......	....	....	....	....
	TOTAL				$

(2) Indicate month-end balances for all major accounts listed above, for the latest period for which data is available. (The letters used to describe the bank accounts correspond to the entries listed above. List amounts in thousands.)

Month	*Account*							*Total*
	(A)	*(B)*	*(C)*	*(D)*	*(E)*	*(F)*	*(G)*	
....	$....	$....	$....	$....	$....	$....	$....	$......
....	....	....	....	....	....	....	....	......
....	....	....	....	....	....	....	....	......
....	....	....	....	....	....	....	....	......
....	....	....	....	....	....	....	....	......
....	....	....	....	....	....	....	....	......
....	....	....	....	....	....	....	....	......
....	....	....	....	....	....	....	....	......
....	....	....	....	....	....	....	....	......
....	....	....	....	....	....	....	....	......
....	....	....	....	....	....	....	....	......
....	....	....	....	....	....	....	....	......
AVERAGE	$....	$....	$....	$....	$....	$....	$....	$......

(3) List all locations through which cash is received or disbursed. This includes any address, building, location, or post-office box at which payments may be rendered or received.

For each location, indicate last year's annual collection and disbursement volumes (in thousands), and approximate number of transactions.

Location	*Agency/ Department*	*Approximate No. of Transactions*	*Annual Volume*	
			Receipts	*Disbursements*
....	....	....	$.......	$...............
....	....	....	....	....
....	....	....	....	....
....	....	....	....	....
....	....	....	....	....
....	....	....	....	....
....	....	....	....	....
....	....	....	....	....
....	....	....	....	....
....	....	....	....	....
....	....	....	....	....
TOTAL			$	$

(4) Obtain a listing showing the key personnel of the cash management function by position level and work location.

Name	*Position*	*Location*
....	....	....
....	....	....
....	....	....
....	....	....
....	....	....
....	....	....

Cash Management Questionnaire

The cash management questionnaire is applicable to most audits. Careful planning and flexibility are needed in large decentralized operations to determine the extent to which subentities need to be reviewed in relation to the entire operation.

The questionnaire comprises the following sections:

- Section I: Organization and Management;
- Section II: Daily Management of Cash Flow—Receipts;
- Section III: Daily Management of Cash Flow—Disbursements;
- Section IV: Banking Relations;
- Section V: Cash Forecasting; and
- Section VI: Investment of Idle Funds.

Section I: Organization and Management

An effective organization to manage cash resources will have a positive effect on cash position. On the other hand, poorly defined assignments can adversely affect cash position and lead to costly delays in the collection and employment of cash resources and deterioration in banking relations.

	Yes	*No*
(1) Does the cash management function have		
(a) An organization chart?	☐	☐
(b) Job descriptions?	☐	☐
(c) Clearly defined assignments and responsibilities?	☐	☐
(d) Job rotation schedules?	☐	☐

	Yes	*No*
(2) Are there written guidelines outlining the objectives, policies, standards, and procedures for the cash management function?	☐	☐
(3) Does the cash management function interact with other operating departments with respect to		
(a) Consideration of unforeseen cash requirements?	☐	☐
(b) Normal receipt/disbursement of funds?	☐	☐
(c) Approved collection/disbursement locations?	☐	☐
(4) Does the entity normally apply for advance funding of grants rather than for reimbursement after the funds have been expended (see Chapter 4, Dollarization Procedure 7: Cost of Idle Funds)?	☐	☐

Section II: Daily Management of Cash Flow—Receipts

The efficient and timely receipt of revenue and the speed to which this cash is put in the financial system are important to the effective management and operation of an entity.

(1) Are due dates for major revenue sources established at the earliest possible point, notwithstanding any applicable statutory limitations (see Chapter 4, Dollarization Procedure 8: Establishing Credit Terms/Progress Payments)?	☐	☐
(2) With respect to the collection of receivable items, does the entity have		
(a) Appropriate penalties and realistic interest rates to nullify any advantage to late payment (see Chapter 4, Dollarization Procedure 9: Delinquency Penalties)?	☐	☐
(b) Appropriate charges for the cost of redepositing and reprocessing checks returned for insufficient funds?	☐	☐
(c) Arrangements for acceptance of "progress payments," whereby partial remittances are received on a monthly or quarterly basis (see Chapter 4, Dollarization Procedure 8:		

	Yes	No
Establishing Credit Terms/Progress Payments)?	☐	☐
(3) Does the entity retain a percentage of contract cost until a contract is completed?	☐	☐
(4) Is taxpayer/customer invoicing conducted		
(a) On an accurate basis (e.g., current tax rates, valuations, addresses, etc.)?	☐	☐
(b) On a timely basis (see Chapter 4, Dollarization Procedure 10: Untimely Invoicing)?	☐	☐
(5) Are bank deposits made on a daily basis (see Chapter 4, Dollarization Procedure 11: Undeposited Receipts)?	☐	☐
(6) Does the entity's cash management system enable easy identification of		
(a) All collection/disbursement locations on remittance/payment documents?	☐	☐
(b) Source and amount of "over the counter" cash receipts and currency remittances?	☐	☐
(c) Drawers of bad checks?	☐	☐
(7) Does the entity act in a timely manner to reconcile and settle discrepancies between amounts invoiced and those actually received?	☐	☐
(8) Does the entity make use of regional or "area concentration" banking (see Chapter 4, Dollarization Procedure 11: Undeposited Receipts)?	☐	☐
(9) If so,		
(a) Does the entity use zero balance or automatic balance accounts, whereby a regional ("participating") bank initiates automatic fund transfers to and from a central bank?	☐	☐
(b) Are participating banks part of a bank wire system?	☐	☐
(10) Does the entity use lock boxes for cash remit-		

	Yes	*No*
tances (see Chapter 4, Dollarization Procedure 11: Undeposited Receipts)?	☐	☐
(11) If so,		
(a) Are banks which receive lock box deposits required to forward deposit slips on a timely basis?	☐	☐
(b) Is there an established daily cutoff time for mailing of funds to lock boxes (see Chapter 4, Dollarization Procedure 11: Undeposited Receipts)?	☐	☐
(12) Has the entity considered pooling all bank account balances into a limited number of general accounts?	☐	☐
(13) Has the entity compared the cost of managing the cash functions (payroll, etc.) in-house with the cost of having a bank perform such functions (see Chapter 4, Dollarization Procedure 12: Cash Maintenance)?	☐	☐

Section III: Daily Management of Cash Flow—Disbursements

Control over the disbursement of funds is necessary for efficient resource management. This section of the questionnaire addresses those controls necessary for effective management of disbursements.

(1) Are major disbursements deferred until the latest possible date?	☐	☐
(2) Are cash discounts taken (see Chapter 4, Dollarization Procedure 13: Cash Discounts)?	☐	☐
(3) Are cash withdrawals avoided on Fridays as a means of gaining week-end interest?	☐	☐
(4) Are bank drafts or warrants used as a payment instrument? (Bank drafts are not charged against an account until the draft is presented and accepted.)	☐	☐

	Yes	*No*
(5) If imprest accounts are used, is their number and balance limited (see Chapter 4, Dollarization Procedure 7: Cost of Idle Funds)?	☐	☐

Section IV: Banking Relations

Formal guidelines for banking relations permit the logical organization of bank arrangements, as well as a competitive approach to bank selection.

(1) Are written specifications maintained for banking services?	☐	☐
(2) Is borrowing authority centralized and well controlled?	☐	☐
(3) If compensating balances are required, are balances maintained as low as possible?	☐	☐
(4) Are banks required to bid competitively for the entity's account?	☐	☐

Section V: Cash Forecasting

A meaningful cash forecast is necessary for a viable cash management program.

(1) Does the entity prepare long-term forecasts by functional activity?	☐	☐
(2) Does the forecast list the significant sources and uses of funds, taking into consideration changes in working capital?	☐	☐
(3) Does the forecast show cash flow by intervals long enough to reveal cyclical patterns?	☐	☐
(4) Is the long-term forecast correlated to an overall financing/investment plan (see Chapter 4, Dollarization Procedure 14: Cash Investment)?	☐	☐
(5) Does the entity use the short-term forecast in determining day-to-day cash needs?	☐	☐
(6) Is actual cash flow compared to forecasts?	☐	☐

Section VI: Investment of Idle Funds

Clear objectives, well-defined assignments, and attention to the employment of cash result in proper utilization of a highly liquid resource.

	Yes	*No*
(1) Has the entity developed formal directives regarding investment of funds?	☐	☐
(2) If so,		
(a) Are specific responsibilities delineated (see Chapter 4, Dollarization Procedure 7: Cost of Idle Funds)?	☐	☐
(b) Are specific procedures outlined?	☐	☐
(3) Does the entity, by means of management reports or other such data, have an accurate idea of cash available for investment at any given time (see Chapter 4, Dollarization Procedure 7: Cost of Idle Funds)?	☐	☐
(4) Does the entity perform periodic analyses of the yield obtained on available cash balances (see Chapter 4, Dollarization Procedure 14: Cash Investment)?	☐	☐
(5) Do cash investments appear to be yielding a reasonable return (see Chapter 4, Dollarization Procedure 14: Cash Investment)?	☐	☐
(6) Has the entity considered the employment of idle cash for forward or strategic purchasing of equipment, raw materials, or other regularly purchased items which are subject to dramatic price fluctuations?	☐	☐
(7) Are investments pooled from all available funds to maximize return and reduce overhead charges (see Chapter 4, Dollarization Procedure 15: Investment Expenses)?	☐	☐
(8) Does the entity use state investment pools to obtain higher yield and greater flexibility in making		

	Yes	No
investments (see Chapter 4, Dollarization Procedure 14: Cash Investment)?	☐	☐
(9) Has the entity considered joint investment with other surrounding entities (see Chapter 4, Dollarization Procedures 14: Cash Investment, and 15: Investment Expenses)?	☐	☐

CHAPTER 9

Operational Controls Review–Procurement

Part I—General Discussion

Part II—The Questionnaire

Part I—General Discussion

Effective procurement involves planning, organizing, and managing to obtain goods and services in an efficient and economical manner. If volume is substantial, the cost of ineffective procurement practices may be significant. Conversely, effective practices facilitate smooth operations and result in efficiency and economy.

In government, the organization of procurement functions varies widely. In some agencies, each department does its own purchasing, while in others, purchasing is done by a separate purchasing department or committee.

In state and city governments, the procurement function derives its authority from several different sources, the most common being statutes, charters, local ordinances, administrative codes and edicts, and legislation. For example, in city government, the final purchasing authority may rest with the city manager, purchasing agent, city council, mayor, administrator, user agency, or a committee, depending on where the function obtains its authority.[1] On the county level, the purchasing department or agent may report to the finance director, controller, chief administrative officer, or chief elected official.[2]

Centralized or cooperative purchasing has gained increased acceptance because it frequently results in volume purchase discounts, reduces duplication of effort, and permits better use of resources. Centralized buying is being adopted in states, counties, municipalities, hospitals, colleges, school districts, and utility districts. Accordingly, many of the preferred practice questions in this questionnaire are in keeping with a centralized purchasing operation. If an entity does not have a centralized purchasing operation, purchases should be aggregated to determine total volume and to evaluate the potential for improvement through centralization aspects.

The Procurement Process

A good understanding of the procurement process is essential for an evaluation of the procurement function. The procurement process consists of the following steps [3]:

- Determination of product specifications, quantities required, and delivery requirements;
- Authorization to purchase requisitioned items;
- Selection of vendor/contractor;
- Delivery in accordance with purchase-order terms; and
- Payment of invoice.

Determination of Product Specifications, Quantities Required, and Delivery Requirements

A sound procurement system includes systematic procedures for determining what items are needed, based on technical and perform-

---

[1] *1975 Municipal Year Book* 192–199 (International City Management Association 1975).

[2] *1975 County Year Book* 80 (National Association of Counties 1975).

[3] The following discussion is based on an explanation of the procurement process in Brink, Cashin & Witt, *Modern Internal Auditing—An Operational Approach* 124–149 (Ronald Press 1973).

ance specifications, how much should be purchased, and how the item should be purchased. Since most procurements involve estimations of future needs, requirements must be stated as accurately as possible.

To aid in the selection of vendors and products, most government entities develop and maintain a list of vendors and certain available items that have been satisfactory in the past. Eligibility for the vendor list must be carefully established. Moreover, the list must be reviewed regularly to remove unsatisfactory vendors.

The purchasing department must make certain that the item it selects from the list is the one envisioned by the user. To prevent misunderstandings, many purchasing departments provide users with lists of materials, supplies, and equipment relating to their areas of responsibility for use in preparing purchase requisitions.

The procurement of specially designed items requires close coordination between the purchasing department and the user. The purchasing department must advise the user as to how his requirements can best be met within the constraints of the budget.

The determination of the quantity of an item to be purchased requires the best available data on the usage and the life of the item. The replacement of equipment and spare parts should be based on estimates of the rate at which equipment or parts will wear out. The purchase of materials and supplies which are repetitively used should be based on an inventory control system. If inventory controls are used as the basis for purchasing, management will usually establish reorder points and economic order quantities at least for those items which are significant from a financial or operating point of view. Reorder points will usually be computed based on safety stock plus the quantity expected to be used during the replenishment period. Economic order quantities will be computed so as to represent an optimal quantity which results in the lowest aggregate acquisition cost and carrying charges. It is apparent that complete and accurate records are necessary to develop the information required for the design and maintenance of an inventory control system.

Establishing when an item is needed is an essential part of the procurement process. Untimely procurements, whether too early or too late, can be costly. Procuring an item before it is needed may be a cause of poor cash management; late procurements may adversely affect the economy and effectiveness of operations because of disruptions caused by out-of-stock conditions or because premium prices may have to be paid. The purchasing department must make certain that user requirements are met in a timely manner.

Authorization to Purchase Requisitioned Items

Establishing a need for an item may not in itself justify its purchase. Procurement policies must be in line with the entity's goals and objectives and established priorities. Procurement priorities must be consistent with the entity's activities. Other factors that should be considered are:

- *Possibility of repairing the item.* Has the cost of repairing an item been compared with the cost of buying a new one? This consideration is especially important in procurements of high unit-cost items or specially designed equipment.
- *Excesses in other departments.* Is the item available from another department? Excess property lists from other departments should be reviewed and availability of an apparently desirable item confirmed.
- *Availability of substitutes.* Are less costly substitutes available?

The purchasing agent must make certain that these factors have been considered before final authorization of a purchase.

Selection of Vendor/Contractor

An important step in the procurement process is selecting a vendor or contractor. The purchasing department should have well-defined procedures for soliciting bids and for evaluating prospective vendors/contractors.

Government procurements are usually accomplished by either of two methods—formal advertisement or negotiation. These methods are sometimes combined; formal advertisements are often followed by a negotiation process with the most qualified bidders.

Formal advertising normally includes the following steps:

- The purchasing department requests bids. These requests contain detailed technical and performance specifications describing the item desired and related information.
- Vendors/contractors submit sealed bids by the date specified in the request.

- The purchasing department opens the sealed bids at a public opening.
- The purchasing department evaluates the bids and awards the contract to the lowest bidder whose proposal conforms to the established requirements.

Negotiation, on the other hand, cannot be accomplished in formalized procedural steps. The negotiation process consists of a series of proposals and counter-proposals in contrast to the "one-shot" approach of formal advertising. Negotiated procurements can be competitive or sole-source, as follows:

- *Competitive.* The purchasing agent encourages competition between potential suppliers with respect to the technical specifications and price of the item to be procured. When he receives the proposals, the agent negotiates the price, delivery, and sale terms with one or more of the vendors/contractors and awards a contract on the best terms.
- *Sole-source.* One vendor/contractor may be the only source for a unique or proprietary item or service. The purchasing agent is at a disadvantage in these circumstances; however, he must negotiate the best offer he can obtain.

Once the vendor/contractor has been selected, the procurement is finalized by a contract, or is evidenced by issuance of a purchase order. Two types of contracts—the fixed-price contract or the cost-plus-fixed-fee contract—are generally used.

- The fixed-price contract provides for a fixed cost and allows only limited adjustments to the contract price. In some circumstances, the contract price may be adjusted for inflation or for meeting predetermined goals. If obtainable, this type of contract is often preferable.
- The cost-plus-fixed-fee contract allows a vendor/contractor to receive reimbursements for allowable costs in addition to a fixed fee. Occasionally, these contracts include incentive clauses to compensate vendors/contractors for exceptional performance.

Delivery in Accordance With Purchase-Order Terms

The signing of a purchase agreement, either by contract or purchase order, does not terminate the purchasing department's involvement in the procurement process. The purchasing department must make certain that the item is delivered in accordance with the purchase agreement. They must ensure that the vendor is meeting required performance standards and that the item is delivered on time. On occasion, a purchasing agent will have to visit a vendor to check on progress and to verify the quality of the vendor's performance. In the event that a problem occurs, the purchasing agent will act as a liaison between the user department and the vendor.

In most government purchasing departments, purchasing agents are required to file periodic status reports for procurements they have initiated. Any cost overruns or performance deficiencies should be noted in these reports so that management can take appropriate action. The reports also provide management with an overview of its purchasing operation.

Payment of Invoice

The accounting department pays the vendor. Controls over disbursements must be organized to provide all practicable and reasonable assurance that no unauthorized payments are made, payments are made on time, and an accurate record is made of each payment. Payment should be preceded by an approval from the receiving department and the inspection department, where appropriate.

Auditing the Procurement Function

The auditor should be concerned with the reasonableness and appropriateness of the purchasing department's actions and the overall effectiveness of the procurement process. The auditor must also consider if any laws and regulations have been violated and, if deficiencies are noted, whether a need for revision of a practice is indicated. If the auditor feels that a regulation contravenes sound business practice, he may propose revision of the regulation to the appropriate entity official.

The procurement function can be measured by the volume of activity in terms of dollar value of products acquired, number of transactions, contracts or purchase orders issued, requisitions processed, quantities on order, reduction in delivery time, and savings achieved. An understanding of the procurement function's priorities and objectives is essential.

Part II—The Questionnaire

Background Information

To facilitate the understanding of a purchasing department, the following pertinent background information should be obtained:

(1) Obtain analysis, by fund, of purchasing volume for supplies, services, and capital outlays. (Use figures for the latest year.)

	Supplies	*Services*	*Capital Outlays*
General fund	$..........	$..........	$..........
Special revenue fund	....	....	....
Capital project fund	....	....	....
Enterprise fund	....	....	....
Intergovernmental service fund	....	....	....
Others (identify)	....	....	....
TOTAL	$	$	$

(2) Obtain an estimate of the annual volume of the major types of procurements. (Major trade-ins or sales of surplus material should be considered as a purchasing function.)

	Amount
Materials and supplies	$..........
Equipment	....
Equipment leases	....
Outside repair services	....
Outside professional services	....
Construction contracts	....
Real property purchases and leases	....
TOTAL	$

(3) Obtain an estimate of the annual purchase volume of major categories of supplies and services (such as fuel oil, gasoline, cleaning supplies, stationery, etc.).

Category	*Amount*
....	$..........
....	....
....	....
....	....
....	....
....	....
....	....
....	....
....	....
TOTAL	$

(4) With the assistance of purchasing department employees, summarize legal requirements, if any, relating to competitive bidding. Consider state laws, local constitutional or ordinance requirements, and any federal or state grant requirements. Refer to any emergency or waiver provisions for the bidding process.

....

....

....

....

....

....

....

....

....

....

(5) Obtain approximate workload statistics for the purchasing department.

	No. Annually
Requisitions	....
Purchase orders	....
Bids received	....
Salesmen interviewed	....
Blanket purchase orders	....
Purchase contracts	....

(6) Obtain personnel data for the purchasing department.

	Number
Purchasing agents, buyers	....
Expediters (of transactions with vendors)	....
Others	....
TOTAL	

(7) Obtain a listing showing the key personnel of the purchasing department by position level and work location.

Name	*Position*	*Location*
....	....	....
....	....	....
....	....	....
....	....	....
....	....	....
....	....	....

(8) Describe any significant purchasing not conducted through the centralized purchasing department. . . . .

. . . .

. . . .

. . . .

. . . .

. . . .

. . . .

Consider the costs and benefits of making separate reviews of such buying activities and of preparing separate questionnaires for each activity. Document conclusions. . . . .

. . . .

. . . .

. . . .

. . . .

. . . .

. . . .

(9) Obtain maintenance contract data.

Vendor/Contractor	*Service*	*Period*	*Amount*
. . . .	. . . .	. . . .	$. . . . .
. . . .	. . . .	. . . .	. . . .
. . . .	. . . .	. . . .	. . . .
. . . .	. . . .	. . . .	. . . .
. . . .	. . . .	. . . .	. . . .
. . . .	. . . .	. . . .	. . . .
. . . .	. . . .	. . . .	. . . .
. . . .	. . . .	. . . .	. . . .
TOTAL			$

(10) Procurement
Summarize (estimate, if necessary) procurement volume by:

Purchasing inside the purchasing department	$.........	...%
Purchasing outside the purchasing department	....	...%
TOTAL	$_____	100%

Procurement Function Questionnaire

The questionnaire includes preferred practice questions for the following sections:

- Section I: Organization and Management; and
- Section II: Procurement Policy and Practice.

Section I: Organization and Management

Since procurement results in major commitments of funds, inefficiencies or uneconomical practices within the procurement function can have a detrimental effect on an entity. Practices such as failure to shop the market or to negotiate favorable contract terms can result in cash drains.

	Yes	*No*
(1) Does the purchasing department have		
(a) An organization chart?	☐	☐
(b) Job descriptions?	☐	☐
(c) Clear-cut buying assignments?	☐	☐
(2) Is there a formal manual of purchasing policy?	☐	☐
(3) If so, does it cover		
(a) Department relationships, particularly buying responsibilities?	☐	☐
(b) Competitive buying and source selection, with particular attention to		
(i) legal solicitation of bids?	☐	☐

	Yes	*No*
(ii) public opening of bids?	☐	☐
(iii) resolution of tied bids?	☐	☐
(iv) preference for local vendor?	☐	☐
(c) Maintenance of multiple buying sources to protect the continuity of supply?	☐	☐
(d) Rules of commitment and contracts?	☐	☐
(e) Conflicts of interest?	☐	☐
(f) Selection of vendors eligible to receive bidding invitations?	☐	☐
(g) Provisions for development of written product specifications?	☐	☐
(h) Purchases from manufacturers, rather than distributors?	☐	☐
(i) Insurance coverage?	☐	☐
(j) Professional service contracts?	☐	☐
(k) Disposal of surplus and scrap?	☐	☐
(4) Do procedures for repetitive purchases provide for the more economical approach of—either stocking materials and supplies through a central stores organization, or providing for drop shipments to different locations (see Chapter 4, Dollarization Procedure 16: Multiple Stocking)?	☐	☐
(5) Do the department's procedures require the purchasing agent to develop a cost estimate for use in evaluating bids received where such estimates are a useful tool (e.g., construction or maintenance contracts)?	☐	☐
(6) Do the department's procedures provide for control over changes to purchase orders and contracts?	☐	☐
(7) Do the department's procedures		
(a) Encourage purchasing agents to specialize?	☐	☐
(b) Provide that the head of the purchasing department approve significant orders placed by purchasing agents?	☐	☐

Section II: Procurement Policy and Practice

Procurement efficiency and economy depends upon consistent implementation of procurement policies. The failure to adhere to an established procurement policy or practice is an indication that resources may have been wasted.

Purchasing

	Yes	*No*
(1) Does the procurement system provide reasonable and timely estimates of needs on a periodic basis?	☐	☐
(2) Are requisitions based on one of the following:		
(a) Calculated reorder points (see Chapter 4, Dollarization Procedures 17: Extra Cost for "Rush" Deliveries, and 18: Excessive Inventories)?	☐	☐
(b) Stock status ordering when availability reaches zero?	☐	☐
(c) Period planning?	☐	☐
(3) In deciding how much to buy, does the purchasing department calculate economic order quantities (see Chapter 4, Dollarization Procedure 18: Excessive Inventories)?	☐	☐
(4) Do requisitions indicate when material will be required (see Chapter 4, Dollarization Procedure 18: Excessive Inventories)?	☐	☐
(5) Does the purchasing agent receive enough lead time so that he can properly "shop the market" (see Chapter 4, Dollarization Procedure 19: Noncompetitive Buying)?	☐	☐
(6) Is the purchasing agent provided with technical and performance specifications so that he knows what to buy?	☐	☐
(7) Does the purchasing agent keep up to date on advances in technical equipment (as evidenced by booklets, manuals, and minutes of meetings with suppliers)?	☐	☐

	Yes	*No*
(8) Does the purchasing agent negotiate purchase contracts and blanket purchase orders (see Chapter 4, Dollarization Procedure 20: Lost Quantity Discounts)?	☐	☐
(9) Does the purchasing department participate in (see Chapter 4, Dollarization Procedure 16: Multiple Stocking)		
(a) Standardization?	☐	☐
(b) Value analysis?	☐	☐
(c) Make or buy decisions?	☐	☐
(d) Price trend analyses?	☐	☐
(10) Does the purchasing agent receive summaries of (see Chapter 4, Dollarization Procedure 20: Lost Quantity Discounts)		
(a) Commodity buying volumes?	☐	☐
(b) Vendor buying volumes?	☐	☐
(11) Are excess property lists of other departments reviewed before a purchase order is generated (see Chapter 4, Dollarization Procedure 18: Excessive Inventories)?	☐	☐
(12) Does the system provide for evaluation of repairs or replacement decisions prior to major purchases (see Chapter 4, Dollarization Procedure 21: Repair Versus Replace)?	☐	☐
(13) Does the system provide for evaluation of product substitution where appropriate?	☐	☐
(14) Does the nature of emergency purchases seem appropriate as to		
(a) Amount?	☐	☐
(b) Frequency?	☐	☐
(c) Vendor?	☐	☐
(15) Does the system provide that annually recurring purchases (e.g., salt for snow removal) are planned and contracted for rather than handled on an "as needed" basis?	☐	☐

	Yes	No
Vendor/Contractor Selection		
(16) Has the department established		
(a) A roster of qualified vendors/contractors eligible to receive bidding invitations?	☐	☐
(b) Procedures for qualifying additional vendors/contractors in terms of		
(i) capacity to perform?	☐	☐
(ii) financial responsibility?	☐	☐
(iii) past experience?	☐	☐
(iv) proposed work schedule?	☐	☐
(v) compliance with an entity's specifications and material requirements?	☐	☐
(c) Procedures to eliminate vendors/contractors		
(i) with consistently poor performance records?	☐	☐
(ii) who have not responded to previous bid requests?	☐	☐
(iii) who have substituted key personnel?	☐	☐
(17) Has the department established procedures to identify a sufficient number of potential vendors/contractors?	☐	☐
(18) Does the purchasing department maintain vendor/contractor evaluation files, which indicate the adequacy of their performance in relation to		
(a) Quantity?	☐	☐
(b) Quality?	☐	☐
(c) Delivery?	☐	☐
(d) Cost?	☐	☐
Bidding		
(19) Does the purchasing agent actively solicit competitive bids from vendors (see Chapter 4, Dollarization Procedure 2: Bidding)		
(a) When required by law?	☐	☐
(b) When not required by law, but suggested		

	Yes	No
by good business practice (see Chapter 4, Dollarization Procedure 19: Noncompetitive Buying)?	☐	☐
(20) Are potential vendors/contractors provided the opportunity to submit a bid?	☐	☐
(21) Do bid solicitations contain the information necessary to enable prospective vendors/contractors to prepare proposals properly?	☐	☐
(22) Are procedures in effect whereby		
(a) Potential bidders are allowed sufficient time to develop their bids?	☐	☐
(b) Requests call for submission of bids in sealed form?	☐	☐
(c) Bids received are controlled (e.g., by time stamps, custody of bids by a responsible official, and simultaneous public opening of bids)?	☐	☐
(23) Is the number of competitive bids requested reasonable in relation to the dollar volume and nature of the article being purchased (see Chapter 4, Dollarization Procedure 2: Bidding)?	☐	☐
(24) When bids are not obtained, is the purchasing agent required to document the reason?	☐	☐
(25) Does the purchasing agent perform a detailed analysis of the cost and other data supporting the bidder's proposal?	☐	☐

Negotiations

	Yes	No
(26) Is periodic rebidding required of long-term purchase orders or contracts to prevent "ever-green" contracts?	☐	☐
(27) Does the purchasing agent negotiate complete terms with vendors/contractors, including prices, FOB points, routing instructions, cash discounts, delivery terms, and adjustments (see Chapter 4,		

	Yes	No
Dollarization Procedure 22: Purchase-Order Completeness)?	☐	☐
(28) When negotiations are not conducted, is the purchasing agent required to document why they were waived?	☐	☐
(29) Does the department require that any significant changes to a basic contract be negotiated?	☐	☐
(30) Do purchase orders or contracts include audit clauses when appropriate?	☐	☐
(31) Does the purchasing agent consider trade-in allowances in negotiating equipment replacement?	☐	☐

Termination Clauses

(32) Is the cost versus benefit of having a termination clause evaluated for each contract? (In some instances having a termination clause increases the contract price.)	☐	☐
(33) If so, does the termination clause protect the entity in the event of default?	☐	☐

Performance

(34) Does the purchasing department have an orderly system to ensure the delivery of materials within the time specified on purchase orders?	☐	☐
(35) When a contract calls for progress payments, is the vendor/contractor's performance evaluated prior to each payment?	☐	☐
(36) Are property items inspected and tested prior to final acceptance?	☐	☐
(37) Is the final acceptance or rejection of the item documented?	☐	☐
(38) Are contractors required to comply with the government entity's labor and material standards?	☐	☐

	Yes	*No*
(39) Are contractors required to use government contracted material and supplies on hand?	☐	☐
(40) Is the performance of contractors periodically assessed?	☐	☐

Inventory Receipt and Storage

	Yes	*No*
(41) Is there a central receiving activity (see Chapter 4, Dollarization Procedure 16: Multiple Stocking)?	☐	☐
(42) Are receipts of items properly documented?	☐	☐
(43) Are items received promptly inspected		
(a) To ensure that the item ordered is the one received?	☐	☐
(b) For damage?	☐	☐
(44) Are there procedures for returning rejected items?	☐	☐
(45) Is accounting control established over damage and other claims to protect the entity's interest?	☐	☐
(46) Is an attempt made immediately to renegotiate prices on overshipments and on damaged or otherwise unsatisfactory items, before steps are taken to return such items to the vendors?	☐	☐
(47) Is there a system for controlling inventory items in storage?	☐	☐
(48) Do the storage facilities		
(a) Preclude unauthorized access to storage areas?	☐	☐
(b) Provide adequate storage space?	☐	☐
(c) Provide specialized storage where needed?	☐	☐
(d) Have an effective security system?	☐	☐
(e) Facilitate the receipt and disposition of items in storage?	☐	☐

	Yes	*No*
(49) Is withdrawal of high-priced inventory items from storage areas made only upon submission of properly authorized requisitions?	☐	☐
(50) Does the entity avoid maintaining comprehensive inventory records on minor, expendable supply items?	☐	☐
(51) Does the insurance program cover inventory items?	☐	☐

CHAPTER 10

Operational Controls Review–Public Works

Part I—General Discussion

Part II—The Questionnaire

Part I—General Discussion

The purpose of a public works department is to maintain public facilities and provide services to the general public. The department's responsibilities usually include such functions as highway and street construction and maintenance, maintenance of street signs and signals, refuse collection and disposal, and maintenance of public facilities such as libraries or parks.

The extent of the services provided by the public works department makes it a major spender of government funds. Accordingly, it is imperative that effective management techniques are employed within the department to ensure maximum utilization of resources and achievement of targeted objectives. The preferred practice questions in this chapter are designed to aid in evaluating the effectiveness of the public works department. To facilitate such evaluation, an understanding of the organization and activities of a public works department is essential.

Organization

Because of the size and diversity of its operations, a public works department is normally divided into several divisions. In large government entities, these divisions are normally organized on a functional basis; specific individuals are usually assigned responsibility for particular geographic areas within the cities, counties, or states. This organization facilitates the operation of the public works department because divisional employees can be given clearly defined responsibilities and held accountable for performance. Administrative functions, such as budgeting, revenue and expenditure control, and workload management are also more easily controlled on a functional basis. Each division may have its own accounting, purchasing, and personnel function, or these functions may be provided at the department level.

Most public works departments are organized so that the planning, budgeting, revenue and expenditure control, and similar functions are the responsibility of the operating divisions. The overall management of the public works department usually rests with a single individual, often referred to as the city, county, or state engineer. This individual, who is concerned primarily with long-range planning, review, and coordination, should report directly to the chief executive of the entity.

In reviewing the organization of a public works department, the primary concern of the auditor is to ensure that the structure of the department facilitates the most effective and efficient operation possible. For example, it is not appropriate for each division to do its own recruiting and hiring if it would be more efficient to have the function performed at the departmental or entity level.

Activities

Before auditing a public works department, the auditor must understand the activities of the department. However, not all of the activities discussed here will be found in every public works department. Generally, activities fall into the following functional areas:

- *General services.* This includes the management of publicly owned service activities and, in some instances, the regulation of privately owned utilities.
- *Property and facility management.* This includes maintenance, acquisition, and construction of government facilities and the upkeep of public grounds.
- *Management of highways and streets.* This encompasses the maintenance of the present highway and street system and the planning and construction of new systems to meet current and future needs.

General Services

One of the most important functions of a public works department is providing essential services and utilities to the public. These services include electricity, water, refuse removal, and sewage. Basic elements of a service division are:

- Effective organization;
- Planning process;
- System for rate determination;
- Clearly defined operating standards; and
- Quality control system.

Organization

An unexpected breakdown in a general service function has a tremendous impact upon the public. Accordingly, the organization of a service function must provide for prompt identification of problems, as well as timely and effective response.

The management of a general service function must consist of a mix of public administrators and technical personnel. Further, the department should have a system for direct input of public complaints.

Planning

Most service organizations are greatly affected by external factors, such as population growth or shifts, technological breakthroughs, environmental restrictions, and availability of natural resources. Therefore, to make certain that current and future service needs can be met, an effective planning function must be in operation.

Rate Determination

Most public services are revenue producing and can be self-sustaining. Therefore, a system for rate determination must exist to ascertain whether proper charges are made for services and to ensure that current, as well as anticipated costs are properly funded. In most situations, the setting of rates rests with a board or commission, whose function is to review and rule on any changes to the rate structure as recommended by the public services' management. In essence, the board represents the public and serves as a link between the public and the entity. Therefore, it is imperative that the public be able to express its views to the board and that these views are considered in the board's deliberations. This is usually accomplished through public hearings, where individuals and groups have an opportunity to express their views and to hear the views of the entity. The board's final decision should be communicated to the public with appropriate explanation and justification.

Operating Standards

It is important that a public service organization has clearly defined operating standards. These operating standards should encompass the following:

- *Administrative standards.* Administrative standards for a public service organization are comparable to those found in any organization. They include the establishing of budgetary requirements and proper accounting and inventory records.

- *Service standards.* Service standards provide guidance for the distribution of services to the public. Criteria must be established for the level of service, as well as the distribution of service to users. For example, refuse collection may be provided twice weekly for residences and daily for businesses.
- *Health, safety, and environmental standards.* In this era of federal intervention in health, safety, and environmental matters, service organizations have been required to become increasingly responsive to various regulatory agencies. Each organization must make certain that its standards comply with regulatory criteria and that a reporting system has been set up to document this compliance.
- *Revenue management standards.* As previously mentioned, most public services are revenue producers. Therefore, standards comparable to those of any profit-motivated entity are essential to ensure that billings are timely, accurate, and properly controlled. Delinquent accounts should be acted upon and appropriate penalties set. Innovative techniques, such as the use of estimated billings, should be used where appropriate.

The primary concern of the auditor is that management has established and implemented operating standards, and that these standards are periodically reviewed and evaluated. The auditor should also be concerned that management has a system for monitoring actual performance.

Quality Control

The last basic element of an effective service organization is a system for evaluating the quality of service performed. Such a system should determine the extent to which overall operating standards are met and the causes for any deviation from the standards. Quality control, which should be an integral part of every service organization, and may be supplemented by an independent function, is a continuing process that provides follow-up to ascertain that management's action is timely and responsive.

Property and Facility Management

Property and facility management is a major division of most public works departments. This division is responsible for the maintenance and construction of government facilities and for the upkeep of public grounds, such as parks and recreational areas. Because of the large investment most governments have in land and buildings, it is important that the property and facility management division be well managed.

Probably the most important function of a property and facility management division is maintenance. This includes daily housekeeping duties and the maintenance of systems, such as heating and air-conditioning, within the facilities. A breakdown in maintenance directly affects operations and can seriously impair the effectiveness of the operating departments. (Because of the importance of this segment of a public works department, preferred practice questions dealing with maintenance are presented in detail in Chapter 11.)

The property and facility management division also manages the acquisition of new property and facilities and additions to existing facilities.

In managing government facilities, the division normally has responsibility for defining space needs and for allocating space to other government agencies. Accordingly, to prevent disruption of operations, the division must have a system for monitoring the use of available space, defining future space needs, and acquiring any needed space.

When acquiring additional space, the best method of acquisition —lease, purchase, or construction—must be determined. This entails detailed analyses of the costs and benefits of the various acquisition methods. Whatever method of acquisition is selected, the property and facility management division must be involved throughout the acquisition process to ensure that needs are met and that the interests of the government are protected. If the decision is made to construct a facility, either by government or by an outside contractor, the division's involvement will be prolonged. Therefore, it is important that a sound system is set up to monitor the project throughout the construction process. (Preferred practice questions applicable to the procurement function are presented in detail in Chapter 9.)

Once a facility is acquired, the division must see that it is properly used. This requires a reaffirmation of the need for space as originally defined, proper allocation of space, and provision of adequate office equipment, services, and utilities.

Highway and Street Construction and Maintenance

The last major activity of a public works department to be discussed is the construction and maintenance of highways and streets. We live in a highly mobile society that has become extremely dependent on the automobile and other highway transportation for travel and transporting goods. The planning, constructing, and maintaining of highways and streets is a prime responsibility of the public works department.

A sound planning and scheduling process is essential to the maintenance and repair of highways and streets. Routine maintenance and repairs should be scheduled when they least affect the public and far enough in advance to maximize utilization of personnel and equipment. Though emergency repairs cannot be planned, the public works department can develop procedures for responding to emergencies. For example, certain work crews can be designated to respond to particular types of emergencies.

Major improvements are an integral part of highway and street maintenance. These include such tasks as resurfacing roads, installing guard rails and street lights, etc. These projects should be systematically planned and scheduled to facilitate their performance and completion as well as their financing.

Another aspect of highway and street management is the construction of new highway and street systems. The costs involved in constructing new highways and streets have increased to the point where many local governments can no longer afford them. Federal funds have become a major source of revenue for constructing new highway systems. These funds, along with those provided by the local government, must be appropriately managed in compliance with requirements imposed by the federal government. The department must have an effective planning process and an effective system for monitoring and controlling construction and its costs. The planning process must give recognition to federal requirements for funding to avoid interruption of the flow of federal funding.

Part II—The Questionnaire

Background Information

An audit of a public works department can be a very difficult segment of a government audit. Public works involves diverse considerations, is inherently complex, and is difficult to control. To facilitate the understanding of a public works department's activities, the following background information should be obtained:

(1) Obtain a copy of the department's organization and procedures manual.

(2) Obtain an analysis of the funding and expenditures for the current and prior fiscal years. (The purpose is to obtain an indication of the relative size of the public works department.)

	Total Government Budget		*Public Works Dep't Budget*	
Fund	*Current Year*	*Prior Year*	*Current Year*	*Prior Year*
General	$..........	$.........	$..........	$.........
Special assessment	....	....	....	....
Capital projects	....	....	....	....
Special revenue	....	....	....	....
Enterprise	....	....	....	....
Others (identify)	....	....	....	....
TOTAL	$	$	$	$

(3) Obtain an analysis of public works expenditures by division for the current and prior fiscal years.

	Expenditures		*Amount Per Employee**	
Division	*Current Year*	*Prior Year*	*Current Year*	*Prior Year*
....	$..........	$.........	$..........	$.........
....	....	....	....	....
....	....	....	....	....
....	....	....	....	....
....	....	....	....	....
....	....	....	....	....
TOTAL	$	$	$	$

* Where there are geographic locations within a division, the auditor may find it useful to compare expenditures by employees by geographic locations. This gives a general view of the workload distribution per employee.

(4) Obtain a summary of the facilities and property managed by the public works department.

Division	*Item***	*Method of Acquisition*†	*Date of Acquisition*	*Useful Life*	*Cost*	*Depreciated Value*††
....	......	....	....	......	$.....	$.........
....	......	....	....	......	.....	....
....	......	....	....	......	.....	....
....	......	....	....	......	.....	....
....	......	....	....	......	.....	....
....	......	....	....	......	.....	....
	TOTAL				$	$

** Identify item: Building, vehicles, land, etc.
† Indicate method by using following legend:
Purchase –A
Rental/lease –B
Transfer from another division–C
Constructed –D
†† Where applicable, especially enterprise funds.

(5) Obtain the most recent statistical data on the highway and street systems managed by the public works department.

	Miles		
Type	*Current Year*	*Next Year*	*Five-Year Projection*
Interstate highway	....	....	....
Primary state highway	....	....	....
Secondary roads	....	....	....
City streets	....	....	....
Others (identify)	....	....	....
TOTAL			

(6) Obtain the most recent statistical data on the general service functions managed by the public works department.

Service	*Customers Served*	*Revenue*	*Expenditures*	*Customers Served Five-Year Projected Growth*
......	....	$......	$..........	....
......	....	......	....	....
......	....	......	....	....
......	....	......	....	....
......	....	......	....	....
......	....	......	....	....
	TOTAL	$	$	

(7) Obtain personnel data for the department.

	Number Employed		
Division	*Current Year*	*Next Year*	*Five-Year Projection*
....	....	....	....
....	....	....	....
....	....	....	....
....	....	....	....
....	....	....	....
....	....	....	....
....	....	....	....
....	....	....	....
....	....	....	....
....	....	....	....
....	....	....	....
....	....	....	....
....	....	....	....
TOTAL			

(8) Obtain a listing showing the key personnel of the public works department by position level and work location.

Name	*Position*	*Location*
. . . .	. . . .	. . . .
. . . .	. . . .	. . . .
. . . .	. . . .	. . . .
. . . .	. . . .	. . . .
. . . .	. . . .	. . . .
. . . .	. . . .	. . . .
. . . .	. . . .	. . . .

(9) With the assistance of public works department officials, summarize the significant legal requirements relating to the department. . . . .

. . . .

. . . .

. . . .

. . . .

. . . .

. . . .

. . . .

Public Works Questionnaire

This questionnaire consists of the following categories:

- Section I: Organization and Management;
- Section II: Management Information System;
- Section III: General Services;
- Section IV: Facility Management;
- Section V: Property Management;
- Section VI: Highways and Streets; and
- Section VII: Traffic Engineering.

Section I: Organization and Management

Because the public works department provides support and services to most government entities, it is one of the most important functions in state and local governments. The diversity of the department's activities makes the tasks of organization and management extremely difficult, but essential to the effectiveness of the department.

Procedures

	Yes	*No*
(1) Does the public works department have		
(a) An organization chart?	☐	☐
(b) Divisions responsible for major areas?	☐	☐
(c) Clear-cut divisional or functional assignments?	☐	☐
(2) Does the department have a formal policy and procedures manual?	☐	☐
(3) If so, does it cover		
(a) Relationships with other departments?	☐	☐
(b) Relationships between divisions within the public works department?	☐	☐
(c) Standards and procedures for the various divisions within the department?	☐	☐

Planning

	Yes	*No*
(4) Does the department have a short- and long-range planning function?	☐	☐
(5) If so, does the planning function		
(a) Involve the various divisions in the planning process?	☐	☐
(b) Establish short- and long-range goals and objectives for the department?	☐	☐
(c) Make appropriate revisions to department goals and objectives when required by legislation?	☐	☐

Budgeting

These questions are intended only to give an overview of the budgeting function in a public works department. (Chapter 6 contains a detailed discussion of the budgeting area and should be used where appropriate.)

	Yes	*No*
(6) Does the department have a budgeting function?	☐	☐
(7) If so, does the budgeting function		
(a) Involve divisions in the planning process?	☐	☐
(b) Provide the public works department's input to the government entity's overall budgeting process?	☐	☐
(c) Assist in the allotment of expenditure authority to divisions?	☐	☐
(d) Keep the department head informed as to actual results versus budget (performance and financial)?	☐	☐
(8) Does the budget function periodically reevaluate its needs in accordance with overall goals and objectives?	☐	☐
(9) If so, are the results of these reevaluations used as inputs to the entity planning and budgeting functions?	☐	☐

Personnel

The following questions provide only an overview of the personnel function in a public works department. (Preferred practice questions dealing with personnel are presented in detail in Chapter 7.)

(10) Does the department have a system for allocating personnel to divisions (see Chapter 4, Dollarization Procedure 1: Personnel Allocation)?	☐	☐
(11) If so, does the personnel allocation system give consideration to		
(a) Seasonal fluctuations in personnel needs?	☐	☐
(b) Rotation of personnel between divisions to offset seasonal demands (see Chapter 4, Dollarization Procedure 1: Personnel Allocation)?	☐	☐
(c) Matching of skills to job requirements?	☐	☐

	Yes	*No*
(12) Are personnel ceilings established for divisions?	☐	☐
(13) Are these ceilings in compliance with the legislative ceiling established for the department?	☐	☐

Section II: Management Information System

Management needs an information system if it is to be effective in responding to day-to-day demands. Lack of adequate information invites loss of revenue or excessive costs. The diverse nature of the operations of the public works department makes the need for an information system especially important.

Data Collection and Processing

(1) Is there a unit for determining and updating the information needs of management?	☐	☐
(2) Does the system provide for the accumulation of both financial and operational data?	☐	☐
(3) Does the system provide a reasonably complete picture of the department's resources and activities?	☐	☐
(4) Is the system designed to facilitate current and long-range planning?	☐	☐
(5) Does the system provide information on		
(a) Total resources of the department (personnel, facilities, equipment, and any revenue generated)?	☐	☐
(b) Allocation of resources to the various divisions (see Chapter 4, Dollarization Procedure 1: Personnel Allocation)?	☐	☐
(c) Costs and outputs for the various functional elements of the department (for example, number of miles repaired by road operations and the related cost?	☐	☐
(6) Does the system provide historical, current, and projected data?	☐	☐

	Yes	*No*
(7) Does the department use a computer-based system where justified (see Chapter 4, Dollarization Procedure 4: Computer Utilization)?	☐	☐
(8) Is the information base kept current through a mandatory reporting system?	☐	☐
Reporting		
(9) Has the department defined its reporting requirements on the basis of its organizational structure?	☐	☐
(10) Have reporting responsibilities been assigned to the divisions?	☐	☐
(11) Do the reports appear to be		
(a) Complete and up to date?	☐	☐
(b) Submitted on a timely basis?	☐	☐
(c) Prepared in a standard format?	☐	☐
(d) Acccurate?	☐	☐
(12) Does the department periodically evaluate reports to determine that the appropriate information is provided?	☐	☐
Records Management		
(13) Has the department established policies and procedures for the retention and disposition of		
(a) Financial records and reports?	☐	☐
(b) Operational and cost information?	☐	☐
(c) Program and budgetary data?	☐	☐
(d) Historical data?	☐	☐
(14) Does the department have adequate storage facilities for records?	☐	☐
(15) Are often-used records and reports easily accessible? (For computerized records, is the information easily retrieved?)	☐	☐
(16) Are copies of critical master files maintained off-site?	☐	☐

	Yes	No
Communication		
(17) Does the department have a system for distributing communications and directives to the divisions?	☐	☐
(18) Does the department have manuals and other administrative documents that describe the policies and procedures of the divisions?	☐	☐
(19) Is information generated by the system used in the decision-making process?	☐	☐
(20) Is the information gathered used to support and justify capital expenditures?	☐	☐

Section III: General Services

The public works department in most county, city, and state governments has responsibility for managing certain essential services provided to the public. The critical nature of the services, which include water, refuse removal, and sewage treatment, require that the department develop an effective management system both from an administrative and from a technical standpoint. The department has to be concerned with long-range service requirements as well as the day-to-day operation of the services.

This section addresses the operational controls of any division providing general services to the public. The approach is to review the functional elements of the system, which include planning, rate determination, operating standards, quality control, and capital expenditures.

Planning		
(1) Does the general services division have short- and long-range plans?	☐	☐
(2) If so, do the plans		
(a) Project future service requirements?	☐	☐
(b) Make use of technological advances in determining long-range requirements?	☐	☐
(c) Determine future physical and financial		

	Yes	*No*
needs (for example, the type of facilities needed and their cost)?	☐	☐
(d) Consider federal and state standards and requirements, especially pollution standards?	☐	☐
(e) Coordinate with the zoning function?	☐	☐
(3) In planning long-range service requirements, does the division		
(a) Perform studies to obtain population information?	☐	☐
(b) Collect data on current and past service requirements?	☐	☐
(c) Use the above information?	☐	☐
(d) Coordinate its programs with other activities of the public works department?	☐	☐
(4) Does the division perform cost versus benefit analyses to determine the most cost-effective way to meet future needs?	☐	☐
(5) Has the division determined the future availability of natural resources to meet long-range demands (for example, availability of fresh water and land fill)?	☐	☐

Rate Determination

(6) Does the division have authority for establishing a rate structure for services provided?	☐	☐
(7) Does the division have written guidance as to the		
(a) Procedures followed in establishing the rate structure?	☐	☐
(b) Documentation required to support requests for rate changes?	☐	☐
(8) In developing the rate structure, does the division recognize the need for obtaining sufficient revenue to		
(a) Provide for operational and maintenance costs?	☐	☐

	Yes	*No*
(b) Amortize bond indebtedness?	☐	☐
(c) Provide for contingencies?	☐	☐
(d) Provide for modifications required to meet federal and state environmental standards?	☐	☐
(9) Does the division use the same rate structure within a user class?	☐	☐
(10) If not, are the exceptions reasonable?	☐	☐
(11) Does the division submit requests for proposed rate changes to a board or commission?	☐	☐
(12) Are public hearings conducted on proposed rate changes?	☐	☐
(13) Are these hearings adequately publicized?	☐	☐
(14) Are individuals and civic organizations provided adequate time to respond to proposed rate increases?	☐	☐
(15) Has the division established a review board for evaluating and recommending action on proposed rate changes?	☐	☐
(16) Where appropriate, are rate changes approved by the state regulatory commission?	☐	☐
(17) Does the division evaluate the economic impact of rate increases on		
(a) Revenue?	☐	☐
(b) Services?	☐	☐
(18) Are approved rate changes publicized well in advance of their effective date?	☐	☐

Operating Standards

General:

(19) Has the division established operating standards for service functions?	☐	☐

	Yes	No
(20) If so, do the standards address		
(a) Administrative requirements?	☐	☐
(b) Quality of service?	☐	☐
(c) Health, safety, and environment?	☐	☐
(d) Revenue management?	☐	☐
Administrative requirements:		
(21) Has the division defined the record-keeping and reporting requirements for general services?	☐	☐
(22) Does the system provide for a comparison of actual results to budget?	☐	☐
(23) Are major variances adequately explained and documented?	☐	☐
(24) Does the division have contingency plans to meet emergency situations?	☐	☐
Quality of service:		
(25) Have minimum service standards been established?	☐	☐
(26) If so, do these service standards provide		
(a) Guidance on how services are to be provided to the various classes of users?	☐	☐
(b) Operating criteria for abnormal periods?	☐	☐
(c) Operational requirements for users (for example, certain entities may be required to place refuse in special containers to facilitate collection)?	☐	☐
(d) Criteria for the level of service provided (for example, the frequency of refuse collection)?	☐	☐
(27) Does the division periodically evaluate service standards?	☐	☐
(28) Is appropriate management action taken on results of the evaluation?	☐	☐

	Yes	*No*
(29) In planning for expanded services, does the division use (its own or outside) technical consultants to determine the most effective distribution system? (For example, the distribution of water and sewage service to a residential area requires a different system from that used for an industrial park.)	☐	☐
Health, safety, and environment:		
(30) Has the division developed health, safety, and environmental standards?	☐	☐
(31) Has the division compared its standards to federal, state, and local regulations?	☐	☐
(32) Does the division have a report and review system to assure compliance with these standards?	☐	☐
(33) Do inspection reports indicate that violations are appropriately resolved?	☐	☐
(34) Do reports indicate that the division has met the goals established by the Environmental Protection Agency for modifying existing sewage and refuse disposal facilities?	☐	☐
(35) Does the division coordinate with local civic groups in establishing and implementing health and safety standards?	☐	☐
(36) Has the division given consideration to establishing recycling centers?	☐	☐
(37) Does the division have a conservation program? (Such a program is especially critical during the months when shortages may occur. For example, a summer dry spell can reduce the available water supply.)	☐	☐
Revenue management:		
(38) Has the division considered the use of estimated billings (see Chapter 4, Dollarization Procedure 23: Estimated Billing)?	☐	☐

	Yes	No
(39) Does the division use the most favorable billing cycle for low-cost services (see Chapter 4, Dollarization Procedure 24: Billing Frequency)?	☐	☐
(40) Are deposits required or are services billed in advance (see Chapter 4, Dollarization Procedure 23: Estimated Billing)?	☐	☐
(41) Are the service activities self-sustaining?	☐	☐

Quality Control

	Yes	No
(42) Does the division have a system for evaluating the quality of service provided?	☐	☐
(43) If so, does the system provide for		
(a) A determination of the extent to which overall operating standards are met?	☐	☐
(b) A review and update of operating criteria?	☐	☐
(c) A reporting system of actual performance?	☐	☐
(44) Does the control function		
(a) Make use of employee productivity analysis (see Chapter 4, Dollarization Procedure 1: Personnel Allocation)?	☐	☐
(b) Develop plant utilization data (see Chapter 4, Dollarization Procedure 25: Equipment Utilization Review)?	☐	☐
(c) Compare actual service with standards?	☐	☐
(d) Determine causes of performance variances?	☐	☐
(45) Are productivity results (for example, the pounds of refuse collected per employee) compared with those of other municipalities and standards?	☐	☐
(46) If so, does the division determine the reason for significant variances and institute corrective actions?	☐	☐
(47) Does the division solicit user reaction in evaluating the quality of service?	☐	☐

	Yes	No
(48) Are user complaints reviewed and appropriately resolved?	☐	☐
(49) Is the user informed of the disposition of his complaint?	☐	☐
(50) In addition to the continuous monitoring of performance, does the division periodically conduct an overall evaluation of service?	☐	☐
(51) If so, does this study include an analysis of how the		
(a) Quality of service might be improved?	☐	☐
(b) Level of service might be improved?	☐	☐
(c) Return on investment might be improved?	☐	☐
(52) Are recommendations resulting from the quality control function implemented by management?	☐	☐
(53) Are recommendations followed up to ensure they are implemented properly?	☐	☐

Capital Expenditures

These questions address the planning, approval, and management of capital expenditures. (Procurement methodology is addressed under the "Facility Management" and "Property Management" sections of this questionnaire and in detail in Chapter 9.)

(54) Does the division have policies and procedures for capital expenditures?	☐	☐
(55) Does the division require that major expenditure projects be approved by top management?	☐	☐
(56) In submitting a project for approval, does the division require that the proposed package contain		
(a) Preliminary estimates of the cost of the project?	☐	☐

	Yes	No
(b) Detailed justification for the expenditure?	☐	☐
(c) Explanation of the method of procurement (see Chapter 4, Dollarization Procedure 26: Lease Versus Purchase)?	☐	☐
(d) Discussion of the probability of grant reimbursement?	☐	☐
(57) Does the capital expenditure justification documentation include		
(a) An explanation of the anticipated demand for services that necessitates the expenditure?	☐	☐
(b) An analysis of the cost versus benefit of the expenditure?	☐	☐
(c) An indication of the impact the expenditure will have on present and future revenue?	☐	☐
(d) Alternatives for the chief executive to consider?	☐	☐
(58) After the project proposal is approved, does the division require that a firm estimate of the project costs be developed?	☐	☐
(59) If so, does the estimate show the costs of alternative courses of action? (For example, if a new treatment plant is proposed to replace an old one, does the estimate show the cost of modernizing the old facility?) (See Chapter 4, Dollarization Procedure 21: Repair Versus Replace.)	☐	☐
(60) Has the division established guidelines for evaluating the return on capital investments?	☐	☐
(61) Is the final authorization to proceed with a major project the responsibility of the chief executive?	☐	☐
(62) Is the division's procurement methodology applied consistently to all major capital expenditure projects?	☐	☐
(63) Has the division determined that the financing method used (e.g., lease, installment purchase,		

Yes *No*

etc.) is the one that is most advantageous to the entity? ☐ ☐

(64) Are capital expenditures planned well in advance to avoid unexpected drains on cash? ☐ ☐

(65) Does the division have a system for

(a) Monitoring the progress of project planning? ☐ ☐

(b) Evaluating post completion results to ensure that established financial and administrative goals are met? ☐ ☐

Section IV: Facility Management

Facility management consists of the administration of buildings and grounds owned by the government. Because most governments have a large investment in real estate, an effective, efficient system must be employed to manage the facilities.

Organization and Management

(1) Is the facility management division centralized? ☐ ☐

(2) Has the division developed policies and procedures for managing the entity's facilities? ☐ ☐

(3) If so, do they cover

(a) The maintenance of detailed inventory records? ☐ ☐

(b) Insurance practices? ☐ ☐

(c) A cost distribution system? ☐ ☐

(d) The maintenance of facility utilization records? ☐ ☐

(e) Procedures for justifying additions and new construction? ☐ ☐

(f) Maintenance criteria? ☐ ☐

(4) Do the inventory records contain information on kinds and numbers of facilities, their location, and condition? ☐ ☐

	Yes	*No*
(5) Has the division defined the entity's facility management workload (for example, square feet of daily cleaning, moving, etc.)?	☐	☐
(6) Are workload statistics developed and used to determine personnel requirements?	☐	☐

Building Operations

Space requirements:

(7) Has the division performed a study to determine space requirements and allocation of space to organizational units?	☐	☐
(8) Has the division considered future plans and anticipated workloads in determining space requirements?	☐	☐
(9) Does the division monitor the utilization of available space? Consider such matters as		
(a) Does space layout promote effective and efficient performance?	☐	☐
(b) Is space being used for the purpose for which it was designed?	☐	☐
(c) Has available space been appropriately allocated?	☐	☐
(d) Are facilities well maintained?	☐	☐
(e) Are vacant areas minimized?	☐	☐
(f) Is excess space promptly rented at competitive rates?	☐	☐
(10) Are adequate parking facilities available for employee and public use?	☐	☐

Layout of space:

(11) Has the division established standards for office sizes and work stations? (Standards should be based on level of management, physical limitations imposed by the building, and equipment requirements.)	☐	☐

		Yes	*No*
(12)	Has the division performed a study to determine the most effective and efficient layout of office space?	☐	☐
(13)	Have environmental conditions been considered in the layout arrangement?	☐	☐
(14)	Are reception areas and counter service functions situated to facilitate public access?	☐	☐
(15)	Does the division use temporary walls and partitions to facilitate changes in layout necessitated by functional or organizational changes?	☐	☐
(16)	Has space been provided for conference rooms and lounge areas?	☐	☐
	Building services:		
(17)	Is space made available for employee facilities (cafeterias, rest areas, etc.)?	☐	☐
(18)	Has the division established utility standards (for example, amount of lighting, temperature, etc.) in government buildings?	☐	☐
(19)	If so, do the standards appear to be in line with federal and state standards?	☐	☐
(20)	Are service facilities provided in the building grounds, parks, and recreation areas (rest rooms, public telephones, park benches, and litter containers)?	☐	☐
(21)	Are facility entrances and exits clearly marked? (Clearly marked entrances and office directions can often obviate the need for using a receptionist or security personnel for this purpose.)	☐	☐
(22)	Has the division determined the support services needed to ensure an effective, productive operation?	☐	☐

	Yes	*No*
(23) Do the services provided include		
(a) Mail and messenger?	☐	☐
(b) Reception?	☐	☐
(c) Special communication facilities?	☐	☐
(d) Reproduction facilities?	☐	☐
(24) Has the division made a cost versus benefit analysis regarding the frequency of mail pickups and distribution?	☐	☐
(25) Is the mail-room schedule coordinated with the local postal service schedule?	☐	☐
(26) Where appropriate, does the division use a numbering system to handle intergovernmental mail? (For example, each field location or subelement should have an identification number to facilitate the processing and delivery of mail.)	☐	☐
(27) Is before- and after-hours traffic to and from the building controlled? (For example, are employees asked to sign in or sign out?)	☐	☐
(28) Has the division evaluated its need for special communications facilities, such as special telephone features, teletype, and public address systems?	☐	☐
(29) Is the cost versus benefit of such facilities evaluated periodically (see Chapter 4, Dollarization Procedure 25: Equipment Utilization Review)?	☐	☐
(30) Has the division evaluated its copying, reproduction, and printing needs?	☐	☐
(31) Are these needs periodically reevaluated (see Chapter 4, Dollarization Procedure 25: Equipment Utilization Review)?	☐	☐
(32) Are acquisitions of reproduction equipment based on identified needs?	☐	☐
(33) Has the division established controls to prevent unauthorized use of reproduction equipment?	☐	☐

	Yes	*No*
(34) Are office copiers located to facilitate their use?	☐	☐
(35) Are logs used with the office copiers to identify the user and the number of copies made?	☐	☐
(36) Has the division evaluated the cost versus benefit of having the reproduction and printing services performed by an outside contractor?	☐	☐
Insurance program:		
(37) Does the division have an insurance program in effect?	☐	☐
(38) If so, does the program		
(a) Adequately define insurance needs?	☐	☐
(b) Provide adequate and up-to-date coverage?	☐	☐
(c) Require competition in selection of insurers?	☐	☐
(d) Provide for determination of appropriate deductible clauses?	☐	☐
(e) Provide for periodic review of coverage?	☐	☐
(39) Has the division evaluated the feasibility of being a self-insurer?	☐	☐
Building security:		
(40) Has the division evaluated facility security requirements?	☐	☐
(41) If so, did the evaluation consider such matters as		
(a) Incidence of theft and vandalism?	☐	☐
(b) Adequacy and cost of a security force?	☐	☐
(c) Controls over entrances to restricted areas?	☐	☐
(d) Controls over entrances to storage areas?	☐	☐
(e) Coordination with law enforcement officials?	☐	☐
(42) Is there a formal fire-protection program?	☐	☐
(43) Does the division have an emergency plan in the event of a riot, bombing, or similar disturbance?	☐	☐

	Yes	No
Facility Additions		
Planning:		
(44) Has a master plan that shows the size, location, and use of new facilities or major additions been developed?	☐	☐
(45) Is the master plan reviewed and approved by the chief executive and legislative body?	☐	☐
(46) Has a study been performed to determine future facility needs?	☐	☐
(47) If so, does this study include		
(a) A location analysis?	☐	☐
(b) Projected usage?	☐	☐
(c) Cost and method of financing?	☐	☐
(d) Analysis of public need (for example, need for public health unit)?	☐	☐
(48) After a project is authorized, does the division follow up to ensure that the final facility layout, equipment, and specifications are in line with original plans?	☐	☐
(49) Does the division (or the authorized planning group) take action, prior to initiating construction, to assure that adequate funding will be available for a new facility? (For example, action might be needed to get a bond referendum approved.)	☐	☐
(50) Are efforts made to obtain federal and state financial assistance?	☐	☐
Method of acquiring:		
(51) Has the division determined the most efficient method (e.g., eminent domain, purchase, condemnation, etc.) of acquiring real estate for additional facilities?	☐	☐

	Yes	*No*
(52) In determining the method of acquisition, does the division take precautions to avoid conflict-of-interest situations?	☐	☐
(53) Is the planned addition and the method of its acquisition publicized?	☐	☐

Construction:

The general practice among cities and states is to contract for major facility construction projects. The following questions assume construction by an outside contractor.

(54) Are bids for construction solicited		
(a) On a timely basis?	☐	☐
(b) With distribution adequate to ensure access to capable contractors?	☐	☐
(55) Is widespread public notice given to stimulate bidding?	☐	☐
(56) Are notices clear as to where to obtain bid packages?	☐	☐
(57) Does the division strive to obtain fixed price contracts whenever feasible?	☐	☐
(58) Are prospective bidders provided with the basic specifications, construction methods, and materials required?	☐	☐
(59) Is this data sufficient for the prospective contractor to prepare his bid? (This is especially necessary for fixed-price contracts.)	☐	☐
(60) Does the division maintain adequate control over specifications, drawings, etc.? (The high cost of preparing specifications and drawings requires that the division control these items.)	☐	☐
(61) Does it appear that the number of bids received is reasonable in relation to the size of the project (see Chapter 4, Dollarization Procedure 2: Bidding)?	☐	☐

	Yes	No
(62) When the bidders do not respond to a bid solicitation, does the division		
(a) Attempt to determine why?	☐	☐
(b) Readvertise?	☐	☐
(63) Does the division use sealed bidding procedures?	☐	☐
(64) Are the bids		
(a) Properly controlled before opening?	☐	☐
(b) Opened on a specified hour and day?	☐	☐
(c) Publicly read?	☐	☐
(65) To assure the validity of bids, does the division require a bid deposit? (General practice is to require a certified check at a set amount or percentage of the bid. The checks are returned to the unsuccessful bidders when the contract has been signed and the successful bidder furnishes a surety bond. Bidders' bonds are sometimes used in lieu of certified checks.)	☐	☐
(66) Has the division developed an adequate estimate of the project for use in evaluating the bids received?	☐	☐
(67) Has the division developed a process for evaluating the bids received?	☐	☐
(68) Does the division require the successful bidder to supply a surety or performance bond?	☐	☐
(69) Does the division negotiate with the leading bidders for a lower price?	☐	☐
(70) Does the contract provide for an audit of the contract costs when appropriate?	☐	☐
Construction control:		
(71) Does the division designate a supervising engineer to represent the city or state with the contractor?	☐	☐
(72) Is the engineer supported by a group of inspec-		

	Yes	No
tors whose duty it is to see that the contractor meets all plans and specifications?	☐	☐
(73) Do inspectors perform tests of materials and techniques used?	☐	☐
(74) Does the division require the contractor to complete the project by a certain date or within a specified number of days?	☐	☐
(75) Is the contractor required to pay a penalty when he does not meet the contract time constraints?	☐	☐
(76) Do inspectors have the authority to reject defective materials as well as improper methods?	☐	☐
(77) Do inspectors		
(a) Inspect certain materials prior to delivery to the contractor?	☐	☐
(b) Submit periodic reports to the project engineer?	☐	☐
(c) Adequately support claims of defective materials or improper practices?	☐	☐
(78) Do the inspector's reports provide adequate data for the engineer to evaluate the progress of the project and the contractor's performance?	☐	☐
(79) Does the project engineer make periodic field visits?	☐	☐
(80) Are periodic financial and performance reports required from the contractor?	☐	☐
(81) Are these periodic reports used to evaluate the progress of the project from the standpoint of both cost and performance?	☐	☐
(82) Are inspectors screened to avoid possible conflicts of interest?	☐	☐

Office Equipment

The office equipment function covers the activities involved in developing policies and standards for the

	Yes	*No*
many kinds of office equipment needed to support an entity's activities.		
(83) Is the office equipment and supplies function centrally managed?	☐	☐
(84) If so, are significant purchases made by the centralized group?	☐	☐
(85) Are volume purchases made where practical (see Chapter 4, Dollarization Procedure 20: Lost Quantity Discounts)?	☐	☐
(86) Are employees informed of the procedures for requisitioning office equipment and supplies?	☐	☐
(87) Does the centralized group review and evaluate the requests for the procurement of office equipment and supplies?	☐	☐
(88) If so, does this evaluation establish that the office equipment requested is appropriate for the task to be performed?	☐	☐
(89) Are the cost versus benefits of leasing versus buying considered in obtaining major office equipment (see Chapter 4, Dollarization Procedure 26: Lease Versus Purchase)?	☐	☐
(90) Are inventory records maintained for major office equipment (including furniture and fixtures)?	☐	☐
(91) Are physical inventories taken on a periodic basis?	☐	☐
(92) Are the storage areas for unused office equipment properly secured?	☐	☐

Section V: Property Management

This section of the questionnaire is designed for use in the review and evaluation of an entity's system for acquiring, using, and disposing of property. Some programs require a substantial investment in property, while others, usually in the service area, require very little. Accordingly, the following background data should be obtained to provide an overview of the property management function:

(1) Obtain a summary of the facilities and property managed by the public works department. (See p. 189.)

(2) Obtain a schedule of planned property additions and disposals.

Property	*Additions Estimated Cost*	*Planned Method of Acquisition**	*Planned Disposals*
Land	$........	....	$........
Machinery and equipment	....	....	....
Test equipment	....	....	....
Vehicles	....	....	....
Supplies	....	....	....
Other (identify)	....	....	....
TOTAL	$		$

* Indicate method by using following legend.
Purchase —A
Rental/lease —B
Transfer from another division—C
Constructed —D

Management and Records Control

Adequate control over property begins with an effective system of controls that applies to all of the function's aspects and ensures accurate accounting for significant items.

	Yes	*No*
(1) Does the division have guidelines concerning the acquisition, use, and accounting for property items?	☐	☐
(2) If so, do they cover		
(a) Maintenance of detailed inventory records?	☐	☐

	Yes	*No*
(b) Identification of items purchased with federal funds?	☐	☐
(c) Requirements for physical inventories?	☐	☐
(d) Maintenance of utilization records?	☐	☐
(e) Action to be taken with regard to damaged and lost items?	☐	☐
(f) Procedures for justifying procurement of new items?	☐	☐
(3) Does the division maintain detailed inventory records for significant items?	☐	☐
(4) Do inventory records contain information on kinds and amount of items on hand, their location, condition, and value?	☐	☐
(5) Are periodic physical inventories conducted?	☐	☐
(6) If so, are they conducted in accordance with written instructions?	☐	☐
(7) Are inventory differences explored to determine their causes?	☐	☐
(8) Do records segregate federal property from state, city, or county property?	☐	☐
(9) Are machinery and equipment tagged with metal plates or other identification?	☐	☐

Acquisitions and Replacements

Control over the acquisition and replacement of property items should include justification of the need for the items by user group; determination of appropriate means of acquisition; review and approval of justification by higher management; and inspection of property items before they are accepted.

(10) Has the division established acquisition and replacement criteria for the various classes of property items?	☐	☐

	Yes	No
(11) Do justifications for new equipment items contain information as to anticipated use and past use of items being replaced?	☐	☐
(12) Do procedures require that consideration be given to other techniques for acquiring property, e.g., outright purchase, sale leaseback, installment purchase, etc. (see Chapter 4, Dollarization Procedure 26: Lease Versus Purchase)?	☐	☐
(13) Are written reports analyzing alternative methods for acquiring major property items prepared?	☐	☐
(14) If so, are the decisions resulting from these studies approved by the appropriate authority?	☐	☐
(15) Have terms for lease transactions been standardized? (Standard terms facilitate the comparison of alternative arrangements.)	☐	☐
(16) If terms have been standardized, are departures from standards explained in writing and approved?	☐	☐
(17) Are significant nonstandard lease terms reviewed by the		
(a) Legal department?	☐	☐
(b) Accounting department?	☐	☐
(18) Do leases include "capture options" where appropriate? (Capture options allow the lessee to acquire a piece of equipment, usually at a price substantially higher than estimated cost but less than aggregate rentals if the item is leased over an extended period.)	☐	☐
(19) If repairs or other operating expenses are to be shared by lessor and lessee, do leases identify which of the items are for the lessee's account?	☐	☐
(20) Do rental agreements incorporate the condition of the equipment where pertinent to the rates charged?	☐	☐

		Yes	No
(21)	If condition is pertinent to rates, is condition evaluated upon equipment delivery?	☐	☐
(22)	Is the condition evaluation performed by qualified personnel?	☐	☐
(23)	Is the evaluation documented in writing?	☐	☐
(24)	Is the evaluation report forwarded to personnel concerned with processing lessor invoices?	☐	☐
(25)	Do the equipment operators maintain logs of operation that can be used to verify rental invoices?	☐	☐
(26)	Are the equipment operators' logs subject to spot-checking by timekeepers?	☐	☐
(27)	Do the equipment operators maintain detailed records of maintenance performed to ensure compliance with rental agreements?	☐	☐
(28)	Has responsibility been assigned for seeing that rental equipment is appropriately used?	☐	☐
(29)	Are formal reports prepared on a timely basis when equipment is no longer required?	☐	☐
(30)	Is there a procedure for speedy removal of rental equipment no longer needed?	☐	☐
(31)	Are explanations and approval required for keeping leased equipment that remains idle for extended periods (see Chapter 4, Dollarization Procedure 3: Equipment Downtime Evaluaation)?	☐	☐
(32)	Do accounting personnel perform checks of		
	(a) Equipment use as shown by operators' logs, timekeepers' logs, or others?	☐	☐
	(b) Rates against contracts or control documents abstracted from the contracts?	☐	☐

	Yes	*No*
(33) Are items replaced when they become uneconomical to maintain (see Chapter 4, Dollarization Procedure 21: Repair Versus Replace)?	☐	☐
(34) Are property acquisitions subjected to the normal procurement process?	☐	☐
(35) If not, do the reasons for deviation appear valid?	☐	☐
(36) Has the division established a policy for determining when property items should be expensed rather than capitalized?	☐	☐
(37) If so, are the criteria for capitalizing reasonable?	☐	☐
(38) Are property items inspected and tested before they are accepted?	☐	☐
(39) Is the final acceptance or rejection of an item documented?	☐	☐

Utilization

(40) Does the division have utilization standards for the various classifications of property items?	☐	☐
(41) Are property items assigned to the using organization on an as-needed basis? (The assignment of property items on a permanent basis can result in underutilization and unnecessary procurements.)	☐	☐
(42) When property items are assigned on a permanent basis, are justifications for the assignment reevaluated periodically to ensure that a need continues to exist?	☐	☐
(43) Does the division have a system for monitoring property utilization?	☐	☐
(44) If so, does the system include		
(a) A reporting system to identify underutilized property items?	☐	☐

	Yes	*No*
(b) The requirement that a determination be made of alternative uses for underutilized items?	☐	☐
(c) The requirement that an evaluation be made of differences in actual usage and the estimated usage cited in the acquisition justification (see Chapter 4, Dollarization Procedure 25: Equipment Utilization Review)?	☐	☐
(d) Reassignment of underutilized property items to potential users?	☐	☐
(e) Periodic evaluation of utilization standards?	☐	☐
(45) If the division does not have a formal monitoring system, are under-utilized property items identified and is appropriate action taken (see Chapter 4, Dollarization Procedure 25: Equipment Utilization Review)?	☐	☐

Property Storage

(46) Does the division have a system for controlling property items in storage?	☐	☐
(47) Do the storage facilities		
(a) Deter unauthorized access to storage areas?	☐	☐
(b) Provide adequate storage space?	☐	☐
(c) Provide specialized storage where needed?	☐	☐
(d) Use an effective security system?	☐	☐
(e) Facilitate the receipt and disposition of items in storage?	☐	☐
(48) Does the division's system provide control over the receipt of property from manufacturers and suppliers?	☐	☐
(49) Does the division have a central receiving activity?	☐	☐
(50) Are receipts of items properly documented?	☐	☐

	Yes	No
(51) Are items received promptly inspected		
(a) To assure that the item ordered is received?	☐	☐
(b) For damage?	☐	☐
(c) To assure that the amount ordered is received?	☐	☐
(52) Does the division have procedures for returning rejected items?	☐	☐
(53) Is withdrawal of property items from storage areas made only upon submission of properly authorized requisitions?	☐	☐
(54) Are the property records of items in storage kept up to date?	☐	☐
Property Disposal		
(55) Are property items periodically evaluated with a view towards economical salvage or disposal of items no longer needed because of obsolescence, wear, or lack of use?	☐	☐
(56) Does the division have a procedure whereby potential users are made aware of excess items?	☐	☐
(57) Are the property requirements of other organizational units screened prior to disposal of excess property?	☐	☐
(58) Is federal property that is no longer of use under a program returned to the grantor or sold?	☐	☐
(59) Are attempts made to use excess federal property in other programs? (Federal property may be transferred to other programs without reimbursement to the grantor agency.)	☐	☐

Section VI: Highways and Streets

Planning, constructing, and maintaining highways and streets are prime responsibilities of the public works department. The mobility of modern civilization requires an extensive system of highways and streets. To meet ever-increasing demands, the public works department must be concerned with maintaining and upgrading the present system, and with public needs several years in the future.

The preferred practice questions for highways and streets are divided into two categories: road operations and highway and street construction. These functions are usually performed by separate divisions of the public works department.

Road Operations

Road operations include paving, cleaning, snow removal, improvement, and routine maintenance of the highway and street system.

	Yes	*No*
Planning and scheduling routine maintenance:		
(1) Does the division have a formal system for planning and scheduling recurring maintenance?	☐	☐
(2) If so, does the system		
(a) Provide a detailed schedule of recurring maintenance and the related personnel, equipment, and material requirements?	☐	☐
(b) Consider seasonal needs?	☐	☐
(c) Provide enough flexibility to respond to emergency situations?	☐	☐
(d) Consider the opening of new streets and highways and the closing of old ones?	☐	☐
(3) Is the planning and scheduling process based on past experience supplemented by projected increases and decreases in traffic? (For example, the opening of a new street may change the traffic flow of other streets, thus affecting the maintenance cycle.)	☐	☐
(4) Does the process give consideration to new or improved techniques and equipment that will affect the maintenance cycle?	☐	☐
(5) Is convenience to the public a primary factor in the planning and scheduling process? (For ex-		

	Yes	*No*
ample, repairing major thoroughfares during rush hours should be avoided.)	☐	☐
(6) Does the division assign priorities to the maintenance projects? (For example, major thoroughfares should be given priority.)	☐	☐
(7) Does the division have contingency plans to handle emergency situations?	☐	☐
(8) If so, do the contingency plans identify the personnel, equipment, and materials to be used for an emergency? (For example, if a water main breaks, is a crew designated to respond?)	☐	☐
(9) Is there a mobilization plan for emergencies that provides for quick response with minimum disruption? (Often, it is useful to provide written instructions to those involved so employees know where and when to report and their assigned tasks.)	☐	☐
(10) During the winter season, is close communication maintained with the weather bureau in order to be prepared for changes in weather conditions?	☐	☐
(11) Because of the difficulty in predicting snow, is there flexibility in planning for its removal (for example, in the use of overtime)?	☐	☐
(12) Is equipment periodically evaluated to determine if it meets the needs of the division?	☐	☐
(13) If so, does this evaluation include		
(a) An analysis of the productivity of the equipment (see Chapter 4, Dollarization Procedure 25: Equipment Utilization Review)?	☐	☐
(b) An analysis of how productivity could be improved with different techniques for operating the equipment?	☐	☐
(14) Is information on the results of road mainte-		

	Yes	*No*
nance reviewed with a view toward improvement through the use of different techniques?	☐	☐
(15) If an entity has several maintenance districts, are road maintenance costs for each district compared with the others and variances investigated and adequately explained?	☐	☐

Replacement and improvement program:

(16) In addition to the routine maintenance program, does the division have a short- and long-range program for improving the highway and street system?	☐	☐
(17) If so, does the program include		
(a) Improvement of highway and street lighting?	☐	☐
(b) Construction of rest areas along major highways?	☐	☐
(c) Construction of emergency lanes along major highways?	☐	☐
(d) The widening and straightening of heavily traveled highways and streets?	☐	☐
(e) Improvement in highway safety, such as installation of safety rails?	☐	☐
(18) Does the program assign priorities to replacement and improvement projects?	☐	☐
(19) Does the program give consideration to the cost versus benefits received by the public from the planned improvement?	☐	☐
(20) Are specialists used in planning replacements and improvements? (For example, are street lighting engineers used to ensure that the public receives greatest visibility and protection per dollar invested in street lighting?)	☐	☐
(21) Are the needs for major replacement and improvements adequately documented to avoid approval and funding problems?	☐	☐

	Yes	*No*
(22) Are proposed projects periodically reevaluated as to need and priority?	☐	☐
(23) Is the long-range improvement program closely coordinated with the long-range programs of other divisions and departments to provide a smooth flow of capital expenditures?	☐	☐
(24) Do the long-range improvement projects fully disclose all financial requirements?	☐	☐
(25) Does the public works department head or his staff evaluate the need for and desirability of improvement projects proposed by the various divisions and/or maintenance districts?	☐	☐
(26) Does the department		
(a) Obtain federal and/or state financial assistance for major highway and street improvement projects?	☐	☐
(b) Obtain the maximum amount of federal and state funds available?	☐	☐
Environmental and safety program:		
(27) Is there an environmental and safety program for the highway and street system?	☐	☐
(28) Is the program coordinated with local civic groups?	☐	☐
(29) Have environmental standards been established?	☐	☐
(30) Are these standards in compliance with Environmental Protection Agency regulations?	☐	☐
(31) Are highway and street environmental standards incorporated into new construction and improvement programs?	☐	☐
(32) Does the division have an active antilitter campaign?	☐	☐
(33) Are facilities for litter disposal made available to the public?	☐	☐

	Yes	No
(34) Are efforts made to obtain the assistance of civic groups for large-scale cleanup efforts?	☐	☐
(35) Are studies and accident reports used to direct the safety program efforts?	☐	☐
(36) Is the safety program coordinated with local law enforcement groups?	☐	☐
(37) Is safety literature published by federal and state governments used?	☐	☐
(38) Has the division developed standards for highway and street signs to ensure that they are compatible with		
(a) The entity's beautification program?	☐	☐
(b) Internationally recognized signs or symbols?	☐	☐
(39) Have standards been established for commercial advertisements along highways and streets?	☐	☐
(40) Are commercial advertisements selectively and periodically reviewed to ensure that they comply with established standards?	☐	☐
(41) Are environmental impact studies performed during the planning of new construction and improvements to existing highways and streets?	☐	☐
Outside contractors:		
(42) Has the use of outside contractors for maintenance and improvements of highways and streets been considered?	☐	☐
(43) Has the cost versus benefit of using outside contractors been evaluated?	☐	☐
(44) Are outside contractors subject to the standard procurement procedures?	☐	☐
(45) If not, is there adequate justification for deviating from the procurement standards?	☐	☐
(46) Are outside contractors required to comply with		

	Yes	*No*
the construction specifications and performance standards established by the entity?	☐	☐
(47) Is the performance of the outsider contractor monitored and evaluated?	☐	☐
(48) If so, does management act on the results of the evaluations?	☐	☐
(49) Are potential conflicts of interest considered before a contract is awarded?	☐	☐
(50) Does the agreement with the outsider contractor provide that the division can		
(a) Cancel the agreement for unsatisfactory service?	☐	☐
(b) Suspend the arrangement in the event of large reductions in revenue?	☐	☐
(c) Audit the costs under the contract?	☐	☐
(51) Is the contractor required to submit financial and performance reports?	☐	☐
(52) Are these reports used in monitoring the contractor's performance?	☐	☐
Personnel:		
If personnel policy and procedures are to be reviewed, the preferred practice questions in Chapter 7 should also be addressed.	☐	☐
(53) Has the division or group responsible for maintenance and improvement to highways and streets defined its personnel needs?	☐	☐
(54) When vacancies occur, is the personnel department provided with a description of the skill level needed and the job prerequisites?	☐	☐
(55) Are personnel needs periodically evaluated from the standpoint of number of employees, as well as skill level required (see Chapter 4, Dollarization Procedure 1: Personnel Allocation)?	☐	☐

		Yes	*No*
(56)	If so, do these evaluations include a determination of the impact new maintenance techniques and materials and equipment will have on the personnel requirements (see Chapter 4, Dollarization Procedure 6: New Machine Feasibility)?	☐	☐
(57)	Are labor pools considered to meet workload requirements?	☐	☐
(58)	If used, is the utilization rate high for the labor pools?	☐	☐
(59)	Are there temporary employment programs for assistance during the peak maintenance period?	☐	☐
(60)	Are standards used for recurring jobs? (For example, has a standard been determined for the number of hours required to mow one mile of highway shoulder?)	☐	☐
(61)	If so, are the standards used		
	(a) In developing workload schedules?	☐	☐
	(b) To evaluate the performances of individuals and crews?	☐	☐
(62)	Are the standards periodically reviewed and updated?	☐	☐
	Quality control:		
(63)	Is there a system for evaluating the quality of services provided by the road operations division?	☐	☐
(64)	Have performance standards been developed for evaluating the services provided?	☐	☐
(65)	Has the cause of variation from the standards been determined and corrective action initiated?	☐	☐
(66)	Are the performances of various maintenance divisions compared?	☐	☐
(67)	If so, are the reasons for any variances investigated and corrective actions taken?	☐	☐

	Yes	*No*
(68) Is there a method for measuring the degree of public satisfaction with the services provided?	☐	☐
(69) Are service complaints investigated and appropriately resolved?	☐	☐
(70) Is there a problem identification program whereby the public is asked to assist in identifying highway and street problems (e.g., need for a traffic signal)?	☐	☐
(71) Does the quality control system provide performance data in a timely manner?	☐	☐
(72) Are trend analyses developed to determine		
(a) Frequently occurring public complaints?	☐	☐
(b) Those performance standards which are most often not met?	☐	☐
(c) The cost versus benefit of the particular services provided? (For example, are mowing operations required as often on lightly traveled highways as on heavily traveled ones?)	☐	☐
(73) Is management responsive to the findings and recommendations arising from the quality control function?	☐	☐
(74) Is there follow-up to determine if quality control recommendations are implemented?	☐	☐

Highway and Street Construction

To keep pace with increasing demands, an entity must also have an active construction program. The cost of highway and street construction requires a carefully planned program that balances long-range needs against the constraints of available funding.

Planning:

(75) Is current data maintained on the highway and street system?	☐	☐

	Yes	*No*
(76) If so, do these data show		
(a) Utilization rates?	☐	☐
(b) Utilization trends over several prior years?	☐	☐
(c) Projected utilization rates for several future years?	☐	☐
(d) Street and highway classification (expressways, major arteries, etc.)?	☐	☐
(77) Is a master plan maintained to show the most desirable location of planned highways and streets and their projected utilization rate?	☐	☐
(78) Has the master plan given consideration to		
(a) Population density?	☐	☐
(b) Land development?	☐	☐
(c) Zoning requirements?	☐	☐
(d) Highway safety?	☐	☐
(e) Nature of traffic movement?	☐	☐
(f) Overall entity planning objectives?	☐	☐
(g) Cost of construction?	☐	☐
(h) Revenues available?	☐	☐
(i) Characteristics of future vehicles?	☐	☐
(79) Has the planning process given consideration to the impact the topography will have on construction (number of bridges, grading, etc.)?	☐	☐
(80) Are proposed highways and streets adequately justified and documented?	☐	☐
(81) Has the most favorable method of financing been determined?	☐	☐
(82) Have efforts been made to obtain federal and state financial assistance?	☐	☐
(83) Is the maximum amount of federal and state financial assistance available being obtained?	☐	☐
(84) Are rejected requests for assistance fully investigated to determine the reasons for the rejection?		

		Yes	*No*
	(Such knowledge assists greatly in preparing future requests.)	☐	☐
(85)	Has the financing of highway and street construction been coordinated with other major construction programs, such as facility construction?	☐	☐
(86)	Are the preliminary street and highway construction plans reviewed and approved by the chief executive? (Top management approval should be obtained before detailed plans and specifications are developed.)	☐	☐
(87)	Is the highway and street construction master plan coordinated with other states and cities?	☐	☐
(88)	Are efforts made to develop joint projects, especially between city and state and state and state? (Such joint efforts often facilitate the obtaining of federal assistance.)	☐	☐
	Construction control:		
(89)	Does the division have a project engineer to represent the city or state with the contractor?	☐	☐
(90)	Is the engineer supported by a group of inspectors who are responsible for seeing that the contractor meets all plans and specifications?	☐	☐
(91)	Do the inspectors perform tests of materials and techniques used?	☐	☐
(92)	Do the inspectors have the authority to reject defective materials, as well as improper methods?	☐	☐
(93)	In performing their jobs, do the inspectors		
	(a) Inspect certain materials before their delivery to the contractor?	☐	☐
	(b) Submit periodic reports to the project engineer?	☐	☐
	(c) Adequately support their claims of defective materials or improper practices?	☐	☐

	Yes	*No*
(94) Do the inspectors' reports provide adequate data for the engineer to evaluate the progress of the project and the contractor's performance?	☐	☐
(95) Does the project engineer make periodic field visits?	☐	☐
(96) Does the division require periodic financial and performance reports from the contractor?	☐	☐
(97) Are these reports used to evaluate the progress of the project from the standpoints of timeliness, cost, and quality?	☐	☐

Section VII: Traffic Engineering

Movement of large numbers of vehicles and pedestrians over a limited highway and street system requires an effective system of traffic control. Traffic control is especially important on those city streets that handle large volumes of traffic within a confined area.

This section of the questionnaire is to be used in evaluating a system for controlling vehicle and pedestrian traffic.

Traffic Control

(1) Is there a traffic engineering function?	☐	☐
(2) Are traffic volume studies performed?	☐	☐
(3) If so, do these studies show		
(a) The heavily traveled areas?	☐	☐
(b) Diagrams of major intersections and industrial entrances?	☐	☐
(c) Volume counts for hourly or half-hourly periods?	☐	☐
(d) Types of vehicles using the streets or highways?	☐	☐
(e) Capacity of street and highway intersections (number of vehicles per hour)?	☐	☐
(4) Are the periodic traffic studies summarized into an annual traffic program?	☐	☐

	Yes	No
(5) If so, does the annual traffic program show		
(a) Traffic trends over the past few years?	☐	☐
(b) Hourly, daily, and seasonal variations in traffic volume on major highways and streets?	☐	☐
(c) Traffic patterns for downtown areas?	☐	☐
(6) Has the cost versus benefit of manual traffic counters been compared with that of mechanical traffic counters? (Manual counters should normally be used only when data is needed on the nature of the traffic and number of passengers using the vehicles.)	☐	☐
(7) Are these studies used in determining traffic routes, one-way regulations, parking, standing and stopping restrictions, and street lighting requirements?	☐	☐
(8) Are the studies made available to law enforcement groups?	☐	☐
(9) Are special studies performed for use in		
(a) Establishing traffic zones?	☐	☐
(b) Determining the need for traffic signals?	☐	☐
(c) Determining the proper timing for traffic signals?	☐	☐
(d) Establishing the appropriate speed for intersection approaches?	☐	☐
(10) Are follow-up studies made to determine the impact that changes have on the traffic flow?	☐	☐
(11) Are accident studies performed?	☐	☐
(12) Are the various studies used as input for improving the control of traffic and its flow?	☐	☐
(13) Is management responsive to the recommendations generated by these studies?	☐	☐
(14) Are suggestions for improving traffic control solicited from the public?	☐	☐

	Yes	No
(15) Are traffic control studies and manuals published by public service organizations and the state and federal governments used?	☐	☐
(16) Are various traffic control devices experimented with, especially in problem areas?	☐	☐
(17) Are traffic control devices regularly inspected, cleaned, and replaced?	☐	☐
(18) Is there a program for standardizing all traffic control devices? (The federal government has issued standards for control devices. There should be a program for complying with these standards as control devices are replaced.)	☐	☐

Pedestrian Control

	Yes	No
(19) Is there a program for controlling pedestrian traffic?	☐	☐
(20) Are pedestrian-control devices, including crosswalk markings, regularly inspected and maintained?	☐	☐
(21) Are studies performed to determine		
(a) Pedestrian traffic volume?	☐	☐
(b) Accident-prone areas?	☐	☐
(c) Areas needing sidewalks and street crossings?	☐	☐
(22) Is management responsive to the results of these studies?	☐	☐
(23) Are follow-up studies made to determine the impact that changes have on pedestrian traffic control?	☐	☐
(24) Are electronic devices used to assist pedestrians in highly congested areas?	☐	☐
(25) Are crossing guards used for school zones? (It is often more economical to employ part-time		

	Yes	*No*
crossing guards than to use the police force for these duties.)	☐	☐
(26) Has consideration been given to the special needs of the handicapped in the pedestrian control program? (For example, have ramps been installed on sidewalks at crosswalks to help those in wheelchairs?)	☐	☐
(27) Are suggestions for improving pedestrian traffic and safety solicited from the general public, civic and school groups, and other organizations?	☐	☐
(28) Does the division use slides, manuals, and other information on pedestrian safety?	☐	☐

Parking and Loading Control

Parking and loading control is closely related to street traffic control since free and easy circulation on the streets is largely dependent on parking availability. Therefore, the planning and operation of the street system should include parking control.

	Yes	*No*
(29) Does the traffic-control program encompass parking control?	☐	☐
(30) Have studies been conducted that show		
(a) An inventory of existing parking and loading facilities?	☐	☐
(b) Usage of existing parking and loading facilities at different periods of the day? (Such analyses are useful in determining time restrictions on parking areas.)	☐	☐
(c) Parking and loading zone deficiencies?	☐	☐
(31) In determining bus stop locations, has consideration been given to		
(a) Bus routing?	☐	☐
(b) Number of buses?	☐	☐
(c) Traffic and pedestrian movement?	☐	☐

	Yes	*No*
(d) Traffic control devices?	☐	☐
(e) Major transfer and destination points?	☐	☐
(32) Have the merits of separate lanes for buses been considered?	☐	☐
(33) In determining where to have freight loading and unloading zones, have the following been considered:		
(a) Public need?	☐	☐
(b) Time required to unload and load, and frequency?	☐	☐
(c) Size and type of vehicles used?	☐	☐
(d) Number of businesses to be served?	☐	☐
(e) Hours of delivery?	☐	☐
(34) Are restricted parking and loading zones clearly marked?	☐	☐
(35) In determining the curb parking time limits, has the need for short time limits been evaluated?	☐	☐
(36) Are meters used for curb parking? (While meters are normally a good source of revenue, the cost versus benefit should be determined before installation.)	☐	☐
(37) Are meters adequately maintained and serviced?	☐	☐
(38) Are off-street parking facilities available?	☐	☐
(39) Are the parking and loading requirements periodically reevaluated?	☐	☐
(40) Does the division have a program for maintaining and servicing off-street parking facilities owned by the entity?	☐	☐
(41) Does the division coordinate with law enforcement groups to ensure that parking and loading restrictions are enforced?	☐	☐

CHAPTER 11

Operational Controls Review–Maintenance

Part I—General Discussion

Part II—The Questionnaire

Part I—General Discussion

Maintenance is the repair of equipment and tools after breakdown, work to minimize breakdown, and work to extend the service life of equipment and tools.[1] In an entity that has a large investment

[1] Schiff & Schirger, *Control of Maintenance Cost–Research Report No. 41*, 4 (National Association of Accountants 1964).

in fixed assets, control of the maintenance function becomes increasingly important as technological advances bring more—and more complex—equipment into use.

Even though the diversity of maintenance operations complicates the measurement of the effectiveness of maintenance programs, an operational controls review of such programs may reveal opportunities for improved efficiency and reduced costs.

Maintenance Objectives

As in any other operational area, a maintenance function cannot be effective unless it has clearly defined objectives. The scope and nature of activities performed by a maintenance function vary from entity to entity. But overall maintenance objectives have been summarized as follows:

Functional Objectives

- To maintain equipment so that breakdowns will not interfere with operations;
- To maintain equipment in good condition to prolong its life;
- To keep equipment in condition to produce a high quality of output; and
- To increase productivity of the maintenance function by selecting project work with the greatest benefit.

Cost Objectives

- To keep total maintenance cost constant over time;
- To make maintenance cost follow the trend of activity;
- To keep maintenance cost within a certain percent of the budget; and
- To minimize maintenance work at premium wage rates.[2]

For a maintenance operation to be effective, a balance must be maintained between the functional and cost objectives, i.e., between efficiency and economy. For example, a maintenance program operating on a "least-cost" basis, though apparently achieving a cost objective, does so to the detriment of the physical condition of the assets. On the other hand, an unnecessarily high level of maintenance is also uneconomical.

---

[2] *Id.* at 11.

In establishing the balance between functional and cost objectives, maintenance policy should be coordinated with management's plans and expectations with regard to obsolescence, replacement, and disposal of equipment. Maintenance expenditures are worthwhile if they extend the useful life of equipment. If, however, the useful life of the equipment is short, maintenance expenditures are usually uneconomical.

Maintenance Organization

In most government entities, the maintenance function is part of the public works department. The maintenance function of a large government entity may service such diverse facilities as sanitation, police, fire, or utilities. Due to this diversity, total centralization of the maintenance function may be inappropriate, though some centralization (for vehicle maintenance, for example) is feasible. Decentralization has some advantages:

- The performance of maintenance is facilitated by the proximity of maintenance employees.
- Also, because of proximity, maintenance employees can be provided with clearly defined responsibilities and held accountable for their performance.

Planning

The planning and scheduling of most maintenance operations is achieved through the use of a work-order system. Under this system, long- and short-term maintenance schedules are supported by individual work orders containing estimates of personnel and material requirements for each maintenance task to be performed. The estimates are based on the entity's preventive maintenance policy and on past experience. They are generally developed by a maintenance foreman and approved at an appropriate management level. The work orders are the basis for daily, weekly, and monthly work schedules and provide management with an estimate of personnel requirements and material and equipment needs. These personnel and material estimates also can be used as an informal standard for particular tasks and thereby facilitate management's evaluation of the maintenance function.

Maintenance work orders and schedules should not be developed without consideration of certain external factors such as budget constraints, operational interference, and emergency breakdowns:

- Budget constraints, though usually outside the control of the maintenance organization, directly affect the performance of maintenance through the reduction of personnel and materials. The maintenance organization must be aware of probable budget cuts and have alternative plans to ensure that critical maintenance needs can be met.
- Interference with normal operational activities is an important factor to consider in planning and scheduling maintenance. Maintenance tasks must be scheduled for those periods in which operational activity will be least impaired.
- Emergency breakdowns cannot be anticipated or controlled. The maintenance organization can, however, take steps to ease the burden of emergency breakdowns by building a degree of flexibility into work schedules and by designating specific work crews to respond to certain emergencies. The key consideration in an emergency is the ability to respond quickly; emergencies usually occur when least expected and normally have a significant impact on operational activity.

Preventive Maintenance

A preventive maintenance program calls for systematic servicing of machines to minimize breakdowns and to preserve machine operating efficiency.

Preventive maintenance frequently involves lubrication and minor adjustments. Standard operating instructions should specify when and how these operations are to be performed and who is responsible for them.

Preventive maintenance may also involve the replacement of parts. A replacement schedule should be developed with the assistance of vendors. (It may be of interest that many major oil companies and equipment vendors provide free assistance in the installation of preventive maintenance programs and in the establishment of preventive maintenance records.)

Tickler files—files that indicate that work should be performed or parts replaced and at what time—should be developed. The development of the maintenance file included in the tickler file requires the cooperation of other departments. For example, operating departments must inform maintenance of the identification number and location of machines to be serviced and the purchasing department must participate in establishing reorder points for materials and supplies used in the maintenance function.

Equipment and Supply Management

Most maintenance operations have substantial investments in small tools, equipment, and supplies. Management must weigh the benefits of controlling these items with consideration of the impact the control mechanisms will have on the productivity of the maintenance function. For example, if stringent controls are placed over small tools, maintenance employees may spend considerable time checking out and returning the tools. Although there is no optimum balance of control and productivity for the maintenance function, the following basic practices usually provide control over tools, equipment, and supplies without deterring productivity:

- Management must assure that the purchase, receipt, and issuance of high-cost items are controlled. Periodic inventory counts should be made, inventory location cards should be maintained, and a system of receipt and issue forms should be used.
- Tight control over high-cost items can usually be offset by more relaxed control over frequently used inexpensive items. Management can often enhance productivity by having these items readily available to maintenance personnel.
- Management may have some difficulty deciding upon the degree of control needed for mid-priced items. Often, control over these items is best accomplished by delegating responsibility for them to the employees involved. For example, if certain small tools are often used by a particular individual, they can be issued to him and he can be held accountable for their security and upkeep. In such instances, however, management must provide the employee with means for securing these items, such as tool boxes or lockers.

The extent of control over small tools, equipment, and supplies varies from entity to entity. The important factor is that the degree of control is appropriate for the cost of the items and that controls do not deter the delivery of services.

Part II—The Questionnaire

Background Information

The following background information should be obtained prior to initiating the review of a maintenance function:

(1) Obtain an analysis of the facilities and equipment serviced by the maintenance department. (This information may have been obtained through a review of the public works department. See Chapter 10: Public Works Questionnaire, Section IV.)

(2) Obtain a copy of the maintenance function's organization chart and policies and procedures manual. (In most government entities, the maintenance function is part of the public works department. The chart and manual, however, should be available for the division or branch within the public works department responsible for maintenance.)

(3) Obtain a listing showing the key personnel of the maintenance function by position level and work location.

Name	*Position*	*Location*
. . . .	. . . .	. . . .
. . . .	. . . .	. . . .
. . . .	. . . .	. . . .
. . . .	. . . .	. . . .
. . . .	. . . .	. . . .
. . . .	. . . .	. . . .

(4) Obtain an analysis of the funding for the maintenance function.

	Amount				
Fund	*Personnel*	*Supplies*	*Equipment*	*Other*	*Total*
General	$.	$.	$.	$. . . .	$. . . .
Enterprise	. . . .	. . . . . .	. . . .	. . . .	. . . .
Capital projects	. . . .	. . . . . .	. . . .	. . . .	. . . .
Others (identify)	. . . .	. . . . . .	. . . .	. . . .	. . . .
TOTAL	$	$	$	$	$

(5) Obtain personnel data for the maintenance function.

Function	Number: Employed	Number: Budgeted
Motor pool	....	....
Supply	....	....
Equipment repair (shop)	....	....
Building operation	....	....
Others (identify)	....	....
TOTAL		

(6) Obtain contract data for maintenance performed by outside contractors.

Vendor/Contractor	*Service*	*Period*	*Amount*
....	....	....	$........
....	....	....	....
....	....	....	....
....	....	....	....
....	....	....	....
....	....	....	....
TOTAL			$

(7) Record the approximate ratio of preventive maintenance to emergency repair cost.

Function	*Preventive**		*Emergency*		*Total*	
Motor pool	$....	...%	$....	...%	$....	...%
Supply	....	...	....	...	....	...
Equipment repair (shop)	....	...	....	...	....	...
Building operation	....	...	....	...	....	...
Others (identify)	....	...	....	...	....	...
TOTAL	$	100%	$	100%	$	100%
% of Total		%		%		100%

* Including planned repairs.

Maintenance Questionnaire

The questionnaire covers the following categories:

- Section I: Organization and Management;
- Section II: Planning and Scheduling;
- Section III: Materials and Labor;
- Section IV: Preventive Maintenance Program; and
- Section V: Performance Data.

Section I: Organization and Management

The maintenance function in state and local government may be a part of the public works function (most common), a separate department, or an organizational element of the activity it serves.

	Yes	*No*
(1) Does the maintenance function have		
(a) An organization chart?	☐	☐
(b) Job descriptions?	☐	☐
(c) Clear-cut responsibilities?	☐	☐
(2) Have goals and objectives been established for the maintenance function?	☐	☐
(3) Are these goals and objectives in line with the entity's overall goals and objectives?	☐	☐
(4) Does the function have a maintenance manual?	☐	☐
(5) If so, does it cover		
(a) Maintenance standards or instructions?	☐	☐
(b) Reporting requirements?	☐	☐
(c) Procedures for requesting emergency maintenance?	☐	☐
(d) Relationships with other departments?	☐	☐
(e) Functional relationships within the maintenance organization?	☐	☐
(f) Equipment and supply standards?	☐	☐
(g) Control over maintenance equipment and supplies (see Chapter 4, Dollarization Procedure 27: Deficient Inventory Control)?	☐	☐
(h) Budgeting and planning requirements?	☐	☐

	Yes	*No*
(6) Are personnel requirements based on the planned work load rather than on peak work load (see Chapter 4, Dollarization Procedure 5: Personnel Utilization Evaluation)?	☐	☐
(7) Are salaries and benefits adequate to retain and motivate competent personnel?	☐	☐
(8) Is the maintenance function under the control of one executive?	☐	☐

Section II: Planning and Scheduling

Planning and scheduling are fundamental to the operation of an effective maintenance program. This involves the determination of personnel and job requirements, inventory levels for parts and supplies, priorities, and cost estimates. The maintenance program must also include provisions for emergency situations.

Organization

(1) Does the maintenance function have a planning and scheduling process?	☐	☐
(2) Do maintenance foremen participate in the planning and scheduling of jobs and ensure that such jobs are completed within the established parameters?	☐	☐
(3) Is the planning and scheduling process based on the concept of preventive rather than responsive maintenance?	☐	☐

Work Order System

(4) Does the maintenance function use a work order system in setting up its schedule? (A work order system provides for application of material, supplies, and labor to maintenance jobs.)	☐	☐
(5) Are work orders prepared in advance in planning significant maintenance jobs?	☐	☐

	Yes	*No*
(6) Do the work orders show		
(a) A description of the work to be performed?	☐	☐
(b) Location?	☐	☐
(c) Urgency or priority?	☐	☐
(d) Name of requesting department?	☐	☐
(e) Signature and approval?	☐	☐
(f) Cost code?	☐	☐
(g) Estimated time for completion?	☐	☐
(7) Are work orders approved at an appropriate level?	☐	☐
(8) Are work orders and scheduling based on past experience?	☐	☐
(9) Are work orders or related documents used to make certain that the following will be available when the work is to be performed		
(a) Personnel?	☐	☐
(b) Tools and equipment?	☐	☐
(c) Materials?	☐	☐
(d) Instructions?	☐	☐
(10) Is maintenance scheduling that involves the shutdown of a facility or major equipment coordinated with the affected department?	☐	☐
(11) Is an effort made to delegate minor, routine maintenance tasks to personnel of operating departments?	☐	☐
(12) Is preventive maintenance based on the manufacturer's suggested program as modified by past experience where necessary?	☐	☐
(13) Are standing work orders used to accumulate costs for recurring minor maintenance activities, such as lubrication?	☐	☐
(14) If so, are such standing work orders subject to review to avoid "burial" of excessive expenses?	☐	☐

	Yes	No
Personnel Requirements		
(15) Does the system provide for breaking down projected needs by the skills required?	☐	☐
(16) Are planning schedules met by the work force without idle workers or constant overtime (see Chapter 4, Dollarization Procedure 5: Personnel Utilization Evaluation)?	☐	☐
(17) Are the economics of using temporary employees to meet seasonal demands periodically reviewed (see Chapter 4, Dollarization Procedure 5: Personnel Utilization Evaluation)?	☐	☐
(18) Are the effects of seasonality considered early enough to allow for work force leveling?	☐	☐
(19) Are territories or groups of equipment assigned to specific maintenance personnel for inspection and adjustment?	☐	☐
(20) Is the ratio of supervisors to other maintenance employees regularly evaluated?	☐	☐
Long-Range Planning		
(21) Are long-range maintenance needs projected?	☐	☐
(22) If so, does the long-range plan		
(a) Give recognition to new facilities under construction or to be acquired?	☐	☐
(b) Recognize and allow for changes in work load?	☐	☐
(c) Provide adequate levels of personnel and facilities to meet contingencies?	☐	☐
(23) Is the long-range plan used to determine		
(a) Equipment needs?	☐	☐
(b) Personnel needs?	☐	☐
(c) Supply and material requirements?	☐	☐
(d) Financial requirements?	☐	☐

	Yes	*No*
(24) Is the planning data used as input to the budgeting process?	☐	☐
(25) Is the long-range maintenance plan used as input to the planning processes of other departments?	☐	☐
(26) Does the system provide for evaluation of a decision to repair or replace equipment (see Chapter 4, Dollarization Procedure 21: Repair Versus Replace)?	☐	☐
(27) When unanticipated budget cuts occur, are the planning schedules revised?	☐	☐

Emergency Planning

	Yes	*No*
(28) Are overall work schedules flexible enough to permit emergency repairs and maintenance?	☐	☐
(29) Is a priority system used in reallocating personnel from jobs to make up an emergency force, i.e., are men pulled first from low-priority jobs?	☐	☐
(30) When requests for emergency maintenance are received, does the maintenance organization confirm that an emergency situation actually exists?	☐	☐
(31) Are certain crews designated to respond to specific emergency situations? (For example, a water main break might require a crew with special skills.)	☐	☐

Section III: Materials and Labor

Materials and labor consume most of the funds allocated to maintenance; therefore, control over these items is necessary if maintenance is to make an effective contribution to resource management. This section addresses standards and controls necessary to manage materials and labor costs.

	Yes	No
Materials		
Management:		
(1) Is there a system of inventory control for materials, supplies, equipment, and tools (see Chapter 4, Dollarization Procedure 27: Deficient Inventory Control)?	☐	☐
(2) Have guidelines been issued covering the acquisition, withdrawal, and management of materials, supplies, equipment, and tools (see Chapter 4, Dollarization Procedure 27: Deficient Inventory Control)?	☐	☐
(3) If so, do these guidelines		
(a) Outline procedures for requisitioning items from the storerooms?	☐	☐
(b) Define record-keeping criteria?	☐	☐
(c) Require the establishment of reorder points and economic order quantities (see Chapter 4, Dollarization Procedures 17: Extra Cost for "Rush" Deliveries, and 18: Excessive Inventories)?	☐	☐
(d) Define purchasing procedures for maintenance items not centrally purchased?	☐	☐
(e) Define procedures for receipt of items in the storeroom?	☐	☐
Inventory control—materials and supplies:		
(4) Do maintenance employees have free access to low-cost items?	☐	☐
(5) Are storage areas for these low-cost items located close to the point of use?	☐	☐
(6) Are inventory records maintained for high-cost items?	☐	☐
(7) Are inventory records kept up to date?	☐	☐

	Yes	No
(8) Are physical inventories taken periodically and compared to inventory records?	☐	☐
(9) If so, are inventory counts		
(a) Appropriately controlled?	☐	☐
(b) Taken on a cyclical basis to minimize costs and disruption?	☐	☐
(10) Are inventory records jointly used by purchasing and maintenance in managing inventory?	☐	☐
(11) Is an approved requisition required for items, other than low-cost items, taken from the storeroom?	☐	☐
(12) Do controls over the storeroom ensure that		
(a) Access is limited?	☐	☐
(b) High-cost parts are secure?	☐	☐
(c) Passes are required to move materials off the premises?	☐	☐
(d) Employee parking is restricted?	☐	☐
(e) Gate passes are required for visitors?	☐	☐
(13) When items are returned to the storeroom, are		
(a) Quantities verified?	☐	☐
(b) Checks made to assure that the item has not been damaged?	☐	☐
(c) Credit requisitions prepared and entered in both inventory control and accounting records?	☐	☐
(14) Are material location cards updated for movement of stock from one location to another?	☐	☐
(15) Does the spare parts inventory provide for a minimum stock level adequate for responding to emergency situations?	☐	☐
(16) Are periodic reviews made to determine obsolescence, scrap, and excess materials and supplies?	☐	☐
(17) Are slow-moving articles disposed of on the most favorable basis?	☐	☐

	Yes	No
(18) Does the storeroom issue supplies and materials in standard or predetermined quantities for recurring maintenance jobs?	☐	☐
(19) Are such standards and specifications reviewed periodically?	☐	☐
(20) Do material and supply standards prescribe the technical and performance specifications of the materials to be used on various classes of maintenance jobs?	☐	☐
(21) Is there a system for issuing and assigning tools (see Chapter 4, Dollarization Procedure 27: Deficient Inventory Control)?	☐	☐
(22) Are maintenance tools and equipment properly secured (see Chapter 4, Dollarization Procedure 27: Deficient Inventory Control)?	☐	☐
(23) Are requirements for personal hand tools established and are tool boxes periodically inspected?	☐	☐
(24) Is a regular review made to recover tools outstanding for extended periods?	☐	☐
(25) Are types of tools and equipment evaluated periodically to ensure that the most modern and cost-effective items are used?	☐	☐

Purchasing:

If procurement policy and procedures are to be reviewed, the procurement questionnaire (Chapter 9) should be used. The following questions are directed toward the controls necessary to ensure that effective interaction exists between maintenance and procurement.

(26) Is there communication and coordination between maintenance and procurement?	☐	☐

	Yes	No
(27) Does procurement consult maintenance		
(a) As to the nature of the articles to be purchased?	☐	☐
(b) As to quantities to be purchased for volume procurements (see Chapter 4, Dollarization Procedure 20: Lost Quantity Discounts)?	☐	☐
(c) Prior to making substitutions?	☐	☐
(28) Is maintenance informed immediately of changes in original commitments (for example, delay in shipping date)?	☐	☐
(29) Is maintenance permitted to purchase low-cost items needed on a crisis basis (subject to later review) without going through the normal procurement process?	☐	☐

Labor

Management and work load:

(30) Are maintenance employees performing functions according to their job classifications? (If they perform jobs above their classification, they are usually paid the higher rate. If below, they are paid their regular rate.)	☐	☐
(31) Are enough laborers available to perform non-skilled work?	☐	☐
(32) Are maintenance personnel available or on call to handle weekend and after-hour emergencies?	☐	☐
(33) Have work standards based on motion and time studies been developed where appropriate?	☐	☐
(34) Are these standards used in planning and scheduling the labor force?	☐	☐
(35) Is the foreman aware of what work is being performed by maintenance employees and where it is being done?	☐	☐

	Yes	*No*
(36) Has employing maintenance personnel on an incentive basis been considered?	☐	☐
(37) Are maintenance employees restricted from assignment to make-work projects unless approved by a maintenance foreman (see Chapter 4, Dollarization Procedure 5: Personnel Utilization Evaluation)?	☐	☐
Supervision and control:		
(38) Are time reports required for all employees?	☐	☐
(39) Are time reports reviewed by supervisors based upon actual observation on the job?	☐	☐
(40) Does the foreman complete a daily work report indicating the assignment of maintenance crews?	☐	☐
(41) Does all overtime have to be justified and approved prior to its scheduling (see Chapter 4, Dollarization Procedure 5: Personnel Utilization Evaluation)?	☐	☐
(42) Do the maintenance foreman participate in the evaluation of job candidates' qualifications?	☐	☐
(43) Are all disciplinary decisions reviewed at a higher echelon?	☐	☐
(44) Do maintenance foremen meet periodically to discuss problem areas?	☐	☐

Labor Pools

(45) Has the cost versus benefit of maintaining a labor pool been evaluated?	☐	☐
(46) Is the utilization rate for employees in the labor pool reviewed by skill and by total?	☐	☐
(47) Are employees in the labor pool used for non-maintenance assignments during slack work-load periods?	☐	☐

	Yes	*No*
Contract Services		
(48) Have cost/benefit analyses been made regarding the use of outside contractors for certain maintenance functions such as		
(a) Cleaning services?	☐	☐
(b) Guard services?	☐	☐
(49) Where outside contractors are used, is their selection made as a result of competitive bidding (see Chapter 9, Procurement Questionnaire, Section II, questions 19–25)?	☐	☐
(50) Is the arrangement with a contractor evidenced by a written contract?	☐	☐
(51) If so, do the following appear reasonable based on contract inspection:		
(a) Hourly rates?	☐	☐
(b) Estimated time required?	☐	☐
(c) Pension, health and welfare add-ons, including social security, etc.? (To the degree possible, this information should be verified by reference to other available documentation, e.g., union contracts.)	☐	☐
(d) Profit margin?	☐	☐
(e) Escalator clauses, if any?	☐	☐
(f) Insurance and especially workmen's compensation? (It is particularly important that the nature of any add-on percentages be specified; such percentages could represent estimates subject to later adjustments or actual rates based on earlier experience.)	☐	☐
(52) Are outside contractors required to comply with labor, material, and job-performance standards?	☐	☐
(53) Are outside contractors required to use entity material and supplies on hand or on order?	☐	☐

		Yes	*No*
(54)	Are the performances of outside contractors periodically assessed?	☐	☐
(55)	Does the maintenance function have control over outside contractors?	☐	☐
(56)	Is a review made of contractors' invoices in the light of the original contract terms?	☐	☐

Building Services

(57)	Are building services, whether performed by outside contractors or employees, appropriately supervised? ("Soldiering on the job" should be reasonably evident to the observer.)	☐	☐
(58)	Is the productivity of building services evaluated periodically? (There should be a correlation between the number of employees involved with cleaning and the floor footage involved. Guard services should be appropriate to the type of property being protected.)	☐	☐
(59)	If so, is such evaluation documented?	☐	☐
(60)	Are recommendations resulting from such evaluations implemented?	☐	☐
(61)	Has consideration been given to the use of modern technology to automate building services? (Effective cleaning services require polishing and vacuuming equipment; guard services may be "automated" via electronic eyes, television cameras, etc.)	☐	☐
(62)	Is the adequacy of building security reviewed periodically?	☐	☐
(63)	If so, is such review documented?	☐	☐
(64)	Are recommendations resulting from such reviews implemented to the extent possible?	☐	☐

	Yes	*No*
Shop Layout		
(65) Are garage and shop layouts designed to minimize walking and waiting for tools?	☐	☐
(66) Is an inspection made periodically to ensure that maintenance space is used for its intended purposes?	☐	☐

Section IV: Preventive Maintenance Program

A preventive maintenance program is in effect to some extent in every organization. Its purpose is not only to reduce maintenance costs, but also to ensure that equipment, facilities, and machinery are available for use when needed, and that major repairs are avoided. This section addresses the elements of a preventive maintenance program and the controls necessary to assure its success.

	Yes	*No*
(1) Is preventive maintenance conducted in a planned and organized way?	☐	☐
(2) Are tickler files used to signal jobs to be performed at fixed intervals of time?	☐	☐
(3) If so, do these files include all facilities, machinery, and equipment that require regular maintenance?	☐	☐
(4) Do equipment and machinery records show		
(a) Age and location of item?	☐	☐
(b) Servicing dates?	☐	☐
(c) Warranty details?	☐	☐
(d) Manufacturer servicing record?	☐	☐
(e) Costs and number of hours required for each servicing?	☐	☐
(f) Major parts replaced?	☐	☐
(5) Does the preventive maintenance program make use of product substitution and cost-reduction techniques?	☐	☐
(6) Are potential major problems revealed during the inspection promptly reported to the maintenance supervisors?	☐	☐

	Yes	*No*
(7) Are the departments served responsive to suggestions from maintenance that would lead to reductions in maintenance through changes in operating procedures?	☐	☐
(8) Is a servicing checklist used to guide maintenance efforts? (For example, the 6,000-mile servicing of an automobile would require certain checks and lubrications. A checklist could be used to make certain that all steps are performed.)	☐	☐
(9) If checklists are used, does maintenance require		
(a) An employee to initial each item performed?	☐	☐
(b) An explanation for servicing not performed?	☐	☐
(c) The maintenance foreman to test-check the work performed?	☐	☐
(d) The maintenance foreman to review each checklist and sign it?	☐	☐
(10) Does the preventive maintenance program include scheduled painting of facilities?	☐	☐
(11) Is the technical assistance of the manufacturer obtained in		
(a) Developing preventive maintenance schedules and practices for new machinery and equipment?	☐	☐
(b) Determining the causes for recurring breakdowns?	☐	☐
(12) Are planned major repairs staggered to facilitate both scheduling and funding?	☐	☐
(13) Does the preventive maintenance program include periodic inspection of electrical, plumbing, heating, and air-conditioning systems?	☐	☐
(14) Are these inspections made by competent technical personnel; i.e., is the electrical system in-		

	Yes	*No*
spected by a qualified electrician, the heating and water supply systems by a qualified plumber, etc.?	☐	☐

Section V: Performance Data

Meaningful performance data must be developed to evaluate properly the economy and effectiveness of the maintenance function. This section addresses the type of information needed and its use by maintenance management.

Information

	Yes	*No*
(1) Does a system exist for compiling performance data for the maintenance function?	☐	☐
(2) Does the system provide for the accumulation of financial and operational data?	☐	☐
(3) If so, does the data show		
(a) Comparisons of actual costs and hours to budgeted and/or standard amounts?	☐	☐
(b) Maintenance costs per major item or group (see Chapter 4, Dollarization Procedure 21: Repair Versus Replace)?	☐	☐
(c) Frequency of repair rates for major items of equipment (see Chapter 4, Dollarization Procedure 21: Repair Versus Replace)?	☐	☐
(d) Analysis of unscheduled maintenance and repair?	☐	☐
(e) Analysis of machinery and equipment downtime and facility shutdowns due to repair and maintenance (see Chapter 4, Dollarization Procedure 3: Equipment Downtime Evaluation)?	☐	☐
(4) Are work orders for emergency repairs supported by appropriate justifications?	☐	☐
(5) Does the system accumulate performance data by functional element where appropriate (for		

	Yes	No
example, motor pool, building services, parks, etc.)?	☐	☐
(6) Are standard reporting formats and cost codes used?	☐	☐
(7) Has maintenance information been evaluated to determine if it meets organizational needs?	☐	☐
(8) Are maintenance project reports		
(a) Complete and up to date?	☐	☐
(b) Submitted on a timely basis?	☐	☐
(c) Accurate?	☐	☐
(d) Prepared in the standard or required format?	☐	☐
(9) Are user complaints reviewed and appropriately resolved?	☐	☐

Data Usage

(10) Are the data collected used to evaluate the maintenance function?	☐	☐
(11) Are analyses made of the effectiveness of the preventive maintenance program? (For example, a decrease in emergency work orders may be an indication of the success of preventive maintenance.)	☐	☐
(12) Are breakdown reports analyzed for the detection of failure patterns that might be corrected through preventive maintenance?	☐	☐
(13) Are actual work order results compared to established standards with explanations of variances?	☐	☐
(14) Are the performance reports analyzed with regard to recurring maintenance problems? (Recurring maintenance problems can signify a need for more frequent preventive maintenance, a deficiency in particular pieces of equipment, or a need for replacement.)	☐	☐

	Yes	*No*
(15) Is the cost and performance data used in planning and scheduling future maintenance?	☐	☐
(16) Is the data used to evaluate the results of improvement programs?	☐	☐
(17) Is the data used to perform cost/benefit analyses of work methods and maintenance technology?	☐	☐
(18) Is management in other departments given maintenance data to facilitate changes in operating procedures?	☐	☐

CHAPTER 12

Operational Controls Review–Grant Management

Part I—General Discussion

Part II—The Questionnaire

Part I—General Discussion

A grant (or a grant-in-aid) is a contribution of resources by one government entity to another for the support of a project in which there is substantial public interest or need. The federal government grants billions of dollars each year in support of state or local programs to provide such services as law enforcement, unemployment assistance, parks and recreation, urban renewal, and transportation.

Historical Perspectives

Grants to state and local governments are an increasingly significant item in the federal budget. In 1950, federal grants to state and local governments totaled $2 billion. By 1965, they had risen to $11 billion, and in 1975, they totaled $50 billion. Federal grants have increased at an average annual rate of 18.3 percent since 1965. In comparison, total federal outlays over the same period have increased at an average annual rate of 11 percent.[1]

Figure 12-1 illustrates the recent growth in grant outlays. It is apparent from the figure that federal aid has become an increasingly important factor in the finances of all levels of government over the

Figure 12-1

IMPACT OF FEDERAL GRANT OUTLAYS

(in millions of dollars)

		Federal Grants as a Percent of		
		Federal Outlays		*State and Local*
	Grants	*Total*	*Domestic **	*Expenditures ***
1950	$ 2.253	5.3	8.8	10.4
1955	3.207	4.7	12.1	10.1
1960	7.020	7.6	15.9	11.7
1965	10.904	9.2	16.6	15.3
1969	20.255	11.0	20.1	18.0
1970	24.018	12.2	21.1	19.4
1971	28.109	13.3	21.4	19.9
1972	34.372	14.8	22.8	22.0
1973	41.832	17.0	24.8	24.3
1974	43.308	16.1	23.3	22.7
1975	49.723	15.3	21.3	23.4
1976 estimate	59.787	16.0	21.7	25.2
1977 estimate	$60.523	15.4	21.1	23.0

* Defined for this purpose as excluding national defense and international programs.

** As defined in the National Income Accounts.

SOURCE: Office of Management and Budget, *Special Analysis–Budget of the United States Government—Fiscal Year 1977,* 264 (U.S. Government Printing Office 1976).

---

[1] Office of Management and Budget, *Special Analysis–Budget of the United States Government—Fiscal Year 1977,* 263 (U.S. Government Printing Office 1976).

past two decades. In 1977, federal grant outlays are expected to total $60.5 billion.[2] This represents 15.4 percent of total federal outlays and 21.1 percent of domestic federal outlays. In total, federal aid will finance about 23 percent of state and local expenditures in 1977.[3] The growth of federal grant outlays is further illustrated by Figure 12-2.

Federal Grant-in-Aid Programs by Function and by Agency

In accordance with the Congressional Budget Act of 1974, Congress reviews the budget and sets targets by function. Budgeting by

Figure 12-2

FEDERAL GRANTS TO STATE AND LOCAL GOVERNMENTS

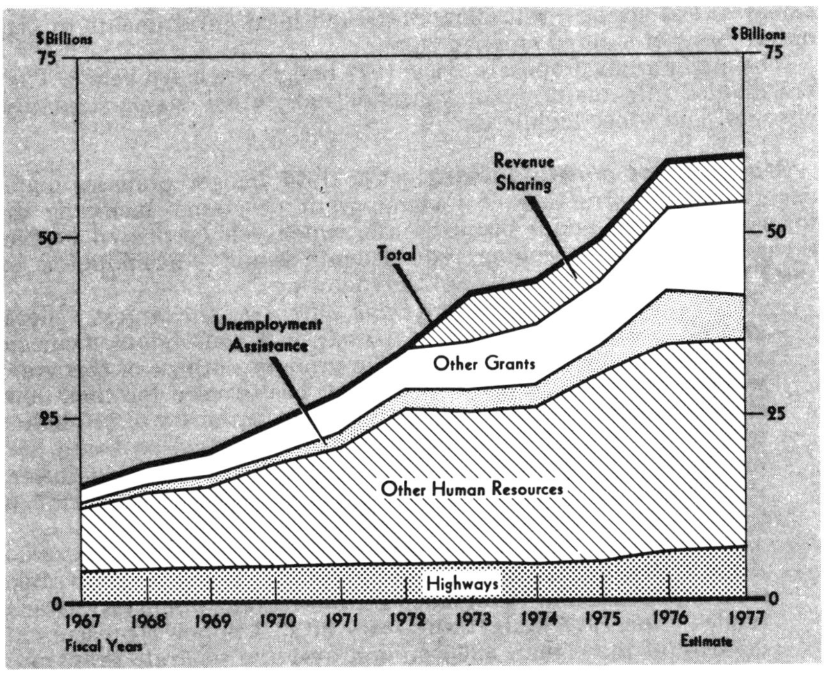

SOURCE: Office of Management and Budget, *Special Analysis–Budget of the United States Government—Fiscal Year 1977,* 255 (U.S. Government Printing Office 1976).

[2] *Id.* at 255.
[3] *Id.* at 263–264.

function provides an important means for analysis and control of federal grants.

Figure 12-3 shows the distribution of federal grant-in-aid outlays by function. Outlays for 1977 are expected to include increases in natural resources, environment, and energy, and a decline in education, training, employment, and social services as the economy improves and spending for programs to alleviate the effects of unemployment decreases.[4] Figure 12-4 illustrates the distribution of federal grant-in-aid outlays by agency. (Details of these grants are presented in Appendix III: Federal Grants to State and Local Governments—Outlays.)

Figure 12-3

FEDERAL GRANT-IN-AID OUTLAYS BY FUNCTION

(in millions of dollars)

Function	*1975 Actual*	*1976 Estimate*	*1977 Estimate*
National defense	74	77	67
Natural resources, environment and energy	2,479	3,088	4,505
Agriculture	404	499	556
Commerce and transportation	5,872	8,227	8,990
Community and regional development	3,335	4,008	3,917
Education, training, employment, and social services	11,638	14,422	12,497
Health	8,810	10,032	10,188
Income security	9,279	11,212	11,434
Veterans benefits and services	32	73	80
Law enforcement and justice	725	838	805
General government	102	145	135
Revenue-sharing and general purpose fiscal assistance	6,971	7,166	7,349
Total outlays	49,723*	59,787	60,523

* Sic.

SOURCE: Office of Management and Budget, *Special Analysis–Budget of the United States Government—Fiscal Year 1977,* 259 (U.S. Government Printing Office 1976).

---

[4] *Id.* at 259.

Figure 12-4

FEDERAL GRANT-IN-AID OUTLAYS BY AGENCY

(in millions of dollars)

	1975 Actual	*1976 Estimate*	*1977 Estimate*
Department of Agriculture	2,936	3,626	3,403
Department of Commerce	299	498	477
Department of Defense—Military	74	77	67
Department of Health, Education, and Welfare	22,010	24,060	24,125
Department of Housing and Urban Development	3,439	4,289	4,769
Department of the Interior	557	618	542
Department of Justice	722	750	717
Department of Labor	4,012	6,888	5,081
Department of Transportation	5,688	8,029	8,797
Department of the Treasury	6,423	6,603	6,883
Environmental Protection Agency	2,025	2,532	3,955
Veterans Administration	32	73	80
Community Services Administration	510	478	339
District of Columbia	226	254	280
Washington Metropolitan Area Transit Authority	175	182	185
Other	595	830	823
Total outlays	49,723	59,787	60,523

SOURCE: Office of Management and Budget, *Special Analysis–Budget of the United States Government—Fiscal Year 1977,* 259 (U.S. Government Printing Office 1976).

Grantee Responsibilities

As shown in Figure 12-5, there are numerous governments in the United States. The structures, priorities, objectives, management practices, and capabilities of these governments differ significantly

Figure 12-5

NUMBER OF STATE AND LOCAL GOVERNMENTS

	1942	*1957*	*1972*
Total	155,115	102,391	78,268
State governments	48	50	50
Local governments	155,067	102,341	78,218
School districts	108,579	50,454	15,781
Other local governments	46,488	51,887	62,437
Counties	3,050	3,050	3,044
Municipalities	16,220	17,215	18,517
Townships	18,919	17,198	16,991
Special districts	8,299	14,424	23,885

SOURCE: U.S. Department of Commerce, *Guide to the 1972 Census of Governments,* Vol. 8, p. 8 (U.S. Government Printing Office 1975).

from one another. But when federal funds are granted to the local governments, the responsibilities for managing the funds are the same. All grantees must:

- Provide adequate stewardship over grant funds received;
- Use the funds efficiently and economically; and
- Use the funds to achieve the purpose of the grant.

These objectives must be accomplished in accordance with the rules and regulations established by the grantor agency and by the U.S. General Services Administration (GSA). GSA requirements are set forth in Federal Management Circulars 74-4 and 74-7 (July 18, 1974; September 13, 1974), and provide overall guidance to state and local governments administering grant programs. (These circulars can be obtained from the General Services Administration (AMF), Washington, D.C. 20405.)

Part II—The Questionnaire

Background Information

In developing his understanding of a grantee's operations, the auditor should obtain the following background information:

(1) Obtain an analysis of the funding and expenditures for the grants administered by the entity. (Use total grant or year-to-date figures. In most cases, the financial information can be obtained from a current financial status report or request for advance or disbursement, when used in lieu of the status report. The funding analysis will provide the auditor with an indication of the dollar significance of the grant program and the relationship between federal and nonfederal funding.)

				Federal Funds				*Nonfederal Funds*		
Agency	*Grant No.*	*Effective Date*	*Function*	*Authorized*	*Rec'd*	*Disbursed*	*On Hand*	*Rec'd*	*Disbursed*	*On Hand*
....	.....	.....	.....	\$.....	\$....	\$.....	\$....	\$....	\$.....	\$....
....	.....	.....	.....	.....	....	.....	....	....	.....	....
....	.....	.....	.....	.....	....	.....	....	....	.....	....
....	.....	.....	.....	.....	....	.....	....	....	.....	....
....	.....	.....	.....	.....	....	.....	....	....	.....	....
....	.....	.....	.....	.....	....	.....	....	....	.....	....
....	.....	.....	.....	.....	....	.....	....	....	.....	....
....	.....	.....	.....	.....	....	.....	....	....	.....	....
....	.....	.....	.....	.....	....	.....	....	....	.....	....
....	.....	.....	.....	.....	....	.....	....	....	.....	....
	TOTAL			\$____	\$____	\$____	\$____	\$____	\$____	\$____

(2) Obtain data on the grant program's personnel and participants. The relationship between the number of participants and the number of operating and administrative employees depends upon the nature of the program. This information may become valuable as an indication of trends when current data are compared with past data and when data for one program are compared with data for programs having similar objectives and resources.

	Number	
	Budgeted	*Actual*
Program Personnel		
Operating	....	....
Administrative	....	....
Program Participants		
Total served to date	....	....
Currently enrolled	....	....

(3) Obtain a listing showing the key personnel of the grantee organization by position level and work location.

Name	*Position*	*Location*
....	....	....
....	....	....
....	....	....
....	....	....
....	....	....

Grant Management Questionnaire

The purpose of the grant management questionnaire is to provide preferred practice questions that measure the efficiency and economy of the management practices of grantee organizations. This questionnaire can be used by an auditor or a grantor agency in evaluating a grantee's performance, or it can be used by a grantee for self-appraisal. Because of the diversity of grant programs and grantee organizations, an all-inclusive operational controls questionnaire in this area is not possible. The principal requirements of most federal grant programs are included in the questionnaire, but the auditor will have to adapt questions to fit the circumstances of particular grantees.

Figure 12-6 is a glossary of key terms applicable to grant management.

The questionnaire covers the following categories:

- Section I: Organization and Management Policies;
- Section II: Program Funding;
- Section III: Program Costs;
- Section IV: Program Participation and Program Results; and
- Section V: Audit.

Figure 12-6

GLOSSARY OF KEY TERMS

Cost allocation plan—A document that identifies, accumulates, and distributes allowable costs under grants and identifies allocation methodolgy.

Grant—An agreement between the federal government and a state or local government whereby the federal government provides funds or other aid to carry out specified programs, services, or activities.

Grant program—Those activities and operations of the grantee that are necessary to carry out the purposes of the grant, including any portion of the program financed by the grantee.

Grantee—The department or agency of the state or local government responsible for administering the grant.

Grantor agency or grantor—Any department, agency, commission, or instrumentality in the executive branch of the federal government that makes grants to state or local governments.

Indirect cost proposal—Cost allocation plan for an individual grantee as opposed to consolidated state-wide cost allocation plan covering all grant programs administered by the state.

Outside organization—A private institution that administers a portion of the grant program under contract from the grantee.

Participant—An individual who qualifies and receives services or takes part in activities of the grant program.

Program funds—All funds received under the grant program, including federal and nonfederal and program income.

Program income—Earnings by the grantee realized from grant support activities, such as sale of commodities and service fees.

SOURCE: General Service Administration Federal Management Circular 74-4 (July 18, 1974).

Section I: Organization and Management Policies

Usually grantor agencies prescribe broad organizational and management guidance to grantees to ensure uniformity and consistency in the administration of federal grant programs by state and local governments. The grantee should use this guidance in developing the grant program's organizational structure and management plans. Even if the grantor agency does not provide such guidance, the grantee must define and implement a sound management system that promotes economy and efficiency in fulfilling program objectives.

	Yes	*No*
(1) Has the grantor provided organizational and management guidance to the grantee?	☐	☐
(2) If so, does the guidance cover		
(a) Establishing agencies for administering the grants?	☐	☐
(b) Establishing planning boards or commissions?	☐	☐
(c) Organizational structure for the program?	☐	☐
(d) Functional activities to be performed by the grantee?	☐	☐
(e) Personnel limitations (number of employees, salary levels, etc.)?	☐	☐
(3) If the grantor agency has not provided organizational guidance, has the grantee		
(a) Coordinated the administration of the grant with similar state programs?	☐	☐
(b) Established a separate organizational structure for administration of the grant?	☐	☐
(c) Provided clear-cut assignments and responsibilities for administering the grant?	☐	☐
(d) Developed written procedures for administering the grant?	☐	☐
(4) Has the grantee assigned accounting responsibility for each project or grant?	☐	☐
(5) Does the grantee have adequate coordination between persons with management and accounting responsibilities to provide for		
(a) Timely submission of requests for expenditure reimbursement?	☐	☐
(b) Documenting of grant reimbursement claims?	☐	☐
(c) Routing and filing of grant claims?	☐	☐
(6) Does the grantee maintain a master listing of federal and state grants?	☐	☐

	Yes	*No*
(7) If so, does it include		
(a) Project descriptions?	☐	☐
(b) Funding sources?	☐	☐
(c) Grant periods?	☐	☐
(d) Federal, state and local contributions?	☐	☐
(e) Reporting requirements?	☐	☐

Section II: Program Funding

This section of the questionnaire is designed to evaluate a grantee's system for managing and controlling program funds. The evaluation is directed toward the budgeting process and compliance with grantor agency requirements.

Budgeting Process

An effective budgeting process is an integral part of a financial management system. The budget provides overall program guidance and assists management in planning its current operations. Absence of an effective budgeting process can result in improper distribution of resources and inadequate planning of program expenditures. (Preferred practice questions dealing with the budgeting process are presented in detail in Chapter 6.)

	Yes	*No*
(1) Does the grantee have a formal budgeting process for the grant program?	☐	☐
(2) If so, does the process		
(a) Involve the various organizational elements in budget formulation?	☐	☐
(b) Allow adequate time for review, revision, and approval prior to implementation of the budget?	☐	☐
(c) Define financial and performance standards for program activities?	☐	☐
(d) Consider funding increases and decreases that may be imposed by the grantor agency?	☐	☐
(e) Provide for periodic review and update throughout the budget period?	☐	☐

	Yes	*No*
(f) Provide for integration with the budgeting process of the overall entity?	☐	☐
(g) Require supporting documents for budget estimates?	☐	☐
(h) Provide for control and evaluation of budgets submitted by organizational elements?	☐	☐
(3) Is budget data developed in a form consistent with accounting and management reports, and federal and grantor agency requirements, so that actual results can be compared to the budget?	☐	☐
(4) Are periodic reviews and analyses made of variances between budget and prior periods?	☐	☐
(5) If so, does management take prompt action to determine causes of variance?	☐	☐
(6) Does management act on such variances?	☐	☐
(7) Does the grantee obtain prior approval from the grantor agency for budget changes involving		
(a) Transfers of nonfederal funds that would substantially alter the scope or purpose for which the grant award was made?	☐	☐
(b) Increases in expenditures of federal funds in a particular budget category?	☐	☐
(c) Expenditures of federal funds that would be made in a budget category for which no funds were approved?	☐	☐

Compliance With Federal Rules and Regulations

Federal Management Circular 74-7 establishes general criteria for use by a grantee in managing federal funds. These criteria are normally incorporated in and supplemented by specific guidance from the grantor agency. The grantee should use both in developing a cash management system for the grant program. (In evaluating a grantee's cash management system, the preferred practice questions presented in Chapter 8 should also be addressed.)

	Yes	*No*
(8) Has the grantor agency provided guidance to the grantee for the management of grant funds and program income?	☐	☐
(9) If so, does the guidance cover		
(a) Method of funding (letter of credit or treasury check)?	☐	☐
(b) Limitations as to amount of funds that can be retained on hand?	☐	☐
(c) Accountability and use of		
(i) interest earned on grant funds?	☐	☐
(ii) royalties received from copyrights and patents produced under the grant?	☐	☐
(iii) other program income earned during the grant period?	☐	☐
(10) Has the grantee determined that its system for managing program funds is in compliance with Federal Management Circular 74-7 and grantor agency guidance?	☐	☐
(11) Do the grantee's bonding and insurance standards meet applicable federal and grantor standards?	☐	☐
(12) Has the grantee complied with federal and grantor requirements with regard to		
(a) Reversionary rights to fixed assets?	☐	☐
(b) Retention of records?	☐	☐

Section III: Program Costs

Principles for determining the allowable costs of programs administered by state and local governments under federal grants are determined by Federal Management Circular 74-4. These cost principles are not applicable to all federal grant programs. Accordingly, the auditor should refer to the grant agreement to determine the applicability of the standards before completing this section.

Federal Management Circular 74-4 establishes three major categories of costs: allowable costs, costs allowable with the approval of the grantor, and unallowable costs. The circular defines the types of costs in each of the categories and any applicable restrictions. The auditor should be familiar with the requirements established by Federal Management Circular 74-4 before he begins this section.

Allowable Direct Costs

For most grant programs, the grantor agency, in accordance with the criteria in Federal Management Circular 74-4, establishes certain categories for accumulating direct program costs and describes the costs that should be accumulated in each of these categories. Allowable direct costs are those that can be identified specifically with a particular cost category and that meet the federal criteria for allowability. These costs may be charged directly to the program costs.

	Yes	*No*
(1) Has the grantor agency provided cost categories for accumulating expenditures incurred in administering the grant?	☐	☐
(2) Does the grantee have a formal system of cost control for direct costs? (Grantee may use a cost coding system or similar arrangement.)	☐	☐
(3) Are costs accumulated consistently throughout the program?	☐	☐
(4) Does the grantee's system provide for		
(a) Prompt identification of unallowable costs?	☐	☐
(b) An early warning to management of possible cost overruns?	☐	☐
(c) Identification of capital requirements?	☐	☐
(5) Has the grantee sought grantor agency approval for inclusion of those costs which upon such approval may become allowable by Federal Management Circular 74-4?	☐	☐

Indirect Costs

As defined by Federal Management Circular 74-4, "indirect costs" are those costs incurred for a common or joint purpose benefiting more than one cost category and that are not readily assignable to a specific cost category. Costs of this type include those originating under a grant program or in another department of a state or local government supplying services to the grant program.

Indirect costs can be allocated to grant programs using any of the following methods:

- Actual costs;
- Predetermined fixed rate; and
- Negotiated lump sum.

Detailed discussion of each method is included in Federal Management Circular 74-4. The grantee should use the most advantageous allocation method, considering any limitations imposed by the grantor agency. The grantee's proposed allocation method and related costs are summarized in an indirect cost proposal, which is reviewed and approved by a designated federal agency. (For a definition of "indirect cost proposal," see Figure 12-6.)

	Yes	*No*
(6) Has the grantee established guidelines for allocating indirect costs to grant programs?	☐	☐
(7) Are the grantee's guidelines in compliance with federal and grantor rules and regulations?	☐	☐
(8) Has the grantee's indirect cost proposal been approved by a federal agency? (Failure to obtain proper approval could result in disallowance of certain costs.)	☐	☐
(9) Does the indirect cost proposal include the grantee's indirect costs, as well as the allocable costs of state or local government departments supplying services to the grant program? (The failure to include all allowable indirect costs could result in a significant loss of revenue.)	☐	☐
(10) Has the grantee used the most advantageous indirect cost allocation method?	☐	☐

	Yes	No
(11) Does the grantee's system for accumulating indirect costs provide		
(a) Inclusion of all allowable indirect costs?	☐	☐
(b) Early warning to management of possible cost overruns?	☐	☐
(c) Prompt identification of costs not included in the indirect cost proposal?	☐	☐

Financial Reporting

Financial reports must satisfy the management needs of the grantee and the grantor. For most grant programs the grantor agency specifies the basic financial reports and the frequency of their preparation. Federal regulations, however, require that a financial status report be prepared at least annually.

	Yes	No
(12) Does the grantee have written procedures for financial reporting?	☐	☐
(13) If so, do they cover		
(a) Federal financial reporting requirements?	☐	☐
(b) State and local reporting requirements?	☐	☐
(c) Financial reporting requirements for subgrantees and outside organizations?	☐	☐
(14) Do the financial reports		
(a) Focus on user needs?	☐	☐
(b) Facilitate interpretation and use?	☐	☐
(c) Provide timely financial results?	☐	☐
(d) Facilitate comparisons with up-to-date budgetary information?	☐	☐
(15) Prior to filing, are grant reports		
(a) Reconciled by accounting personnel to the grantee's financial records?	☐	☐
(b) Approved by the project manager?	☐	☐

Section IV: Program Participation and Program Results

Appropriate controls over the selection, performance, and evaluation of program participants are essential to the effectiveness of a grant program. Participant controls along with a management system for compiling and utilizing information on overall program results often dictate the success or failure of a program.

This section of the questionnaire has been designed for use in the evaluation of the controls over program participation and results. Since the questions are directed towards those programs which have participants, modifications will have to be made when they are nonexistent.

(1) To provide an overview of a program's participants, the following information should be obtained (data can be obtained from performance reports usually prepared for the grantor agency):

	Number of Applicants				*Number of Participants*			
Activity	*Rec'd*	*Pro-cessed*	*No. Quali-fied*	*No. Ac-cepted*	*Pro-gram Goal*	*Currently Participating*	*Com-pletions*	*Drop-outs & Termi-nations*
....	.....	......	......	......	.....	....	....	....
....	.....	......	......	......	.....	....	....	....
....	.....	......	......	......	.....	....	....	....
....	.....	......	......	......	.....	....	....	....
....	.....	......	......	......	.....	....	....	....
....	.....	......	......	......	.....	....	....	....
....	.....	......	......	......	.....	....	....	....
....	.....	......	......	......	.....	....	....	....
TOTALS								

Participant Qualification

A screening process for program applicants is essential to the overall effectiveness of a grant program. The process should include detailed qualification standards, appropriate review and approval of applications, and a system that identifies and accepts the most qualified applicants.

	Yes	*No*
(1) Has the grantee established qualification standards for applicants?	☐	☐

	Yes	*No*
(2) Does the grantee's system for screening applicants		
(a) Incorporate the qualification requirements of the grant agreement and the grantor?	☐	☐
(b) Provide for an evaluation of applicants' ability to participate in the program?	☐	☐
(c) Provide for an evaluation to ensure that the aid provided is commensurate with the participants' needs?	☐	☐
(d) Require documentation of the qualification process?	☐	☐
(e) Establish aid limits?	☐	☐
(3) Are accepted applications reviewed and approved by a second party to determine		
(a) That qualification standards have been met?	☐	☐
(b) If the level of aid provided meets program criteria?	☐	☐
(4) Has the grantee established a priority system for classifying qualified applicants?	☐	☐
(5) If so, does the priority system provide that qualified applicants with greater needs are accepted into the program first?	☐	☐
(6) Does the grantee evaluate the participant selection process on a regular basis?	☐	☐
(7) If so, does management take action to correct any problems uncovered by the evaluation?	☐	☐

Outside Organizations

Commercial, charitable, and educational organizations frequently provide training and education under grant programs. When outside organizations are involved, the grantee's direct control over the participants is reduced. Consequently, additional control mechanisms are necessary.

	Yes	No
(8) Does the grantee have written agreements with outside organizations involved in the grant program?	☐	☐
(9) If so, do the agreements include		
(a) Rules and regulations imposed by the federal government?	☐	☐
(b) Rules and regulations imposed by the grantor agency?	☐	☐
(c) The grantee's program standards, including participant qualification standards?	☐	☐
(d) Reporting requirements (both financial and performance)?	☐	☐
(10) Does the grantee periodically evaluate the performance of outside organizations in relation to		
(a) Adherence to the written agreement?	☐	☐
(b) Achievement of overall grant objectives?	☐	☐
(c) Program administration?	☐	☐
(11) If so, does the grantee take action on the results of the evaluation?	☐	☐
(12) Do the reports (financial and performance) provided by the outside organization provide sufficient data for the grantee to monitor and evaluate the organization's performance?	☐	☐

Program Fund Disbursements

Funding arrangements with program participants and outside organizations should be supported by written agreements, and fund disbursements and subsequent collections should be appropriately documented and reviewed by management.

	Yes	No
(13) Has the grantee established guidelines for the distribution of funds to program participants and outside organizations?	☐	☐
(14) If so, do these guidelines cover		
(a) Level of funding?	☐	☐

	Yes	*No*
(b) Achievement standards?	☐	☐
(c) Reporting requirements?	☐	☐
(15) Where a grant is for an educational loan program, has the grantee established procedures which		
(a) Require the execution of a promissory note conforming with the standards of the grantor?	☐	☐
(b) Provide for the establishment of a repayment period?	☐	☐
(c) Provide criteria for loan deferments and cancellations?	☐	☐
(d) Require charges for late repayments (see Chapter 4, Dollarization Procedure 9: Delinquency Penalties)?	☐	☐
(16) Is the grantee adhering to standards for disbursement of funds to participants and outside organizations?	☐	☐
(17) Are loan cancellations and deferments reviewed by management and documented?	☐	☐
(18) Is the cancellation and deferment action in compliance with the original participant agreement?	☐	☐
(19) Does the system provide for a determination of the correct amount of principal and interest to be cancelled or deferred?	☐	☐
(20) Does the grantee have a billing service for processing loan repayments?	☐	☐
(21) Is timely action taken on delinquent loans?	☐	☐
(22) Are reports periodically issued showing		
(a) Loan deferments?	☐	☐
(b) Cancellations	☐	☐
(c) Deliquent repayments?	☐	☐

	Yes	*No*
(23) Where loan repayments are collected by outside organizations, have procedures been established to		
(a) Ensure immediate transfer of funds to the grantee (see Chapter 4, Dollarization Procedure 11: Undeposited Receipts)?	☐	☐
(b) Provide for immediate reporting of delinquent repayments to the grantee?	☐	☐

Participant Control

Control over participants in a program is necessary to ensure that the objectives of the program are achieved. The control should be directed at early identification of program violators and participants who become ineligible, as well as evaluation of individual performance.

Program violators and ineligible participants:

(24) Does the grantee's system provide for the identification of participants who		
(a) Become ineligible for program benefits?	☐	☐
(b) Violate terms of the participation agreement?	☐	☐
(c) Terminate without notice to the grantee?	☐	☐
(25) Does the grantee have written procedures requiring that management take prompt action against program violators and participants who become ineligible?	☐	☐

Performance evaluation:

(26) Are periodic evaluations made of individual performances?	☐	☐
(27) Are the evaluations reviewed, documented, filed, and retained?	☐	☐

Program Results

	Yes	*No*
In addition to evaluations of individual participants, the grantee should also be concerned with overall program performance. Total program results should be evaluated to determine the extent to which program objectives are being achieved. (A detailed description of a technique for evaluating program results is presented in Chapter 3.)		
(28) Does the grantee monitor program performance to ensure that time schedules are met and that performance goals are achieved?	☐	☐
(29) Are performance reports submitted to the grantor agency?	☐	☐
(30) Do the performance reports		
(a) Compare accomplishments to goals established?	☐	☐
(b) Provide reasons for variances between actual performance and goals?	☐	☐
(31) Are problems, delays, or adverse conditions immediately reported to the grantor along with actions taken or contemplated, and any requests for federal assistance needed to resolve the situation?	☐	☐
(32) Has the grantee responded to recommendations made by the grantor?	☐	☐
(33) Is program progress evaluated periodically?	☐	☐
(34) Does management take corrective action when actual program performance varies from program objectives?	☐	☐

Section V: Audit

The federal laws establishing grant programs normally require audits. The nature and extent of these audits vary from program to program. The following preferred practice questions are directed to a grantee organization. (Where an entity's internal audit function is to be evaluated, the preferred practice questions in Chapter 5 should also be answered.)

	Yes	*No*
(1) Are accounting systems and internal controls reviewed by an auditor prior to receipt of grant funds?	☐	☐
(2) If so, are deficiencies noted acted upon?	☐	☐
(3) Are financial statements audited?	☐	☐
(4) Are these audits conducted in compliance with the requirements of the grantor agency?	☐	☐
(5) Do these audits include outside entities and subgrantees who participate in a grant program?	☐	☐
(6) Have unqualified opinions been issued on the financial statements?	☐	☐
(7) If not, has the grantee taken action (if possible) to correct the problem?	☐	☐
(8) Is the audit scope in accordance with grant requirements?	☐	☐
(9) Are management letter comments		
(a) Provided by the auditors?	☐	☐
(b) Implemented by the grantee?	☐	☐
(10) If an audit is not required, has the grantee evaluated the need for an audit?	☐	☐
(11) Have other reviews of the program been performed, e.g., task force reviews and audits by the General Accounting Office?	☐	☐
(12) If so, has the grantee implemented the recommendations made by the review group?	☐	☐

APPENDIX I

GAO Standards

General Standards

(1) The full scope of an audit of a governmental program, function, activity, or organization should encompass

(a) An examination of financial transactions, accounts, and reports, including an evaluation of compliance with applicable laws and regulations.
(b) A review of efficiency and economy in the use of resources.
(c) A review to determine whether desired results are effectively achieved.

In determining the scope for a particular audit, responsible officials should give consideration to the needs of the potential users of the results of that audit.

(2) The auditors assigned to perform the audit must collectively possess adequate professional proficiency for the tasks required.

(3) In all matters relating to the audit work, the audit organization and the individual auditors shall maintain an independent attitude.

(4) Due professional care is to be used in conducting the audit and in preparing related reports.

Examination and Evaluation Standards

(1) Work is to be adequately planned.

(2) Assistants are to be properly supervised.

(3) A review is to be made of compliance with legal and regulatory requirements.

(4) An evaluation is to be made of the system of internal control to assess the extent it can be relied upon to ensure accurate information, to ensure compliance with laws and regulations, and to provide for efficient and effective operations.

(5) Sufficient, competent, and relevant evidence is to be obtained to afford a reasonable basis for the auditor's opinions, judgments, conclusions, and recommendations.

Reporting Standards

(1) Written audit reports are to be submitted to the appropriate officials of the organizations requiring or arranging for the audits. Copies of the reports should be sent to other officials who may be responsible for taking action on audit findings and recommendations and to others responsible or authorized to receive such reports. Copies should also be made available for public inspection.

(2) Reports are to be issued on or before the dates specified by law, regulation, or other arrangement and, in any event, as promptly as possible so as to make the information available for timely use by management and by legislative officials.

(3) Each report shall

- (a) Be as concise as possible but, at the same time, clear and complete enough to be understood by the users.
- (b) Present factual matter accurately, completely, and fairly.
- (c) Present findings and conclusions objectively and in language as clear and simple as the subject matter permits.
- (d) Include only factual information, findings, and conclusions that are adequately supported by enough evidence in the auditor's working papers to demonstrate or prove, when called upon, the bases for the matters reported and their correctness and reasonableness. Detailed supporting information should be included in the report to the extent necessary to make a convincing presentation.
- (e) Include, when possible, the auditor's recommendations for actions to effect improvements in problem areas noted in

his audit and to otherwise make improvements in operations. Information on underlying causes of problems reported should be included to assist in implementing or devising corrective actions.

(f) Place primary emphasis on improvement rather than on criticism of the past; critical comments should be presented in balanced perspective, recognizing any unusual difficulties or circumstances faced by the operating officials concerned.

(g) Identify and explain issues and questions needing further study and consideration by the auditor or others.

(h) Include recognition of noteworthy accomplishments, particularly when management improvements in one program or activity may be applicable elsewhere.

(i) Include recognition of the views of responsible officials of the organization, program, function, or activity audited on the auditor's findings, conclusions, and recommendations. Except where the possibility of fraud or other compelling reason may require different treatment, the auditor's tentative findings and conclusions should be reviewed with such officials. When possible, without undue delay, their views should be obtained in writing and objectively considered and presented in preparing the final report.

(j) Clearly explain the scope and objectives of the audit.

(k) State whether any significant pertinent information has been omitted because it is deemed privileged or confidential. The nature of such information should be described, and the law or other basis under which it is withheld should be stated.

(4) Each audit report containing financial reports shall

(a) Contain an expression of the auditor's opinion on whether the information contained in the financial reports is presented fairly. If the auditor cannot express an opinion, the reasons therefor should be stated in the audit report.

(b) State whether the financial reports have been prepared in accordance with generally accepted or prescribed accounting principles applicable to the organization, program, function, or activity audited and on a consistent basis from one period to the next. Material changes in accounting policies and procedures and their effect on the financial reports are to be explained in the audit report.

(c) Contain appropriate supplementary explanatory information about the contents of the financial reports as may be necessary for full and informative disclosure about the financial operations of the organization, program, function, or activity audited. Violations of legal or other regulatory requirements, including instances of noncompliance, shall be explained in the audit report.

SOURCE: U.S. General Accounting Office, *Standards for Audit of Governmental Organizations, Programs, Activities and Functions* 6-9 (U.S. Government Printing Office 1972).

APPENDIX II
Federal Audit Guides

Agency	*Title of Audit Guide*	*Issued*
Department of Agriculture		
Animal and Plant Health Inspection Service	Cooperative State Meat and Poultry Inspection Programs	7/72
Farmers Home Administration	Instructions to Independent Certified Public Accountants and Licensed Public Accountants Performing Audits of Farmers Home Administration Borrowers and Grantees	9/71
Food and Nutrition Service	Federally Financed Child Feeding Programs in Schools and Institutions—State Conducted Audits	11/74
	Food Stamp Program—State Conducted Audits	8/75
Rural Electrification Administration	Audit of REA Borrowers' Accounting Records	1/72
	Audit Working Paper Guide	11/72
Department of Commerce		
Economic Development Administration	Accounting System Survey and Audit Guide for Economic Development Districts	7/75
	Instructions for Audit of Public Works and Development Facility Grant and/or Loan Projects	9/74

Agency	*Title of Audit Guide*	*Issued*
Department of Commerce (cont.)		
National Oceanic and Atmospheric Administration	Accounting System Survey and Audit Guide For Coastal Zone Management Grants	10/75
Office of Minority Business Enterprise	Accounting System Survey and Audit Guide	10/75
Department of Health, Education and Welfare	Audit Guide: Head Start Program and Other Office of Child Development Programs	9/73
	Audit Guide National Direct Student Loan Program (NDSL), College Work-Study Program (CWS) and Supplemental Educational Opportunity Grants Program (SEOG)	9/73
	Supplement to Audit Guide—National Direct Student Loan Program (NDSL), College Work-Study Program (CWS), Supplemental Educational Opportunity Grants Program (SEOG)	8/74
	Audit Guide: Upward Bound Program	7/73
Department of Housing and Urban Development	Audit Guide for the Comprehensive Planning Assistance Program	8/73
	Audit Guide for the Low-Rent Housing Program for Use by Independent Public Accountants	5/72

Agency	*Title of Audit Guide*	*Issued*
Department of Housing and Urban Development (cont.)	Audit Guide for the Neighborhood Facilities Grant Program for Use by Independent Public Accountants	12/72
	Audit Guide for the Urban Renewal Program for Use by Independent Public Accountants	6/73
	Cost Certification Guide for Mortgagors, Contractors, and Independent Public Accountants	4/72
	Independent Public Accountant Audits—Neighborhood Facilities Grant Program	12/72
	Independent Public Accountant Audits—Public Facility Loans Program	1/73
Department of the Interior		
Fish and Wildlife Service	Audit Guide for U.S. Fish and Wildlife Service Grant Programs	8/75
National Park Service	Audit Guide for National Park Service Historic Preservation Grant Program	12/75
Department of Justice		
Law Enforcement Assistance Administration	Audit Guide: Law Enforcement Education Program (LEEP)	9/73
	Audit Guide for Review of State Planning Agencies, Subgrantees and Contractors	9/71
	Research Grants and Contracts Audit Program	9/75

Agency	*Title of Audit Guide*	*Issued*
Department of Labor	Audit Guide for Manpower Administration Contracts	2/73
	Audit Review Procedures and Audit Contracting Procedures	4/75
	CETA Audit Guide	4/75
	CETA Audit—An Overview	4/75
	Contract Closeout Audit Guide	4/75
	Indirect Cost Audit Guide	4/74
	Job Opportunities in the Business Sector (JOBS) Contracts Audit Guide	12/73
	Public Employment Program—Audit Guide	2/73
	Public Employment Program—Audit Guide Addendum	2/73
Department of Transportation		
Federal Aviation Administration	Audit Guide for Airport Development Aid Program	11/74
	Audit Handbook for the Commercial Operator and Air Carrier Financial Evaluation Program	2/66
	Audit Handbook for the Financial Evaluation of Air Taxi Operators	9/72
	Financial Evaluation Program for Air Taxi Operators and Commercial Operators of Large Aircraft	9/75

Agency	*Title of Audit Guide*	*Issued*
Department of Transportation (cont.)	Guides for Grantee Financial Management System Surveys	8/75
	Planning Grant Program (PGP) Audit Handbook	1/75
Urban Mass Transportation Administration	Accounting System Survey Guide	9/74
	Audit Program for Construction Contracts	—
	Audit Program for Cost-Type Contracts	11/73
	Cost Allocation Plan/Indirect Cost Proposal	5/75
	Program Audit Guide for Capital Improvement Grants and Supplement "Audit Guide for Relocation Expense"	8/74
	Program Audit Guide—Demonstrations and Technical Studies	10/74
	Program Audit Guide—Interim Audits	10/74
	Program Audit Guide—Managerial Training Grants	5/71
	Program Audit Guide—Operating Assistance Projects	8/75
	Program Audit Guide—University Research and Training Grants	2/71
Treasury Department	Audit Guide and Standards for Revenue Sharing Recipients	10/73

Agency	*Title of Audit Guide*	*Issued*
Independent Agencies		
ACTION	Audit Program Follow-Up on Interest Audit Reports	7/75
	Audit Program General Provisions	7/75
	Peace Corps Audit Program—Grants and Contracts	—
Appalachian Regional Development	Audit Guide for Grants Made Under Section 302 (a)(1) of the Appalachian Regional Development Act of 1965, as amended	—
Civil Service Commission	IPA Grant Administration Handbook	6/73
	IPA Grant Audit Guidelines for Use by State, Local Governmental, and CPA Auditors	10/74
Community Service Administration	Accounting System Survey and Audit Guide for CSA Grants	1/75
Environmental Protection	Audit Guide for Construction Grant Program	Draft 2/76
	Audit Guide for Nonconstruction Grant Program	Draft 7/75
Office of Management and Budget	The Integrated Grant Administration Program	1/72
Small Business Administration	Audit Guide for Small Business Investment Companies	11/74
	Business Loan Policy	12/75*

* Proposed guideline.

Agency	*Title of Audit Guide*	*Issued*
Independent Agencies (cont.)		
Social Security Administration	Audit Program for Home Health Agencies Under the Health Insurance for the Aged Act	—
	Audit Program for Hospitals Under the Health Insurance for the Aged Act	
	Audit Program for Skilled Nursing Facilities Under the Health Insurance for the Aged Act	—

APPENDIX III

Federal Grants to State and Local Governments–Outlays*

(in millions of dollars)

Agency and Program	*1975 Actual*	*1976 Estimate*	*1977 Estimate*
		Outlays	
National defense			
Department of Defense—Military			
Civil Preparedness Agency	39	42	37
National Guard centers construction	34	35	30
TOTAL	74	77	67
Natural resources, environment, and energy			
Department of Agriculture			
Watershed planning and flood control	94	108	90
Resource conservation and development	9	11	5
Forest service	32	32	27
Department of Commerce			
NOAA coastal zone management	7	17	17
NOAA—Operations research and facilities	18	19	19
Department of the Interior			
Bureau of Reclamation	4	1	*
Office of Water Research and Technology	9	9	9
Land and water conservation fund	157	160	158
Fish and Wildlife Service	72	79	81
Preservation of historic properties	6	7	9
Energy Research and Development Administration	7	9	6
Environmental Protection Agency	2,025	2,532	3,955
Federal Energy Administration		50	60
Tennessee Valley Authority (shared revenue)	37	48	68
Water Resources Council	5	4	
TOTAL	2,479	3,088	4,505
Agriculture			
Coöperative State Research Service	92	108	120
Cooperative Agricultural Extension Work	183	192	185
Commodity Credit Corporation—donations	128	199	251
Agricultural Marketing Service—cooperative projects in marketing	*		
TOTAL	404	499	556

* Less than $500 thousand.

Note: Details in the tables presented in this Appendix may not add to the totals because of rounding.

Agency and Program	*1975 Actual*	*1976 Estimate*	*1977 Estimate*
		Outlays	
Commerce and transportation			
Department of Agriculture: FmHA: Housing	6	10	5
Department of Commerce: EDA—Minority business development	2	4	3
Department of Housing and Urban Development: Urban transportation	*	2	
Department of Transportation			
Grants-in-aid for natural gas pipeline safety	1	2	2
State boating safety assistance	5	6	6
Airport and airway trust fund	292	375	355
Highway beautification	26	46	40
Highway trust fund	4,573	6,170	6,567
Other highway aid	29	48	158
National Highway Traffic Safety Administration	74	87	93
Federal Railroad Administration	*	19	73
Urban Mass Transportation Administration	688	1,276	1,503
Washington Metropolitan Area Transit Authority	175	182	185
TOTAL	5,872	8,227	8,990
Community and regional development			
Funds appropriated to the President:			
Appalachian regional development programs	306	333	321
Disaster relief	131	158	158
Department of Agriculture			
Rural water and waste disposal grants	35	62	84
Rural development grants	4	9	8
Rural community fire protection grants	2	2	
Department of Commerce			
Economic Development Administration	209	204	174
Regional Action Planning Commissions	41	79	42
Department of Housing and Urban Development			
Community development block grants	38	750	1,600
Urban renewal	1,374	1,375	1,000
Other categorical programs replaced by community development block grants	601	444	110
Comprehensive planning grants	96	107	75
New Communities Administration	3	3	5
Department of the Interior: Bureau of Indian Affairs	2	2	2
Joint Federal-State Land Use Planning Commission for Alaska	1	2	*
Community Services Administration	493	478	339
TOTAL	3,335	4,008	3,917

* Less than $500 thousand.

Agency and Program	*1975 Actual*	*1976 Estimate*	*1977 Estimate*
		Outlays	
Education, employment, training, and social services			
Dep't. of Commerce: Job opportunities prog.	22	175	222
Department of Health, Education, and Welfare			
Financial assistance for elementary and secondary education			294
Elementary and secondary education	2,276	2,277	1,925
Indian education	24	24	20
School assistance in federally affected areas	577	438	344
Emergency school assistance	214	232	219
Education for the handicapped	58	96	75
Occupational, vocational, and adult education	653	674	662
Higher education	83	33	25
Library resources	210	128	94
Special projects and training		4	37
Educational development	118	26	3
Work incentives	304	330	243
Social services	2,047	2,358	2,546
Assistant Secretary for Human Development:			
Child development	430	466	458
Youth, aging and vocational rehabilitation programs	1,166	1,122	1,098
Allied services			5
Department of the Interior: Bureau of Indian Affairs, Indian education programs	24	34	28
Department of Labor			
Employment and training assistance	2,504	3,050	2,494
Temporary employment assistance	319	2,331	1,065
Emergency employment assistance	53	4	
Grants for employment services	—19	94	82
Unemployment trust fund: training and employment	481	434	466
Corporation for Public Broadcasting	62	70	70
National Foundation on the Arts and Humanities	14	22	22
Community Services Administration	17		
TOTAL	11,638	14,422	12,497
Health			
Special Action Office for Drug Prevention	10	6	
Department of Agriculture: Animal and Plant Health Inspection Service—meat and poultry	33	34	34
Department of Health, Education and Welfare:			
Health Services Administration	567	595	285
Center for Disease Control	59	56	23
Alcohol, Drug Abuse, and Mental Health Administration	590	508	375
Health Resources Administration	672	613	433
Financial assistance for health care			9,001
Medicaid	6,840	8,184	
Department of the Interior: Mining Enforcement and Safety Administration	1	1	1
Department of Labor: Occupational Safety and Health Administration	37	36	36
TOTAL	8,810	10,032	10,188

Agency and Program	*1975 Actual*	*1976 Estimate*	*1977 Estimate*
		Outlays	
Income security			
Department of Agriculture			
Agricultural Marketing Service—Funds for strengthening markets, income and supply-donations	494	294	—5
Institutional nutrition support			22
Food stamps—administration	136	230	245
Special nutrition supplements			6
Child nutrition and special milk programs	1,565	2,225	291
Food donations		17	
Child nutrition reform			2,000
Department of Health, Education, and Welfare:			
Public assistance—maintenance	5,121	5,898	5,959
Department of Housing and Urban Development:			
Housing assistance	1,326	1,609	1,979
Department of Labor: Unemployment trust fund: administration of payments	636	939	938
TOTAL	9,279	11,212	11,434
Veterans benefits and services			
Veterans Administration			
Medical care	22	25	28
Medical administrative expenses	1	1	1
Grants for construction of State nursing homes	3	6	5
Health training	6	41	42
Grants for State cemeteries			4
TOTAL	32	73	80
Law enforcement and justice			
National Institute of Corrections			1
Department of Justice: Law enforcement assistance	722	750	716
Equal Employment Opportunity Commission	3	6	8
Legal Services Corporation		82	80
TOTAL	725	838	805
General government			
Department of Interior			
Administration of Territories	16	22	25
Trust territory of the Pacific Islands	69	89	80
General Services Administration	2	18	20
Civil Service Commission (intergovernmental personnel assistance)	15	16	10
TOTAL	102	145	135

Agency and Program	*1975 Actual*	*1976 Estimate*	*1977 Estimate*
		Outlays	
Revenue sharing and general purpose fiscal assistance			
Department of Agriculture: Forest Service (shared revenue)	121	91	37
Department of Defense: Flood Control Act (shared revenue)	4	4	1
Department of Interior:			
Bureau of Land Management	178	179	127
Fish and Wildlife-Service	3	3	3
Internal revenue collections for the Virgin Islands (shared revenue)	17	31	19
Department of the Treasury			
Customs receipts for Puerto Rico and the Virgin Islands (shared revenue)	172	216	220
Internal revenue collections for Puerto Rico (shared revenues)	122	114	114
General revenue sharing	6,130	6,272	6,549
Federal payment to the District of Columbia (shared revenue)	226	254	280
TOTAL, revenue sharing and general purpose fiscal assistance	6,971	7,166	7,349
TOTAL, grants and shared revenues	49,723	59,787	60,523

SOURCE: "Special Analysis" *Budget of the United States Government, Fiscal Year 1977,* 268–273 (U.S. Government Printing Office 1976).

APPENDIX IV

Recognition of ADP Operational Problems*

(The following grid has been designed to aid in identifying operational difficulties in ADP systems.)

Absence of the Following Techniques Leads to Adverse Results	*Adverse Results*																			
	Effect on Employees			*Effect on Systems*						*Effect on Equipment*							*Other Effects*			
	Idleness/Unnecessary Staff	*Constant Overtime*	*Turnover*	*Multitude of Projects*	*Delays*	*Limited Savings/Excessive Costs*	*Managerial Needs Unmet*	*Inaccuracies*	*Excessive Programming*	*Idleness*	*Low Utilization*	*Low Production*	*Peaks/Valleys*	*Excess Usage Charges*	*Multitude of Equipment*	*Downtime*	*Risk of Fraud or Vandalism*	*Wastage of Supplies*	*High Purchasing Costs*	*Costly Reconstruction*
Organization and planning:																				
Long-term master plan for systems development	X	X	X	X		X			X	X	X		X	X	X					
Executive support for systems program			X			X	X				X									
Organization charts and job descriptions	X	X	X		X							X					X			
Assignment of responsibilities for:																				
Systems design	X			X	X	X	X		X								X			

Programming—systems changes	X			X	X	X	X		X								X			
Programming—maintenance	X		X		X				X								X			
Programming—standards	X		X					X	X			X								
Forms design							X	X	X						X			X		
Design and development of coding systems							X	X	X											
Keeping abreast of technological changes							X		X	X	X		X							
Computer operations	X	X	X		X					X	X	X	X	X	X	X				
Keypunching	X	X	X							X	X	X	X							
Production planning and control	X	X								X	X	X	X	X						
Library	X				X			X		X							X			
Separation of duties—Analysts-Programmers/ Computer Operators		X			X						X						X			
Authorizations and approval of program changes				X		X			X								X			
Supervisory review of machine logs					X			X			X	X					X			
Systems Analysis and Programming:																				
Project controls relating to:																				
Project objectives				X	X	X	X													
Project benefits						X	X													
Project costs						X														
Testing and/or acceptance							X	X		X							X			
Supervisory review and approval							X	X									X			
Progress review	X		X			X														
Post completion evaluation						X														
Documentation of study and conclusions							X													X
Project priority assignments and backlog controls	X	X	X	X	X															
Participation in projects by users	X				X	X		X									X			
Participation of internal auditors:																				
Planning and development of project proposals							X										X			
Preinstallation review emphasizing internal controls					X			X		X							X			

* A slightly different version first appeared in Coopers & Lybrand Newsletter (Sept. 1972).

Adverse Results

Absence of the Following Techniques Leads to Adverse Results	*Effect on Employees*			*Effect on Systems*						*Effect on Equipment*							*Other Effects*			
	Idleness/Unnecessary Staff	*Constant Overtime*	*Turnover*	*Multitude of Projects*	*Delays*	*Limited Savings/Excessive Costs*	*Managerial Needs Unmet*	*Inaccuracies*	*Excessive Programming*	*Idleness*	*Low Utilization*	*Low Production*	*Peaks/Valleys*	*Excess Usage Charges*	*Multitude of Equipment*	*Downtime*	*Risk of Fraud or Vandalism*	*Wastage of Supplies*	*High Purchasing Costs*	*Costly Reconstruction*
Review of project documentation									X											X
Review of test documentation (for adequacy and control purposes)							X	X									X			
Current operations:																				
Completeness/security of documentation for existing applications:																				
Systems descriptions		X					X	X	X											X
Run manual, including source listing or deck	X										X	X					X			X
Operator instructions	X										X	X					X			
Test data, current and available		X						X	X								X			
Record of changes to programs		X							X								X			
Use of programmed data controls where opportune								X				X					X			X
Use of multi-programming, as appropriate to improve computer utilization		X									X									

Use of outside services to level peak loads	X	X	X			X									X								
Preventive maintenance, and use of related outside services as appropriate	X					X												X					X
Scheduling of computer and of peripheral equipment	X	X				X						X	X		X	X				X			
Planning and supervisory authorization of overtime		X																		X			
Consideration of high-speed input/output devices	X	X											X	X									
Consideration of sectional core													X										
Time and activity reporting system	X							X												X			
Consideration of key-to-tape and/or key-to-disk			X						X					X									
Consideration of source data automation	X								X				X							X	X		
Preparation of periodic summary reports:																							
Computer utilization							X						X	X						X			
Preventive maintenance																		X					
Downtime							X											X					
Rerun time							X		X					X							X		
Production time							X							X						X			
Time charges to users					X	X	X	X												X			
Periodic review of equipment utilization		X					X					X	X			X							
Periodic studies of equipment "balance"							X					X	X			X							
Periodic study to consolidate or decentralize data processing functions							X					X	X										
Use of electronic switching, as appropriate in a network of computers						X							X										
Security:																							
File protection in terms of the storage of copies in loss-proof vaults	X											X								X			X
File reconstruction capabilities	X											X								X			X
Restrictions on access to necessary personnel																		X		X			X
Guards, lockable doors, and other protection devices																		X		X			X
Terminal and access codes									X											X			
"Instant" terminations of data processing employees																		X		X			X

Absence of the Following Techniques Leads to Adverse Results	*Adverse Results*																			
	Effect on Employees			*Effect on Systems*						*Effect on Equipment*							*Other Effects*			
	Idleness/Unnecessary Staff	*Constant Overtime*	*Turnover*	*Multitude of Projects*	*Delays*	*Limited Savings/Excessive Costs*	*Managerial Needs Unmet*	*Inaccuracies*	*Excessive Programming*	*Idleness*	*Low Utilization*	*Low Production*	*Peaks/Valleys*	*Excess Usage Charges*	*Multitude of Equipment*	*Downtime*	*Risk of Fraud or Vandalism*	*Wastage of Supplies*	*High Purchasing Costs*	*Costly Reconstruction*
Emergency power backup	X									X							X			
Emergency computer installation backup	X				X												X			
Buying of computer resources:																				
Observance of sound procurement practices relating to specification of needs, shopping of market, preparation of complete purchase orders, etc.							X					X			X	X	X		X	
Evaluations of financial and performance capabilities of potential vendors																X			X	
Evaluation of vendor contracts by legal department, as appropriate																X			X	
Periodic lease or buy studies																			X	
Periodic studies of independent peripherals versus main-frame manufacturer												X							X	

Miscellaneous:																							
Sale of waste paper and cards																					X		
Program for cleaning and testing and/or replacing magnetic tape						X			X			X											
Controls over computer time sold to outsiders															X					X			

APPENDIX V

Cost Reduction Opportunities*

Techniques	*Objectives*								
	Cut Purchase Costs	*Cut Freight Costs*	*Maximize Working Capital*	*Cut Scrap*	*Cut Production Interruptions*	*Cut Labor Costs*	*Improve Equipment Utilization*	*Cut Admin. Overhead*	*Increase Revenues*
Reduce numbers of different types of articles in stock	X		X					X	
Standardize "preferred" items	X				X			X	
Define roles of purchasing personnel at different levels of large organization	X		X					X	
Evaluate vendor-quality, delivery, and cost performances	X		X		X				
Provide enough time to "shop the market"	X								
Centralize negotiations for major items, including freight	X	X							
Use traveling requisitions								X	
Give purchasing personnel a free hand in vendor selection, based on operating "specs"	X				X				
Issue complete purchase orders for significant transactions	X								
Reduce "rush" procurement	X	X			X			X	
Prescribe preferred routing for incoming bulk items		X			X				
Seek competitive bids for significant transactions	X								
Establish floor below which bids will not be obtained								X	

Subject all buying contracts to periodic review	X								
Develop approved vendor list for highly technical purchases	X				X				
Combine related items on purchase orders								X	
Conduct make-or-buy studies	X						X		
Use purchase order copy as receiving report								X	
Test-weight bulk commodities	X	X							
Authorize telephone releases for minor items bought on contract								X	
Eliminate useless copies made by receiving clerks								X	
Stage incoming loads to eliminate demurrage, and shipping overtime		X				X			
Speed up invoice processing to avoid discount losses	X								
Set up delivery system					X				
Signal vendor overshipments to buyers for bargaining purposes	X								
Negotiate terms with suppliers affecting packaging, pallets, etc.						X			
Reduce distance between receiving and storage facilities						X			
Establish incoming inspection to minimize damage from defects	X			X	X				
Step up billing to vendors of "rework"	X			X					
Bill freight to vendors on rejected shipments		X							
"Pass" minor invoice discrepancies								X	
Control slow-moving inventories and initiate timely disposal actions	X		X	X					
Establish reorder points and economic ordering or production quantities	X		X		X			X	
Plan use of inventory space						X			

* A slightly different version first appeared in the Coopers & Lybrand Newsletter (Nov. 1970).

Techniques	*Objectives*								
	Cut Purchase Costs	*Cut Freight Costs*	*Maximize Working Capital*	*Cut Scrap*	*Cut Production Interruptions*	*Cut Labor Costs*	*Improve Equipment Utilization*	*Cut Admin. Overhead*	*Increase Revenues*
Maintain current locator files in storerooms						X			
Establish technologically significant materials codes	X				X	X			
Shift burden of carrying inventory to suppliers	X		X					X	
Introduce "self-help" storeroom bins for inexpensive items								X	
Install storeroom facilities to cut metals on site	X								
Determine optimum buying sizes for metals	X			X					
Recharge flashlight batteries instead of buying new ones	X								
Clean gloves instead of buying new ones	X								
Use rebuilding services for valves, instruments, etc.	X								
Use nonoriginal equipment sources for spares	X								
Circumscribe addition of new articles to stock	X		X	X				X	
Signal "premium" freight for investigation		X							
Establish timely control over freight claims		X							
Negotiate favorable terms with freight audit agency		X							
Act as self-insurer on rental cars								X	
Use compacts rather than big cars								X	
Use coach class on planes								X	
Use self-checking capabilities of computers								X	
Main order-input clerks to reduce need for editing								X	
Report physical percentage-of-contract completion vs. dollar percentage									X
Avoid emergency inventory transfers from plant to plant		X							

Eliminate duplications on operating and accounting records								X	
Take inventory cycle counts at "low" of stocks								X	
Consider adaptability of current stocks when planning engineering changes				X					
Substitute second shift for overtime						X			
Avoid "split" labor assignments of high-rate men to low-rate jobs						X			
Monitor machine running speeds to avoid breakdowns					X		X		
Stabilize labor force by "level loading"						X			
Plan maintenance jobs						X			
Reduce fire insurance premiums by complying with inspection reports	X								
Sell used ADP cards to scrap-paper dealers									X
Make secured short-term loans of excess cash			X						
Negotiate interruptible rates with utilities where practicable	X								

APPENDIX VI

Anti-Inflation Tactics*

The following tactics are usually found effective for operating in an inflationary environment. Individual situations, of course, may require additional and/or different approaches. The tactics in this checklist are keyed to the following three objectives:

(1) Accelerate cash receipts and reduce receivables.
(2) Delay cash disbursement and increase payables.
(3) Obtain cash and invest for growth and/or yield.

Tactics	*Objectives*		
Coordinate production and financial responsibilities to minimize surprise cash needs and surpluses.	1	2	3
Improve cash management staff and/or systems capabilities.	1	2	3
Review all banking arrangements with respect to current needs, benefits, and costs.			3
Consolidate accounts to reduce aggregate minimum balances.			3
Use automatic transfer accounts and take advantage of bank wire systems and electronic funds transfer arrangements.	1		3
Reconsider needs and cost effectiveness of cashier functions at all locations.	1	2	3
Plan investment of temporary excess cash.			3
Plan for extra borrowing, loan commitments, credit purchases, etc., to fill temporary shortages.	1	2	3

* A slightly different version first appeared in the Coopers & Lybrand Newsletter (Nov. 1974).

Tactics	*Objectives*		
Review fixed investments, properties, etc., for growth or yield potential and liquidation possibilities.			3
Review litigation and other claims receivable for favorable early cash settlement potential.			3
Evaluate rates for possible increase and/or charges to customers for presently free options.			3
Establish or tighten due date and/or terms for all sales or other money sources; provide interest or penalty charges on late or deferred customer payments.	1		
Strengthen credit and collection function.	1		
Include provisions for advance, partial, or progress payments.	1		
Reevaluate effectiveness and rate of cash discount offered to customers to induce early payment.	1		
Shorten billing cycles.			
Enhance invoice clarity and minimize billing errors and/or omissions, particularly in addresses.	1		
Speed up collection efforts and begin them earlier.	1		
Provide preaddressed return envelope with invoice to speed reply mail and identification.	1		
Provide separate turnaround remittance advice to speed payment identification for collections control and deposit.	1		
Speed up preparation and dispatch of deposits to coordinate with bank clearing schedules.	1		
Use lockbox services to obtain instant deposit.	1		
Streamline efforts to recover for checks returned unpaid.	1		
Reevaluate purchases to reduce unit cost and/or order quantities.		2	
Use supplier's inventory; buy on order wherever feasible.		2	
Balance inventory investment risks' and costs, with anticipated availability and price-level effects.		2	3
Reevaluate make-or-buy and lease-or-buy options for maximum growth or yield from cash used.			3

Tactics	*Objectives*	
Negotiate better terms on purchases and other commitments, especially where delivery/construction is delayed.	2	
Review insurance coverage, premium payment timing, and loan availability.	2	3
Limit need for cash advances to employees, e.g., by providing fast reimbursement, use of charge accounts, and drafts.		3
Use drafts for large volumes of small payments so that cash is required only when drafts are presented.		3
Make selective use of cash discounts.	2	
Time cash transactions to take advantage of grace periods, weekend interest, etc.		3
Avoid undue future price commitments or provide escalator clause in sales contracts.		3

Selected Bibliography

American Institute of Certified Public Accountants (AICPA):

Auditing Standards Executive Committee, *The Effect of an Internal Audit Function on the Scope of the Independent Auditor's Examination*. Statement on Auditing Standards No. 9 (AICPA Dec. 1975).

Committee on College and University Accounting and Auditing, *Audits of Colleges and Universities*. Industry Audit Guide (AICPA 1973).

Committee on Governmental Accounting and Auditing, *Audits of State and Local Governmental Units*. Industry Audit Guide (AICPA 1974).

Committee on Health Care Institutions, *Hospital Audit Guide* (AICPA 1972).

Committee on Relations With the General Accounting Office of AICPA, *Auditing Standards Established by the GAO—Their Meaning and Significance for CPAs* (AICPA 1973).

Federal Government Division, *Federal Financial Management: Accounting and Auditing Practices* (AICPA 1976).

MAS Executive Committee, *Guidelines for Participation in Government Audit Engagements to Evaluate Economy, Efficiency and Program Results* (exposure draft, AICPA 1976).

Brink, Cashin & Witt, *Modern Internal Auditing—An Operational Approach* (Ronald Press 1973).

Conference Board, *Staffing Systems—Managerial and Professional Jobs*. Report No. 558 (The Conference Board 1972).

Coopers & Lybrand:

Audit Committee Guide (2nd ed., Coopers & Lybrand 1976).

Cancellieri & Enstrom, *The Expanded Scope of Government*

Auditing: C&L Reports to Management (Coopers & Lybrand 1976).

"Coopers & Lybrand Complete Pilot Program of City Audits Under New Federal Guidelines," Coopers & Lybrand Newsletter, Feb.–March 1974, pp. 1–5.

Improving Performance Through Management by Objectives (Lybrand, Ross Bros. & Montgomery 1970).

Pomeranz, *Auditing by Perception: C&L Reports to Management* (Coopers & Lybrand 1974).

Pomeranz & Steinberg, *Operational Guidelines for Managing Investment Funds: C&L Reports to Management* (Coopers & Lybrand 1974).

Council of State Governments, *State and Local Government Purchasing* (The Council of State Governments 1975).

Defliese, Johnson, & MacLeod, *Montgomery's Auditing* (9th ed., Ronald Press 1975).

Dilley, "Expanded Scope Audits—Untapped Opportunities," *C.P.A. J.* 30–35 (Dec. 1975).

Drucker, *The Practice of Management* (Harper Bros. 1954).

Federal Government Accountants Association, *Proceedings of the Seminar on Sophisticated Auditing Techniques, Federal Government Accountants Association, Washington, D.C., 1972* (Washington Chapter FGAA 1973).

Fowler, "Pitfalls in Assignment of Management Goals." *Managerial Planning* 34–35 (July/Aug. 1974).

International City Management Association (ICMA):

1975 Municipal Year Book (International City Management Association 1976).

Performance Audits in Local Governments—Benefits, Problems, & Challenges: Special Report, Vol. 8 (International City Management Association 1976).

Measuring the Effectiveness of Basic Municipal Services (International City Management Association and The Urban Institute 1974).

Lynn & Freeman, *Fund Accounting—Theory and Practice* (Prentice-Hall 1974).

Maiben & Schwabe, "Government by Objectives: A Management System," *Gov. Fin.* 2–5 (Feb. 1974).

Municipal Finance Officers Association, National Committee on Government Accounting, *Governmental Accounting Auditing, and Financial Reporting* (Municipal Finance Officers Association 1969).

National Association of Counties, *1975 County Year Book* (National Association of Counties 1976).

Owens, "The Values and Pitfalls of MBO," Mich. Bus. Rev. 11–14 (July 1974).

Sawyer, *The Practice of Modern Internal Auditing* (Institute of Internal Auditors 1973).

Scantlebury, "The Broadening Scope of Government Auditing in the U.S.A.," Int'l J. of Governmental Accounting 10–12 (July 1975).

Schiff & Schirger, *Control of Maintenance Cost: Research Report No. 41* (National Association of Accountants 1964).

Singular, "Has MBO Failed?" Master in Bus. Admin. 47–48 (Oct. 1975).

State of Hawaii, Legislative Auditor, *Financial Audit of the Hawaii Housing Authority* (Jan. 1975).

State of New York, Legislative Commission on Expenditure Review, *Construction of Mental Hygiene Facilities* (Oct. 1973).

Swedish National Audit Bureau, *Effectiveness Auditing in Government Administration* (Stockholm: Gateborgs Offsettryckeri 1971).

U.S. Government:

Bureau of the Census, *Guide to the 1972 Census of Governments* (U.S. Government Printing Office 1975).

Department of Commerce, *Statistical Abstract of the United States 1975* (U.S. Government Printing Office 1975).

General Accounting Office

The Adult Basic Education Program: Progress in Reducing Illiteracy and Improvements Needed (U.S. Government Printing Office 1975).

Answers to Frequently Asked Questions (U.S. Government Printing Office 1973).

Audit Guidelines for Audits of Financial Operations of Federally Assisted Programs (exposure draft, U.S. Government Printing Office 1976).

Auditors—Agents for Good Government, Audit Standards Series, No. 2 (U.S. Government Printing Office 1973).

Case Study: How Auditors Develop Findings—Increasing the Productivity of City Water Meter Readers, Audit Standards Series, No. 8 (U.S. Government Printing Office 1976).

Case Study—Illinois' Use of Public Accountants for Auditing State Activities, Audit Standard Series, No. 3 (U.S. Government Printing Office 1973).

The E's of Management—Auditing Efficiency, Economy and Effectiveness in Government: A Bibliography of Recent Articles June 1974 (U.S. Government Printing Office 1974).

Evaluating Governmental Performance: Changes and Challenges for GAO (U.S. Government Printing Office 1975).

Examples of Findings From Governmental Audits, Audit Standards Series, No. 4 (U.S. Government Printing Office 1973).

Illustrative Report Prepared in Accordance with GAO Audit Standards—Air Pollution Control Program, Sassafras County, Maryland, Audit Standards Series, No. 6 (U.S. Government Printing Office 1975).

Increased Intergovernmental Cooperation Needed for More Effective, Less Costly Auditing of Government Programs (U.S. Government Printing Office 1974).

Internal Auditing in Federal Agencies (U.S. Government Printing Office 1974).

Questions and Answers on the Standards for Audit of Governmental Organization, Programs, Activities and Functions, Audit Standards Series, No. 5 (U.S. Government Printing Office 1974).

Standards for Audit of Governmental Organizations, Programs, Activities and Functions (U.S. Government Printing Office 1972).

Using Auditing to Improve Efficiency and Economy, Audit Standard Series, No. 7 (U.S. Government Printing Office 1975).

What GAO Is Doing to Improve Governmental Auditing Standards, Audit Standards Series, No. 1 (U.S. Government Printing Office 1973).

Office of Management and Budget

Special Analysis: Budget of the United States Government—Fiscal Year 1977 (U.S. Government Printing Office 1976).

The United States Budget in Brief—Fiscal Year 1977 (U.S. Government Printing Office 1976).

Yoder, *Personnel Management and Industrial Relations* (6th ed., Prentice-Hall 1970).